DYNAMICS OF NEW PANCHAYATI RAJ SYSTEM IN INDIA

Volume I : SELECT STATES

Dynamics of New Panchayati Raj System in India Series

Vol. I : Select States
Vol. II : Select States
Vol. III : Select States
Vol. IV : Panchayati Raj and Empowerment of Women
Vol. V : Panchayati Raj and Multi-level Planning
Vol. VI : Panchayati Raj and Empowerment of Dalits
Vol. VII : Finance in Panchayati Raj System
Vol. VIII : Panchayati Raj and Common Property Resource Management
Vol. IX : Participatory and Direct Democracy : Gram Sabha
Vol. X : Capacity Building for Panchayati Raj Leaders and Functionaries
Vol. XI : State-Local Body Relationship
Vol. XII : Panchayati Raj and Socio-Political and Economic Transformation
Vol. XIII : Leadership in Panchayati Raj Institution
Vol. XIV : Thinkers Framework on Panchayati Raj
Vol. XV : Theoretical Nuances of Local Bodies

About the Editor

Prof. Ganapathi Palanithurai, Coordinator in Rajiv Gandhi Chair, Gandhigram ural Institute is an academic activist working with the people in rural areas for uilding the capacity of the leaders and people to reinvent sustainable grassroots emocracy. He is heading the Department of Political Science and Development Administration, in Gandhigram Rural University, Tamil Nadu. His policy advocacy role at the governmental level is increasingly felt at present in all the three levels, namely sub-regional, regional and national as he does more field work than theorisation. He has been associating himself with Centre Planning Commission, State Planning Commission of Tamil Nadu, Population Foundation of India, Ford Foundation, UNICEF, Rajiv Gandhi Foundation, CAPART, Ministry of Rural Areas and Employment and DANIDA (Danish-Indo Development Agency) in specific areas of activities in connection with empowerment of people. He is in the network of the Non-Governmental Organisations for Panchayat activities. He involves himself in capacity building exercise for local body leaders. He has evolved training module and manual for local body leaders. He has to his credit twenty-nine books, seventy-five articles in reputed journals, ten working papers, seven monographs, seven review articles on three major areas, namely, Legislative Behaviour, Ethnicity and Panchayati Raj System. He was a recipient of Fellowship from Sastri Indo-Canadian Institute, New Delhi and World Academy of Art and Science, USA. He is the Chairman of the Tamil Nadu Council for Sustainable Livelihoods. He has visited the US and Canada, on academic assignments. He was a visiting fellow in the MiGill University, Canada in 1989. He is a life member of Indian Institute of Public Administration, Indian Association of Public Administration, Indian Association of Political Science, Indian Association of American Studies and Indian Association of Canadian Studies. He is a member of the expert committee constituted by the Government of Tamil Nadu, to monitor the training programme for local body leaders.

DYNAMICS OF NEW PANCHAYATI RAJ SYSTEM IN INDIA

Volume I

SELECT STATES

Edited by
G. PALANITHURAI

CONCEPT PUBLISHING COMPANY, NEW DELHI-110059

ISBN 81-7022-911-1 (Vol. I)
ISBN 81-7022-910-3 (Series)

First Published 2002

Published and Printed by
Ashok Kumar Mittal
Concept Publishing Company
A/15-16, Commercial Block, Mohan Garden
New Delhi-110059 (India)
Phones: 5648039, 5649024
Fax: 091–(11)–5648053
E-mail: publishing@conceptpub.com

TO

THE DIVINE MOTHER

We trust the people
We have faith in the people
It is the people who must
determine their own destinies
and the destiny of the Nation
To the people of India, let us
ensure maximum democracy and
maximum devolution. Let the
people be empowered.

– *Rajiv Gandhi*

PREFACE

Why this multi-volume set on *New Panchayati Raj System in India*? In what way is this multi-volume set different from the other one published by the National Institute of Rural Development, Hyderabad, and the *Status of Panchayati Raj in the States and Union Territories of India 2000* published by the Institute of Social Science and Concept Publishing Company apart from an array of books published by various companies on the same area? Panchayati Raj in India is a vital question to be answered in this volume which will justify the need of the present work. New Panchayati Raj System, though created constitutionally, will work at the grassroots level in different depths and indicate different dimensions and directions. Its activities are the results of the imaginations of the people and their leaders. Interpretations and explanations on the functioning of the New Panchayati Raj System from the perspective of the provisions of the 73rd Constitutional Amendment and the conformity Act of the respective States are abundant. Functioning of the new system is beyond the purview of the provisions of the local bodies acts. This institution is in the hands of the bureaucrats of the State governments and the people. The pattern of the functioning depends on the level of the hold over Panchayats by the State government, bureaucrats and the people. Further perspectives are also different on the same institutions among the scholars, administrators and politicians. Hence one cannot predict accurately in what direction this new system would move. Especially on the functioning of the new system one cannot rely only on the provisions of the Act. It is beyond the provisions of the act, when it works with the involvement of the people.

This work focuses more on the activities of the new system. It looks at the new system not from the perspective of the legal provisions alone. It goes beyond the established order. It touches the vital activity dimensions of the new institution. Hence this work is different from the earlier works. It projects the realities and trivialities of the Panchayati Raj System in various States in India.

Normally when the workload is increased, naturally the problems associated with the quantum of work will also be increased. Hence there may be gaps in this work and the same would be filled up in the follow up volumes at a later date. Bringing out a multi volume set is not an easy task. I have tried my level best to put the substantive issues in a proper perspective. I have contacted the scholars throughout the country in this connection. Responses are very positive and yet there are problems as some of the scholars have promised, but not delivered the article which ultimately delayed the process of finalysing the whole set. This type of delay is unavoidable in the academic world as priorities of the individuals are different due to pressure of works. But many of the scholars who are always busy in their profession have devoted time and energy and they took pain to complete the task which they have undertaken. I profusely thank all the scholars who have contributed to this multi volume set. I would like to place on record my sense of gratitude to Dr. B.S. Bhargava who was instrumental for this task. He has been encouraging and reminding me all through to bring out this multi volume set in time. My faculty and my family are my two legs for my academic journey and these institutions with the presence of committed individuals have helped me immensely to devote much of my time on academic endeavours. Besides all these individuals, the institution in which I work, Gandhigram Rural Institute though a small in size but the spirit it emits made me accomplish this work in Panchayati Raj. Gandhigram Rural Institute is not an institution but a movement of the grassroots democracy which is ultimately responsible for my work. This credit goes to the two disciples of Mahatma Gandhi Dr. Soundaram and Dr. Ramachandran who founded this institute with the lofty ideals of creating a society of the people who live in peace and prosperity by maintaining harmonious relationship with nature. I earnestly register my profound gratitude to them for their noble action of creating the institute which works towards the successful implementation of the Panchayati Raj System in India.

G. Palanithurai

CONTENTS

Preface vii
List of Contributors xi
Introduction xiii

1. Towards Decentralization of Power
 – ***G. Palanithurai*** 1
2. Panchayati Raj Institutions in India
 – ***E.S. Venkataramaiah*** 14
3. The Local Planning Process : Evolution and Transition to a New System
 – ***K.V. Sundaram*** 34
4. The Panchayats of the Scheduled Areas
 – ***B.R. Purohit*** 63
5. Governance from the Grassroots
 – ***M.P. Boraian*** 83
6. The Panchayat System in West Bengal
 – ***Prabhat Datta** and **Chandan Datta*** 93
7. Panchayati Raj, Decentralized Planning and Development in Kerala
 – ***Sunny George** and **K.N. Lelithabhai*** 141
8. New Panchayati Raj System at Work : Karnataka
 – ***N. Sivanna*** 200
9. Rural Local Government in Andhra Pradesh
 – ***M. Sarumathy*** 242

Bibliography 279
Index 287

LIST OF CONTRIBUTORS

M.P. Boraiyan
Reader in Extension Education, Gandhigram Rural Institute,
Gandhigram - 624 302.

Prabhat Datta
Centenary Professor of Public Administration,
Calcutta University.

Chandan Datta
Society for Participatory Research in Asia (PRIA),
42, Tughlakabad Institutional Area, New Delhi - 110 062.

Sunny George
Associate Professor
Kerala Institute of Local Administration, Thrissur - 680 581.

K.N. Lelithabhai
Research Assistant,
Kerala Institute of Local Administration, Thrissur - 680 581.

B.R. Purohit
Professor Emeritus,
Madhya Pradesh Institute of Social Science Research,
Ujjain, Madhya Pradesh.

M. Sarumathy
Faculty Member, Centre for Panchayati Raj,
National Institute of Rural Development,
Rajendra Nagar,
Hyderabad - 30.

G. Palanithurai
Professor and Head,
Department of Political Science and Development Administration, Gandhigram Rural Institute,
Gandhigram - 624 302.

N. Sivanna
Joint Project Director,
Decentralised Governance and Planning,
Institute of Social Science and Economic Change,
Nagarbhavi, Bangalore - 560 072.

K.V. Sundaram
Development Consultant,
641, Sector-A, Pocket-C,
Vasant Kunj, New Delhi - 110 070.

Late Justice E.S. Venkataramaiah
Former Chief Justice of India, New Delhi.

INTRODUCTION

> The village Republic will be managed by a Panchayat which will be living political force and entity. Panchayats will be united in a free and voluntary association by ever widening circle of "village republics". It will not be an "apex sustained by the bottom" but an oceanic circle where centre will be the individual always ready to perish for the village, the latter ready to perish for the circle of villages and so on, sharing the majesty of the oceanic circle which they are parts.
>
> – *Mahatma Gandhi*

Considerable amount of thought has gone into the academic discourses especially in the domain of social science on decentralization of powers after the introduction of new policies throughout the world in the name of globalization, liberalization and privatization. Decentralization of powers in the context of globalization of economy makes every one to think that it is not a logical exercise which is going on in the world. However it seems paradoxical, both globalization and decentralization are both overtly and covertly managing the society, government and the market. Logical arguments have been built up for the introduction of globalization of economy decentralization of powers. It is beyond doubt human aspirations for betterment of life and comforts need growth in economy which propels the State to initiate new course of action. The process of growth has been accelerated with higher speed compared to the process in the previous era. This is called Globalization. Globalization emphasizes the system management and development. Decentralization of powers is being perceived yet another course of action in the development process of the society. Decentralization of powers is oriented towards building the capacity of the people to administer development and social equity by using a new device. The two courses of action are not taking place in the same intensity, dimensions and nature in all the countries of the world. Globalization and decentralization take place at different levels in the countries. One cannot see uniformity in the operation of the two concepts all over the world. They are operationalized and carried out by the countries based on the level of understanding of the people on the two concepts. Further depending on the need of the country the two courses of actions are being activated and carried out with varying degrees.

In India, in the changing global context, decentralization has been taken up with much resistance from various quarters as it breaks the barriers of the institutions to enable the people to have control over the public institutions.

To give concrete shape to the decentralization of power, Constitution of India has been amended. 73rd and 74th Constitutional Amendment Acts have initiated the process of decentralizing powers to grassroots institutions. To operationalize the whole schema, the provincial governments have enacted provincial acts known as conformity acts to confirm the basic principles of the 73rd and 74th Constitutional Amendments. Activities are initiated at different levels to concretize the grassroots institutions at the bottom. Primarily the successful installation of the institutions at the bottom depends on presence of political will on the part of the leader who is managing the affairs of the province, cooperation of the bureaucracy from the level of Secretary to the Village Administrative Officer, Capacity of the Local Body Leaders and the awareness of the people about the new system.

For the past four years the grassroots institutions are in vogue at various levels in terms of their functioning in different States. To give a fair account of the institutions in terms of their structure, function and functional consequences this work is contemplated. It is a multi-volume set. The first volume has articles covering some of the basic principles of decentralization of powers and the same in some of the leading provinces which are known for their commitment towards decentralization of power.

First article by G. Palanithurai, deals with the basic features of decentralization of powers. In his seminal article "Towards Decentralization of Powers" he has underscored the fundamental principles on which powers have been devolved to the grassroots level institutions through out the world. He has taken the principles from the experiences of many of the countries in the world. This article provides a basic framework for analysis. Since broader principles have been given it will be of immense use for the researchers to pursue their analysis in the backdrop of the framework. Illustrations and explanations are given for each and every principle by drawing instances from the Indian experience. In the second part of the article, he has explained the characteristics of the 73rd Constitutional Amendment Act. Thus the first article sets the tone for the entire work by giving an analytical framework.

Second article "Panchayati Raj Institutions in India" written by late Justice. E.S. Venkataramaiah, is a succinct portrayal of historical events from the epic age to the passing of 73rd Amendment to the Constitution of India. This article has given a historical perspective to the concept of decentralization of powers. He had traced the history of the institutions and explained the historical progression of these ideas over the years by crossing various stages upto the enactment of the 73rd Amendment to the Constitution of India.

Third article "The Local Planning Process : Evolution and Transaction to a New System" by K. V. Sundaram addresses the basic issues of decentralization of powers namely administering development and social justice through planning at the grassroots level with the participation of the people. With his rich experience as an adviser in various decision making bodies both at the national and international levels he unequivocally focussed the issue of planning at the micro level in the backdrop of the history of the movements of the people towards participation. This article has covered the entire history of planning at the micro level from community development to the present amendment to the Constitution of India. Adequately needed information and explanation have been given in the article for the concept of local level planning. Substantial amount of attention has been given to the methods and steps to be followed in the exercise in the article. It is almost a practical guide for all multi level planning.

B.R. Purohit, in his article "The Panchayats of the Scheduled Area" highlighted the salient features of the provisions of the act meant for scheduled areas and how it has been operationalised in Madhya Pradesh by drawing inferences from the field. M.B. Boraian, in his suggestive article looked at the issues involved in governance at the grassroots level from the perspective of welfare policies formulated for the development of rustic folk. Under the new dispensation, for effective management of development in rural areas he has suggested a new paradigm of initiatives.

Prabhat Datta and Chandan Datta in their article "The Panchayat System in West Bengal" touched the basic philosophy of decentralization of powers and traced the history of Local Self Government in West Bengal. Though it covers all aspects of the grassroots institutions in West Bengal since inception, it specifically touches the functional aspects of Panchayats. Structures, functions and responsibilities of the Panchayats have been described. Performances have also been analysed in this article. The authors have highlighted the major achievements of the grassroots institutions on the issues which affect the livelihood of the people. The left parties have their own perspectives on dealing with issues. Hence, on major issues how Panchayats have been placed to deal with, has been explained in the article. Since West Bengal is considered as one of the pioneering States in devolving powers, major exercises made in the Panchayats by the State government have been discussed and explained fully well in this article. In this write-up wide coverage has been given to the functional and performance aspects of decentralization of power that take shape in West Bengal.

"Panchayati Raj in Kerala" by Sunny George and K.N.Lalithabhai, is a detailed account of the people's movement in Kerala exhibited through the newly created Panchayati Raj system. In their article they have analysed all those issues akin to the functioning of New Panchayati Raj System in seven sections. The article includes the history of development in Kerala, philosophy of Kerala's decentralization, decentralized planning, detailed account of the Panchayati Raj system in Kerala, implications of the planning exercise and the evaluation of the whole of decentralization of powers. It gives a fair account of the New Panchayati Raj System in Kerala.

Eighth article entitled "New Panchayati Raj System in Karnataka at Work" by N. Sivanna, depicts the whole process of decentralization of powers in Karnataka. It covers the framework of analysis, historical background of the Panchayati Raj System, the process of decentralization of powers from 1983, powers and functions assigned to the institutions, finance devolved to the Panchayats, income and expenditure pattern of Panchayats, planning and decision making of Panchayats and relationship between the officials and non-officials. He has analysed the structure functions, finances and performances of the institutions. All the three institutions have been evaluated in terms their performance. Case analysis has been conducted for this purpose.

M. Sarumathy's article "Rural Local Government in Andhra Pradesh" is a detailed account of the structural arrangements of the Panchayati Raj system under the new dispensation, assigned functions to the three tier Panchayats, Panchayats in the scheduled areas, evaluation of the institutions in terms of their functions, recommendations of the Finance Commission and performance of the women leaders and *Dalit* leaders in the Panchayats.

In this volume the authors by their standing in the field with the institutional background authentically focused their attention on the basic philosophy and principles of decentralization of powers, structure of the Panchayati institutions, functions assigned to the three tier Panchayats and performance of these institutions on the issues of the people. This volume will give a clear picture about the prevailing trends in decentralization of powers in some of the States. The second volume would focus the trends of the same in other States of the Indian Union.

(In India) one should begin with the old Panchayat system in the villages and the work upto the top. The Panchayat system and the guilds are more representative and they have a living contact with people, they are the parts of the people's ideas.

— *Sri Aurobindo*

1

TOWARDS DECENTRALIZATION OF POWER

G. PALANITHURAI

Decentralization

In the recent decades, federal governments in the world have started decentralizing political, financial and administrative responsibilities to lower level institutions and even to the extent of private sectors. Decentralization is more specific and intensive in developing countries as they face a number of problems in governance. But it is ultimately due to the extreme political pressure on the central system of governance with an expectation of proper delivery of services, effective mobilization of resources and allocations, and stability in the macro economic system along with equity.

Variety of experiences have been gained by nations in the whole process of decentralization of power. There are ups and downs in the experiments and a stage has come not to argue or debate on whether decentralization is "good" or "bad" is unproductive since decentralization is a political reality throughout the world. Against this background, India had made a historical and significant attempt through 73rd Constitutional Amendment to decentralize powers to local bodies. This writeup provides basic details about the whole process of decentralization of powers from the stage of introducing 73rd Constitutional Amendment Act to activating grassroots level institutions in the backdrop of the conceptual framework.

Multiplicity of Concepts

For the concept "decentralization of power", a variety of concepts have been used by the academics and administrators and yet the meanings of the concepts are not the same. Using the concepts such as Local Self Government, Local Government, Grassroots democracy, Grassroots institutions, Panchayat Raj, Panchayati Raj, Panchayati Raj System, New Panchayati Raj System, Local Body Institutions, Empowering people, Small Government Approach and Decentralized Governance interchangeably to connote the same meaning of devolving powers and responsibilities from higher level governing institutions to lower level governing institutions. Of course, all the concepts are not the same and semantic differences ought to prevail among the concepts.

Some of the concepts are western in origin and many of them are indigenous in nature. The concepts have contextual meanings too. Academics and administrators have been using those concepts interchangeably to connote a broader meaning that the problems of people at the community level are being tackled through service facilities rendered by legitimately created institutions.

At present "Decentralization of Power" is mostly an accepted concept all over the world and hence it is being used everywhere. But at the same time some of the concepts are used as rhetorics such as empowering people and grassroots democracy.

New Initiative

It is essential to look at the emergence of the new institutional mechanism to perform certain duties and responsibilities in the backdrop of the context. All over the world countries have introspected their development path and initiated the corrective mechanism in the light of the reforms introduced on the domain of economy of the developed countries. The new developments in India is the outcome of an introspection which resulted in the introduction of new policy initiatives which are quite opposite to the path ways of prosperity which India have followed so far.

At present, the three forces state, market and society are at loggerheads because of the increased market oriented economic activities and its resultant activities of controlling over the power of the state and the society. State cannot abdicate its responsibilities as people's participation in the development process has been increased and the influence of the democratic institutions has been expanded. States are not able to control over the influence of the market and hence a parallel organizational setup is needed to contain the activities of the market when they are exploitative in character. To maintain equilibrium in the system it was thought of empowering the people through an organizational mechanism.

Objectives of Decentralization

Objectives vary from country to country depending on their needs and conditions. In India, the objectives are broader and more deeper as they have to create far reaching results in the attitude, behaviour, performance and the life style of the people who live in the rural areas.The objectives are:

(a) Deepening of Democracy

The confined democracy within the framework of the parliament and state legislatures has to be broadened to percolate into the society to the level of the last rung of the society. Collectivities who have been hitherto marginalised and deprived have to be brought into the fold of democracy. More numbers from the women and Dalit have to be brought into the system of governance. This should be an affirmative action by which the marginalised and depressed have been given an exclusive space through reservation of seats in the local bodies. Thus it is a process by which democracy is being widened and deepened.

(b) Ensuring People's Participation

People's participation is *sine qua non* for development. Development initiatives are to come from the people. People are the initiators and government is the facilitator. To make the government as facilitator from the role of a provider, people have to take initiative and accept new responsibilities. Their participation in the development activities will bring accountability on the part of the government. People have to assess their requirement and chalk out schemes and programmes according to their own needs. They should be people's programmes and government has to participate in the programmes by facilitating the people to carry out their programmes on their own.

(c) More Responsibilities to the People

In the past fifty years, all the responsibilities of the people and the community had been taken away from them and vested with government departments. Communities had enormous responsibilities to manage their affairs on their own and they have their own management system. In the name of nation-state, governments have expanded their departments. The expansion of the government has increased only the management cost and not the efficiency in delivery. To deliver the service worth of one rupee, government takes six rupees as delivery charge. Moreover the quality of service is also poor. In this structural expansion of the government, people had lost their orientation towards the responsibilities that have to be discharged by themselves as citizens. Ultimately what we find in the society, is that people have voters orientation and they do not have the citizens orientation. In order to make the people as responsible citizens, more responsibilities have to be given to them. Hence development works could be allowed to be done with the involvement of people.

(d) Reduction of Government Structure

Many of the countries in the world are facing crisis as a result of the expansion of the Departments of Governments. Bigness of Government is a burden on the society. It will pave way for the disintegration of the nations. The unwieldy expansion of government departments becomes a threat to elected representatives. Moreover people are terrorised by the government through its procedures, rules and regulations. Larger the size of the government lesser the contact with the people. Hence there will be a gap between the people and the government. In order to avoid this complication of the bigness of the government, it was felt that the structure of the government could be reduced to the minimum level and this could be possible only by giving more responsibilities to the people through the institutions created legitimately.

(e) Harnessing the Human Energy

It is a truism that the way in which the human energy is being utilised development could be achieved accordingly. Human energy has different forms and different levels. The state should find a way to raise the level of the energy of people and more particularly the state should work out a detailed mechanism through which the energy of people could be utilised. The developed nations have demonstrated to the world as to how best the energy level of people could be enhanced and how best the enhanced energy could be utilised for activities to accelerate economic growth. To utilise the energy of people, space could be created approximately. It was thought of as an institutional arrangement to utilise the energy of people. At energy level, institutional mechanism could be created for this purpose. Local Body institutions are one such institutional device or mechanism to make use of the human energy for productive functions.

(f) Administering Development and Social Justice

It is a well known fact that countries which are in the process of decentralizing powers have different objectives. But in India, it was a conscious decision of the central government that Panchayati Raj institutions have to work for administering development and social justice by evolving their own plan of action. Traditionally, Panchayati Raj has been looked at as an institution meant for providing services and facilities. But in the new context, it is meant for not only services and facilities but also growth with equity.

(g) Planning from the below

So far, planning exercise had been done at the central level which resulted in large scale demands of the people unmet. In the fifty two years of governance, the centralised planning has achieved tremendous results in macro economics of this country and yet the rural realities have not been changed drastically towards achieving development. Still people are living in sub-human living conditions in the rural and urban areas. In order to provide basic facilities, to make use of the facilities to growth and to bring economic activities planning exercise has to be done at the micro level. This exercise had been thought of many times in independent India. Whether planning institutions could be created at the bottom either at the block level or at the district level. Now this concept gained currency and planning exercise has to be initiated at different levels starting from Gram Panchayat.

(h) Building the Capacity of People

It is an imperative in decentralization of power that people should take more responsibilities and discharge the same effectively and efficiently to deliver the services with quality to the people. To perform the new responsibilities, capacity of the people have to be increased. Till date, people have developed an attitude that the government would provide everything and people have to receive the same. Now the role has been reversed. People have to manage their affairs on their own. Therefore, the new system envisages a new task of building the capacity of the leaders and the people. In a market driven economy for every act people require skill and efficiency. People with skills are to be updated and upgraded to match the requirement of the market. Against this background capacity building assumes significance.

(i) Establishing the Principle of Subsidiarity

The whole exercise has to revolve around the principle of subsidiarity. Activities that could be carried out at the lower level could be allowed to be carried out at that level and things that could not be carried out at that lowest level could be allowed to be carried out at the next higher level and likewise, activities are to be carried out at the appropriate levels depending on the capacity of people. Based on the above principle, powers are to be devolved.

Putting the Last First

The fifty years of development in India demonstrates a postulate that development could not be achieved without the involvement of the people in the development process as a stake holder. In all these years, development programmes are the programmes and schemes of the government and not of the people. In the whole development process one would find the people as the last beneficiaries. Nonetheless, development was not achieved as planned. Now programmes should not be generated by the government but they have to be evolved by the people. Programmes and schemes are to be owned by the people. Governments have to participate in the programmes and schemes of the people. Thus, people come first and the government comes next.

Establishing Good Governance

Administration demonstrates to the people that it would alienate people and it is very difficult to understand. Proliferation of administrative procedures, norms and regulations has made the system totally non-transparent. As long as administration is being run on nontransparent way corruption will continue to entrench every nook and corner of the society. To avoid such malaise, the administration could simplify the procedures, norms and regulations. The whole process has to be initiated from below. This administration should be transparent. Further, it would accommodate every segment of the society and especially women and marginalised.

It should be Pro-Nature

The alarming environmental problems and global warming cautioning our policy makers and administrators that unless serious actions are not taken our life will become problematic. Hence the global scenario needs local action to protect the environment. Activities of the people should be oriented towards protecting the environment and maintaining the natural order. While taking decisions at the micro level and implementing schemes and programmes for rural development adequate care should be taken to protect the flora and fauna. All the ponds, wells, tanks, channels and lanes are to be protected and maintained properly. All the commons are to be well secured and managed. There is a close link between environmental problems and poverty. Green is the lifeline of the poor. By protecting the green, the poor can be given life.

It should be Pro-Poor

All the activities are to be decided on the basis of equity. While taking decisions and fixing priorities for rural development activities, Panchayat has to decide whether the benefits would reach the poor. Normally in the absence of basic facilities and amenities, rich does not bother about it, because they could afford to purchase the same. Poor men's life will be miserable in the absence of public facilities and basic amenities. Hence priority has to be given to the poor. 'Unto the last' has to be the policy of the Panchayat. Poorest of the poor has to be given priority in deciding benefits.

It should be Pro-Women

This is yet another important sector which needs care and attention. Panchayat activities have to be carefully designed so as to provide enough scope for women both in terms of participation and benefits. Hitherto the neglected section of the society is women, who could be integrated into the mainstream of economic and political activities. Further, among the problems faced by the rural society, 70 to 80 per cent of them are being faced directly by the women in the absence of basic amenities, facilities and services. Hence the decentralized political institutions nearer to the people should have resilience to accommodate women folk in their activities.

With the above posited objectives, an amendment has been introduced in the parliament to amend the Constitution of India so as to create systematic structure at the lowest level of the socio-political system. The following are the characteristics of the 73rd Constitutional Amendment Act.

73rd Constitutional Amendment Act

73rd Amendment to the Constitution of India is a guideline and a basic framework evolved to guide the state governments to take initiative of organising grassroots democracy as a system of governance to administer development and social justice. It opens up a new chapter in the modern political history of India. It has certain key characteristics which cannot be set aside by the state governments. They are:

(a) Constitutional Entity

The New Panchayati System came into being as an institution of governance with the approval of the Constitution and it is placed in the third stratum of the hierarchy of the institutions of governance. It enjoys the status as enjoyed by the parliament and state legislature in terms of its existence and conduct of election. It is a permanent institution with earmarked role and responsibilities to be discharged by the newly created institutions.

(b) A New Phenomenon in Federalism

In a federal structure there should be two constituent units to maintain their relationship in administering development and peace through the institutional mechanism. There shall be division of powers between the central government and the provincial governments. Likewise, there shall be sharing of resources between the central and state governments. But now, there is a third institution which has come into being as institution of self governance with distinct and categorical political, financial and administrative powers to administer development and social justice. Now the concept of federalism brings a new meaning which explains the relationship among the three institutions namely federal, regional and local. Hence, 73rd Constitutional Amendment brought a new phenomenon in Indian federalism.

(c) From Representative Democracy to People's Democracy

Indian Democracy has the character of a representative form of government and the decision making has been based on the representations made by the representatives of the people both in the Parliament and state legislatures. It is an irony that hundred crore people are being represented by around four thousand and seven hundred representatives of the people through state legislatures and national parliament. It is natural that a representative cannot represent millions of people. Hence, even after fifty years of Independence, basic facilities and amenities have not been provided to the people. Now the concept of representation has been changed to direct participation of people in the governing process and thereby an institutional mechanism namely Gram Sabha was created to enable the people to participate in the development process. Gram Sabha is the basic institution created for the benefit of the people to participate and administer development. To make the people associate themselves with the community in order to discuss about the problems of the community and to find out solutions to the problems it has been created. It should be an absolute organization of the people. This body will nurture democratic principles in the community. Gram Sabha is giving meaning to the concept "Empowerment of People". Cutting across caste, creed and colour, people will participate in the meeting on equal footings.

(d) Three-tier Structure

The new system envisages a three-tier structure namely gram, block and district Panchayats. The entire Panchayati system is operating in the area of a district. To administer development, the entire development administration is being divided into three units. All the three units are independent in certain respects and inter dependent in certain respects. Gram Panchayat will function at the lowest level and Block Panchayat will function at the Block level and District Panchayat will function at the district level. Roles and responsibilities, powers and duties for each tier will be clearly demarcated and they have to function as per the powers conferred upon them. Development activities have to be carried out by lower level units and planning, coordination, monitoring and supervision activities have be carried out by the district level body namely District Panchayats.

(e) 11th Schedule and Earmarked 29 Subjects

The New Panchayati System is grounded perfectly in the domain of governance authoritatively only through the 11th Schedule conferring 29 subjects to the rural local bodies. As indicated in the constitution the state subjects, central subjects, Panchayat subjects have indicated 29 items of work. Of the 29 subjects, which of the subjects are to be allocated to Gram Panchayat and other tiers could be spelt out by the state government through legislation. The role of the state government is to allocate appropriate duties and responsibilities to each tier of the Panchayats. 73rd Constitutional

Amendment has indicated the suggestive items. It is not an exhaustive list. If the state government wants to give more powers to the local bodies there is no bar. It is more appropriate if the 11th Schedule is given in the fourth list as central list, state list, concurrent list and Panchayat list.

(f) Reservation of Seats for Women

Reservation of seats for women in all the tiers of local bodies is a new phenomenon in governance. When Rajiv Gandhi brought the 64th Amendment bill only 25% of the seats were earmarked for women. The one-third reservation of seats for women had been the contribution of P.V. Narasimha Rao.The one third reservation of seats for women has propelled the whole nation to moot out another demand of the same proportion of reservation of seats for women in the State Legislatures and National Parliament. It is a moot question as to why the reservation of seats for women only in the local bodies? It is unequivocal from the reply given by many in the authoritative bodies that in the absence of basic facilities the worst sufferers are the women. The sufferings of the women are not felt by the policy makers since they are mostly men. By giving the opportunity of taking decision to the women, they would reduce the burden of the women. There is yet another argument that the women have a legitimate space in governance which should be ensured to them. All along they had been marginalised and now it is felt that it should be given to them. It is their space which is being occupied by men. The next explanation is that while deepening democracy, deprived sections have to be included in the fold of the governing bodies and hence they are included by making exclusive reservation of seats for women.

(g) Reservation of Seats for Dalits

Reservation of seats for Dalits in the state legislatures and national parliament is not so difficult as these institutions are far away from the communities. Hurdles are not so high for them to function as members of legislative institutions. They are always looked at from the party perspective and not on caste perspective. But it is very difficult for the Dalits to emerge as they are seen by the society from the caste perspective. The whole of human rights violations, discriminations and social injustice are the frequent occurrence at the grassroots level. Voices are raised vociferously from the marginalised. Both centre and state governments have not fulfilled the objective of administering social justice. Hence it is felt that the responsibilities of administrating social justice could be handed over to lower level institution of governance and thereby it has been handed over to local bodies. This process starts from providing reservation of seats to the Dalits in the local bodies as it has been done to women, proportionate to their population. By creating this clause in the constitutional amendment, the marginalised has been properly given adequate representation. This is yet another revolutionary step taken by the government knowing fully well that the caste ridden Indian society has to pass through the social conflict for some time.

(h) Creation of Finance Commission

It is a well known fact that the Panchayats had been crippled in the past only by reducing the financial allocation to Panchayats as that power was vested with the state government. In order to overcome this eventuality the amendment has incorporated a provision and by which a Finance Commission has to be constituted in every state to suggest ways and means to share the resources between the local bodies and the state government and in the same way, how local body finance could be strengthened. By creating this provision in the amendment act, financial flow to local bodies has been ensured regularly and this provision enables the local body institutions to keep themselves on a permanent footing.

(i) Creation of Election Commission

To elect about 4,700 representatives for State Legislatures and National Parliament, an independent election commission has been created and which functions in all the states at present. As per the new provision, representatives to the tune of 30 millions have to be elected and for which a massive machinery is needed. Against this backdrop, a permanent election commission has been created. Conducting the election to the local bodies is the main earmarked function of the State Election Commission.

(j) District Planning Committee

Though planning is a much loaded concept and publicised word among the people since the days of Jawaharlal Nehru, the Planning Commission at the centre and the state are not the constitutional entity. But the District Planning Committee is the constitutional creation.This district planning committee has come to stay with a specific purpose of altering the planning process. As per the new dispensation, planning exercise has to be initiated from below. For the development of the whole district, the planning committee has to prepare a perspective development plan. Thus, the central concept of planning has been recognized at all the three levels as institutions of governance function at all the three levels to administer development.

Ensuring Regular Election to Panchayati Raj System

Election to Local Bodies was the will and pleasure of the state governments. That is why election was not conducted for Local Bodies for about fifteen years in the past. Any number of reasons could be projected for postponing the election. But through the new dispensation election has been ensured as it has been ensured to parliament and state legislatures. The provision which is applicable to the election of Lok Sabha and state legislature is applicable to New Panchayati Raj system. Hence, New Panchayati Raj System has become a permanent entity. No state government can withhold election beyond six months. The above stated features are the key characteristics of the 73rd Constitutional amendment act and the spirit of the above act has to be carried out by enacting a suitable conformity act at the provincial level.

2

PANCHAYATI RAJ INSTITUTIONS IN INDIA

E.S. VENKATARAMAIAH

I have selected the subject "Panchayati Raj Institutions in India" for discussion here, because, I consider that there is no other socio-political programme launched by any government in independent India, which has generated so much public enthusiasm and opportunity for the participation of the people as the establishment of Panchayati Raj Institutions and Municipalities which constitute a back bone of the Local Self Government in the country. Parts IX and IX-A of the Constitution of India which were introduced in 1993, require the State governments to establish such institutions.

Mahatma Gandhi wrote in *Harijan* in 1942, defining his vision of village Panchayat in the following words:-

> "My idea of village *swaraj* is that it is a complete republic, independent of its neighbours for its own vital wants and yet interdependent for many others in which dependence is a necessity ..... The Government of the village will be conducted by the Panchayat of five persons annually elected by the adult villagers, males and females, possessing minimum prescribed qualifications. These will have all the authority and jurisdiction required. Since there will be no system of punishment in the accepted sense, the Panchayat will be the legislature , judiciary and executive combined to operate for its year of office. Any village can become such a republic today without much

> interference even from the present government whose sole effective connection with the villages is the exaction of the village revenue. Here there is perfect democracy based upon individual freedom. The individual is the architect of his own Government"

In the United Kingdom there are local authorities — county councils, county borough councils, administrative councils of county district and Parish councils. They enjoy a good deal of autonomy as the local bodies. In the United States of America too there are local bodies exercising both legislative and Executive powers in respect of matters of local interest such as education, health, poor relief, sanitation, maintenance of local roads, lighting up of streets and thoroughfares. Promotion of local safety in respect of fire and other accidents, regulation of building activities, functions relating to cultural development such as maintaining and supporting of Art. galleries, museums, zoos, libraries and places of public recreation such as parks and gardens and centres of games and sports, preservation of environment, disposal of wastes, regulation of food supplies through well maintained markets are some of the activities of the local bodies in the West. These local bodies no doubt function under the National Government. Their role in the administration of the country has led to great appreciation in the hands of leading authors in Political Science. Sidgwick writes that the term Local Self Government in a Unitary State means organs, which though completely subordinate to the legislature, are independent of the Central Executive in appointment and to some extent in their decisions and exercise partially independent control over certain parts of public finance. As regards the Constitutional relationship between the Central Government and Local Government, the latter derives its powers from the former and is subordinate to the authority that created it but, though a subordinate body, yet it has certain independence of action. Within the sphere assigned to it, it can make its own rules or regulations or bye-laws to perform its functions and to control its finances. Harold Laski says that "Local Self Government offers the best opportunity to people to bring knowledge, interest and enthusiasm to bear on the solution of their local problems". R.M. Mac Iver writes in his book *The Modern*

State that local interests merge into national interests in variant degrees and particularly with the emergence of the welfare State there are hardly any matters, of local concern that are not matters of national concern. The real problem is to assure at once the reality and responsibility of the local government. Willoughby, De Tocqueville, Carl Friedrich, A.Robson, John Stuart. Mill and several others have all written about the need for establishing and encouraging local authorities. There are local authorities functioning in France and other States in the continental Europe. It is believed that democracy can be nourished and sustained only by maintenance of local bodies which constitute the "grassroots" of democracy. They alone provide the necessary atmosphere for the sustenance of democratic spirit which every liberty loving person cherishes.

In India, several centuries ago, there were small village bodies which had some sort of organised local government discharging various functions including maintenance of law and order under the aegis of the Imperial Government which was functioning from the capital of the country in which these villages were situated. These village institutions gradually withered away and went out of existence on account of several foreign invasions. At any rate after the advent of the British during the regime of Lord Ripon, who was kindly disposed towards the establishment of self-government institutions, a Resolution on Local Self Government was passed in 1882. Self governing institutions which were so far confined to towns and cities were liberalised and extended to rural areas. District Boards were established with jurisdiction over Taluks and Tehsils and with controlling powers vested in the Provincial Governments. This development was considered desirable as an instrument of political and popular education and, therefore, the strength of official element was reduced to not more than 1/3 in both rural and urban local boards and elective principle was adopted for filling non-official seats. In 1883-84, many British Indian Provinces passed Local Self Government Acts to give effect to the policy laid down by the Resolution. The object of the Resolution, it was obvious, was the development of public spirit and training in the exercise of political power. The bureaucracy which was running the government was however alarmed at the liberal tendency of the Acts and worked for the containment of their operation. The Boards were handicapped from the beginning by their narrow functions, their limited powers and their inadequate representative character and ultimately owing to the illiberal attitude of the bureaucracy which was operating the levers of administrative power at the beginning of the present century, the experiment failed to realise the aims set by Lord Ripon. Consequently, the District Boards, Taluk Boards, Village Panchayats, Municipalities and Municipal boroughs and corporations which had been established in the British Indian Provinces and in many Indian States under various local laws and which were functioning on the eve of India's independence were under the control of the bureaucracy and the provincial governments and had very little freedom in the management and the execution of even the limited functions entrusted to them, some of which were obligatory and some optional. The efficiency of these local bodies primarily depended upon the meagre financial resources that were available and the character of men elected to these local bodies.

When the Constitution was enacted, the Constitution makers visualised a federal structure of government for the country — the Central Government functioning at the level of the Union and the State Governments functioning at the level of the States. The laws governing the Local Self Government bodies like the Municipal corporations, improvement trusts, District Boards, Sanitary Boards and village Panchayats which were in force immediately before the commencement of the Constitution were continued by Art. 372 of the Constitution with certain adaptations. The subject of "Local government" that is to say, the Constitution and powers of Municipal Corporations, Improvement Trusts, District Boards, Mining Settlement Authorities and other local authorities for purpose of Local Self Government or village administration" was assigned by the Constitution to be dealt with by the States by entry 5 in List II of the 7th Schedule to the Constitution. The entry was a very wide one and it empowered the State legislatures to legislate with respect to all matters relating to local government including the Constitution and establishment of such local authorities. The Constitution also empowered the State Legislature to confer such powers upon a local authority including the power to levy taxes which the State could levy under the State list, subject to the general control of the State Legislature of the State Government.

Entry 52 of List II of the 7th Schedule of the Constitution which reads as "taxes on the entry of goods into local area for consumption, use or sale therein" empowered the State Legislature to levy a tax commonly known as Octroi, for the benefit of local authorities. The expression 'local area' in the said entry was interpreted by the Supreme Court in DIAMOND SUGAR MILLS Vs STATE OF U.P. (AIR 1961 SC 652) as meaning an area administered by a local body like a municipality, a district board, a local board, a union board or a Panchayat or the like. Art. 277 of the Constitution provided that any taxes, duties or cesses which immediately before the commencement of the Constitution were being levied by the Government of any State or by any municipality or other local authority or body for purposes of the State, municipality, district or other local areas as the case may be, may notwithstanding that such taxes, duties, cesses or fees were mentioned in the Union list would continue to be levied and applied to the same purposes until provision to the contrary was made by Parliament by law.

Apart from the above Constitutional provisions, there was an important directive principle of State policy incorporated in Art. 40 of the Constitution, which read as follows:

40. Organization of Village Panchayats

The State shall take steps to organise village Panchayats and endow them with such powers and authority as may be necessary to enable them to function as units of self government.

This directive was broadly followed by the State governments resulting in the establishment of a network of the village Panchayats all over the country and also in the strengthening of the local self government by replacing the old Local Self Government bodies which had lost their vitality. At the end of March 1956 there were about 123, 670 Gram Panchayats covering more than half the number of villagers in the country. The Second Five Year Plan envisaged that according to the tentative programme drawn up by them, the number of village Panchayats would increase to 2,44,564 which would cover almost the whole of the country side by the end of 1960-61. All the States except Tripura had legislation to establish statutory Panchayats in the rural areas. The pattern of organization, Constitution and jurisdiction of Panchayats however varied from State to State. The interplay of needs, resources available, and administrative convenience had produced a variety of policies under given local conditions. In areas covered by the former States of Saurashtra and Madhya Bharath there were three tiers of Panchayats. Assam and primary village Panchayats which acted as agents of the Rural Panchayat organization constituted by indirect election and comprising of a number of primary Panchayats. West Bengal had a two tier system namely Gram Panchayats and Anchal Panchayats, the latter comprising number of Gram Sabhas. The pyramidal structure of Panchayats in Madhya Bharat had Gram Panchayats at base, Kendra Panchayats above them, at the block level and Mandal Panchayats at the District level, the three layers being organically inter-linked. In some States, eg. Tamil Nadu and Madhya Pradesh Panchayats were classified into two categories on the basis of population and revenue. The Government of India felt that it was necessary to introduce a scheme of community project and national extension service to bring about rural upliftment which was one of the principal objects of the Directive Principles of State Policy. In order to introduce such a scheme, and to make appropriate provisions regarding organization for implementing the proposed scheme, on the recommendation of the committee on plan projects, the Government of India constituted a team for the study of community project and National Extension Service and to make appropriate recommendations to the Government of India to enable it to take suitable action. The decision to constitute such a team and the names of members of that team were communicated to all the ministries on January 16, 1957. The team consisted of Sri Balwantrai G. Mehta, a distinguished Member of Parliament, as the leader and Sri S.D. Sharma who was then serving as Minister in Madhya Pradesh and (later holding the office of the President of India), Thakur Phool Singh who was serving as Deputy Minister in Uttar Pradesh and Sri B.G. Rao, ICS, who was formerly the Chief Secretary, Government of Madhya Bharat, as members, Sri.G. Ramachandran, Director, working Committee, Gandhigram was later on included as a member of the team with effect from 3rd May 1957. The terms of reference of the said committee required the team to study and report on the community projects and national extension service scheme having regard to the economy and efficiency with special reference to following aspects:

(i) The content of the programme and the priorities assigned to different fields of activity within it;
(ii) The arrangements for the execution of the programme with special reference to;

   (a) Intensification of activities in the sphere of agricultural production;
   (b) Co-ordination between
      (1) the different Ministries/Departments at the Centre;
      (2) the centre and the States; and
      (3) the different agencies within the community projects Administration and other State Government organizations and Departments;
   (c) the organizational structure and method of work with a view to securing a greater speed in the despatch of business;

(iii) the assessment of the requirements of personnel for community Projects and National Extension Service and examination of existing training facilities in order to meet the growing requirements of personnel for extending the coverage of the programme.
(iv) the assessment of the extent to which the movement has succeeded in utilising local initiative and in creating institutions to ensure continuity in the process of improving economic and social conditions in rural areas.
(v) the methods adopted for reporting upon the results attained by the Community Projects and National Extension Service.
(vi) Any other recommendation that the Team may like to make in order to ensure economy and efficiency in the working of the community projects and the National Extension Service".

The recommendation of the above team headed by Balwantrai Mehta, made in the year 1957 that public participation in community work should be organised through statutorily organised bodies gave a fillip to the nationwide movement for decentralization of administration. The resolution of the National Development Council passed immediately thereafter affirmed the basic principle of democratic decentralization and it urged the States to work out structures suitable to each State. Accordingly the States took action to inaugurate Panchayati Raj through appropriate Acts passed by the State Legislature. Rajasthan and Uttar Pradesh took the lead in passing such Acts. S.K. Dey, Minister for community Development in Pandit Nehru's Government was the architect of Panchayati Raj. He elevated the whole of Panchayat system to a philosophical level and viewed it as an instrument which linked the individual with the universe. Due to the interest generated by the Panchayati Raj institutions in some States, several other States also set up their own committees to assess the working of their own Panchayat institutions and to recommend measures for improving them. Unfortunately owing to the lack of political will and growing social, communal and caste differences the Gram Sabhas at Panchayat level could not function properly. Elections to Panchayat bodies had to be postponed. The critical problem was the domination of Panchayati Raj institutions by economically and socially privileged classes. In Tamil Nadu itself it is stated that no elections could be held to local bodies for a period of 16 years until they were held in 1986. It is interesting however to note certain beneficent social consequences generated by the holding of elections in 1986. For instance, it is stated that in Kamudi Town Panchayat in Ramanathapuram District, the Muslims and Nadar Communities had been arch enemies for the previous 50 to 60 years. Over the past 30 years, they had opposed each other in the elections to the local bodies. But in 1986, it is stated contrary to the earlier behaviour, they got together and fielded a common candidate and got him elected. This shows that if regular elections are held, traditional rivalries will disappear and issue oriented groupings emerge. It was precisely this beneficial process that had been arrested for years by government by frequently postponing or not holding elections at all. The committee set up by the National Planning Commission with Shri G.V.K. Rao, as the chairman had stated in its report;

> "Apart from inadequate resources, elections to these bodies have not been held regularly. In fact, elections have become overdue for one or more tiers of the Panchayati Raj Institutions in eleven States and in eight States even elections to Gram Panchayats are overdue. Elections have been put off on one pretext or another ... and the term of the existing bodies have been extended or the bodies have been superseded". (CAARD 1985:41)

In 1978, the Union Government, finding that the States had not managed the Panchayati Raj Institution properly, set up a Committee with Sri Ashok Mehta as the Chairman to review the working of Panchayati Raj Institutions and in particular, among other things, to delineate their true role in the task of integrated rural development. The terms of reference of the Ashok Mehta Committee required it to suggest measures for reorganising the Panchayati Raj System and its institutions to enable them to play an effective role in the sphere of Integrated Rural Development. The terms of reference were in brief to review the existing situation regarding democratic decentralization in the States and the Union Territories, and the working of the Panchayati Raj Institutions from the district to the village level, so as to identify shortcomings and defects; to examine, in particular, the working of these institutions in respect of mobilization of resources; the nature of the machinery needed for looking after the interests of the weaker sections of society; methods of constituting the Panchayati Raj Institutions, including the system of elections, the true role of Panchayati Raj Institutions in integrated rural development, the type of relationship that should exist between the Panchayati Raj Institutions, the official administrative machinery, and the co-operative and other voluntary institutions involved in rural development, and to make such other recommendations, including those on financial matters as may be necessary to ensure adequate availability of funds for the discharge of the responsibilities that may be entrusted to the Panchayati Raj Institutions.

The Ashoka Mehta Committee submitted its report in August 1978, making 123 recommendations to revitalise Panchayati Raj as a living and integral part of the democratic continuum. The most significant recommendation of the Committee was for the creation of a two tier system of Panchayati Raj as against the three tier system recommended by the committee on Panchayati Raj Institutions, Ministry of Agriculture (1978). As regards taxation, the Ashoka Metha Committee wanted the Panchayati Raj Institutions to have compulsory powers of taxation to mobilise necessary resources of their own thereby reducing the dependence on devolution of funds from the State Government. A remarkable feature of the Ashok Metha Report was its recommendation favouring open participation of political parties in Panchayati Raj Affairs. The Committee also made some very interesting recommendations favouring the creation of certain monitoring forums to safeguard and promote the interests of the vulnerable social and economic groups in the village. An important recommendation of the Committee was that the State Government must not supersede the Panchayati Raj Institutions on partisan grounds. If, however, the suppression of a body became necessary there should be an election within six months. The Ashok Mehta report emphasised the functional necessity for the decentralization of administration in a truly democratic supervision of the work of Panchayats. Taking into consideration the paucity of service oriented people, to run the Panchayati Raj Institutions and the lack of competent democratic leadership at the village level, the Ashoka Mehta Committee made certain specific recommendations with regard to Human Resources Development. The following were the recommendations on the said question:

> "The human factor is not only a component of growth but also shapes the texture of the society. In many ways, therefore, the human resources is more vital than the financial. Development of human resources should be, therefore, a primary feature of Panchayati Raj Institutions.
>
> There should be three types of training: (i) for officials; (ii) for elected representatives; and (iii) combined courses for both

officials and elected representatives together. The programme content may vary as suited for each participating group.

The training programmes, covering officials as well as non-officials, should be of a staggering dimension. This would require not only the activation of the existing institutions, but also considerable augmentation of their resources. Suitable remedial measures should be taken to resuscitate and revitalise State level training institutions.

The National Institute of Rural Development should be the apex all-India Institution for training of trainers, field studies, developing consultancy capabilities, research work and improvement in the level of training in the States. Its faculty should be strengthend and upgraded for this purpose. The Government of India has an important role to play in this regard. There should be an evaluation for each of the training programme so that it will be possible to make necessary modulations from time to time.

Importance should be attached to the programmes for adult education to develop the latent civil consciousness in all the people and thus strengthen the faith in the working of the Panchayati Raj Institutions. The Panchayati Raj Institutions should have major role in organising such programmes.

As a large segment contributing for the successful operation of a democratic system, special attention is to be paid to the role of women in Panchayati Raj Institutions. Their role could be strengthened in two ways; by allowing them to participate in the election processes more actively and also by giving them opportunities for decision making.

To secure their participation in elections, for the two seats reserved for women in the Zilla Parishad and Mandal Panchayats any women who gets the highest number of votes in the election, even if she does not win, should be taken in as a coopted member.

There should be a committee of women to operate and look after specific programmes which largely concern women and children. This would ensure that they do not become victims of the processes of change and that decisions are made by women themselves on priorities and choices involved in their programmes. Such a committee should have powers of the Mandal Panchayat with reference to the programmes specifically assigned to them.

In designing the rural industrialization programmes there should be special efforts to concentrate on programmes to provide gainful employment to rural women. This will also strengthen their management capabilities.

The formation of Mahila Mandals should be encouraged. The present and the future success of the democratic process through Panchayati Raj Institutions lies with the rural youth. Rural youth is not yet fully covered by the Yuvak Mandals; this weakness has to be attended to. Young farmers' clubs can be formed to activate the interest of the rural youth both in Panchayati Raj Institutions and rural development.

The Yuvak Mandals should be given the status of an associate body in Panchayati Raj Institutions through suitable legislative measures.

Panchayati Raj Institutions have a motivational task in organising Nehru Yuvak Kendras.

The role of voluntary agencies in mobilising people's support for Panchayati Raj will be crucial. They should be strengthened and encouraged to supplement the efforts of the Panchayati Raj Institutions. The motivational and promotional role of the Panchayati Raj Institutions should be clearly spelt to build up and facilitate the work of voluntary agencies and women's organizations.

Voluntary agencies with requisite expertise proven standing and well-equipped organization can assist Panchayati Raj Institutions in the planning process. They can be involved in formulation of projects and to create strong public opinion in support of measures aimed at social change".

Taking into account the several reports and recommendations regarding the working of Panchayati Raj Institutions, the Government of India introduced two amendments to the Constitutions of India. The first one related to the introduction of Part IX into the Constitution consisting of Art. 243 and Art. 243-A to Art. 243-E proposing to make the establishment of Panchayati Raj Institutions in all the States obligatory and insisting that the pattern of Panchayati Raj Institutions should conform to the various provisions introduced into the Constitution by that part The statements and objects of the 64th Constitutional Amendment Bill, introduced during the Prime Ministership of Shri. Rajiv Gandhi, which proposed to introduce part IX relating to Panchayats read as follows;

"A review of the working of Panchayati Raj Institutions has shown that in many States they have become weak and ineffective owing to a variety of reasons, including the failure to hold regular and periodical elections, prolonged supersessions, inadequate representation to the weaker sections like the Scheduled Castes, the Scheduled Tribes and women, lack of financial resources and inadequate devolution of powers and responsibilities on them.

2. Having regard to the inadequacies in the existing system, and keeping in view the Directive Principles of State Policy enshrined in article 40 which aims at endowing Panchayats with such powers and authority as are necessary to enable them to function as units of self-governments, it is proposed to add a new part to the Constitution relating to the Panchayats.

3. The Bill proposes, *inter alia* to:-

   (a) make it obligatory for all States to establish a three-tier system of Panchayats at the village, intermediate and district levels; however, States having a population of less than 20 lakhs would not be obliged to establish Panchayats at the intermediate level;

   (b) provide for all seats in Panchayats at all levels to be filled by direct election; however, the State legislatures may provide for the representation in Panchayats without voting rights of members of the House of the people and the Legislatures of States and Chair Persons of Panchayats at the immediately lower level;

(c) provide for reservations to ensure the due representation in the Panchayats of the Scheduled Castes, Scheduled Tribes and women;

(d) ensure a fixed tenure of five years for the Panchayats. However, if a Panchayat is dissolved before the expiry of its term, provision is made for the conduct of election within a period of six months of the dissolution to reconstitute the Panchayat for the remainder of the term;

(e) provide for the devolution by State Legislatures of powers and responsibilities upon the Panchayats with respect to the preparation of plans for economic development and social justice and for the implementation of development schemes;

(f) provide for the sound finance of the Panchayats by securing authorization from State Legislatures for grants-in-aid to the Panchayats from the Consolidated Fund of the State, as also assignment to or appropriation by the Panchayats of the revenues of designated taxes, duties, tolls and fees;

(g) provide for the Constitution of Finance Commissions in the States every five years to review the finances of the Panchayats and recommend principles, on the basis of which State Legislatures may determine the taxes to be appropriated by, or assigned to the Panchayats, as also grants-in-aid to the Panchayats from the Consolidated Fund of the State.

(h) vest in the Election Commission the superintendence, direction and control of election to the Panchayats at all three levels;

(i) empower the Comptroller and Auditor General of India, to cause the accounts of the Panchayats audited in such manner as he may deem fit; and

(j) exempt certain States and tribal areas and other territories from the application of the provisions of Part IX or empower the President and the Governor to modify them in their application to Union territories and Scheduled areas, respectively."

The above Bill could not be passed as the requisite majority in the Parliament was not available and as a consequence, Shri Rajiv Gandhi tendered his resignation in October 1989. Then again, after the Congress Party was able to form the Government, it introduced two Bills more or less with the same provisions, found in the 62nd and 63rd Constitution Amendment Bills and on this occasion, the two Bills were passed. By the Constitution (73rd Amendment) Act, 1992, part IX was introduced into the Constitution and by the Constitution (74th Amendment) Act, 1992, Part IX-A was introduced. Part IX contained provisions relating to Panchayats and Part IX-A contained provisions relating to the municipalities. Part IX came into effect from 24th of April 1993 and Part IX-A came into effect from 1st June 1993. Two more schedules were added to the Constitution, by these amendments — the XI Schedule to the Constitution containing the subjects over which the Panchayats could be permitted to exercise powers and the XII the Schedule contained the subjects which the municipalities could be permitted to administer, Broadly, the provisions contained in Part IX relating to Panchayats summarised thus:

Part IX requires every State to constitute Panchayats at the village level and at intermediate and district levels in accordance with its provisions. It however provides that if the population of State does not exceed 20 lakhs, such a State is not required to constitute Panchayats at the intermediate level. All the seats in the Panchayats have to be filled by persons chosen by direct election from territorial constituencies in the Panchayat area, and for this purpose each Panchayat area has to be divided into territorial constituencies, in such manner that the ratio between each constituency and the number of seats allotted to it shall, so far as practicable will be the same throughout the area. It is also provided that the Legislature of the State may, by law provide for representation of the Chair Persons of the Panchayats at the village level in the Panchayats in the intermediate level and in the case of a State not having Panchayats in the intermediate level in the Panchayats in the district level of the chair persons of the Panchayats in the intermediate level in the Panchayats at district level and of the members of the House of People and of the members of the

Legislative Assembly of the State representing constituencies which comprise wholly or partly a Panchayat area at a level other than the village level in such Panchayats, and of the members of the legislative council of the State where they are registered as electors within a Panchayat area at the intermediate level, in Panchayat at intermediate level and within a Panchayat area in district level.

The chair person of a Panchayat and other members of Panchayat, whether or not chosen by direct election, from territorial constituencies, in the Panchayat area, have a right to vote in the meetings of the Panchayats. The chair person of a Panchayat at the village level shall be elected in such manner as the Legislature of the State may, by law provide and the chair person of the Panchayat at intermediate level or district level shall be elected by and from amongst the elected members thereof. It is further provided that the seats shall be reserved for Schedule Castes and Schedule Tribes in every Panchayat and the number of seats so reserved shall bear, as nearly as may be , the same proportion to the total number of seats to be filled by direct election in that Panchayat as the population of the Scheduled Castes in that Panchayat area or of the Scheduled Tribes in that Panchayat area, bears to the total population of that area and such seats shall be allotted by rotation to different constituencies in a Panchayat. Not less that 1/3rd of the total number of seats reserved for Schedule Caste and Schedule Tribes shall be reserved of women belonging to the Scheduled Castes or as the case may be the Scheduled Tribes.

Not less that 1/3rd (including the number of seats reserved for women belonging to Schedule Castes and Schedule Tribes) of the total number of seats to be filled by direct election in every Panchayat shall be reserved for women and such seats shall be allotted by rotation to different constituencies in a Panchayat. The offices of the chair persons in the Panchayat at the village or any other level shall be reserved for the Scheduled Castes, Scheduled Tribes and women in such manner, as Legislature of the State may by law, provide. The legislature of a State may also make provision for reservation of seats in any Panchayat or offices of chair persons in the Panchayat at any level in favour of backward class of citizens. The reservation of seats for the Scheduled Tribes and the Scheduled

Castes and the reservation of the office of the chair persons other than the reservation for women shall cease to have effect on the expiration of the period specified in Art. 334 providing for reservation of seats for Scheduled Castes and Scheduled Tribes, in the Legislative Assemblies of the State and in the House of the people.

One of the serious defects in the earlier laws was that it was possible for the State governments not to hold elections to village Panchayats for a long time and that was remedied by the introduction of the provision in the Constitution, which directs that every Panchayat, unless sooner dissolved under any law for time being in force shall continue for five years from the date appointed for its first meeting and no larger, and an election to constitute a Panchayat shall be completed before the expiry of its duration as mentioned above or before the expiration of six months from the date of its dissolution. The disqualifications prescribed by any law for the time being in force, for the purposes of elections for the Legislatures of the States are also the disqualification for being chosen as and for being a Member of a Panchayat. Art. 243-G expressly declares the powers , authority and responsibilities of Panchayats. It says that subject to the provisions of the Constitution, the Legislature of a State may, by law, endow the Panchayats with such powers and authority as may be necessary to enable them to function as institutions of self-government and such law may contain provisions for the devolution of powers and responsibilities on Panchayats at the appropriate level. Subject to such conditions, as may be specified therein with respect to (a) the preparation of plans for economic development and social justice and (b) the implementation of the schemes for economic development and social justice as may be entrusted to them including those in relation to the matters listed in the XI schedule. XI Schedule to the Constitution contains 29 subjects such as agriculture, minor irrigation, social forestry, rural electrification, education, health and sanitation, social welfare of the weaker sections etc. It is hoped that the Legislatures of the States would be liberal in this regard and transfer as much power as possible to Panchayats. The legislature of a State by law authorise a Panchayat to levy, collect and appropriate such taxes, duties, tolls and fees in accordance with such procedure and subject to such limits. The legislature can also assign to the Panchayat such taxes, duties, tolls, and fees levied and collected by the State government for such purposes and subject to such conditions and limits. The law also can provide for making such grants-in-aid to the Panchayats from the Consolidated Fund of the State and provide for Constitution of such funds for crediting all monies received, respectively by or on behalf of the Panchayats and also for the withdrawal of such monies therefrom. Art. 243-I requires the Governor of a State to constitute as soon as may be within one year from the commencement of the Constitution (73rd Amendment) Act, 1992 and thereafter the expiration of every fifth year a finance commission to review the financial position of the Panchayats and to make recommendations to the Governor as (a) the principles which should govern (i) the distribution between the State and Panchayats of the net proceeds of the taxes, duties and tolls and fees leviable by the State, which may be divided between them under part IX and allocation between the Panchayats at all levels of their respective shares of such proceeds, (ii) the determination of the taxes, duties, tolls and fees which may be assigned to or appropriated by the Panchayats and (iii) and grants-in-aid to the Panchayats from the Consolidated Fund of the State; (b) the measures needed to improve the financial position of the Panchayat, and (c) any other matter referred to the commission by the Governor in the interest of sound finance of the Panchayats. The recommendations made by the Finance Commission is required to be laid before the State Legislature.

The elections to the Panchayats are required to be held under the superintendence, direction and control of the State Election Commission to be appointed by the Governor.

These provisions which are applicable to the Panchayats in the States are also made applicable to the Union Territories.

The provisions contained in Part IX-A which relate to the municipalities are more or less similar to the aforesaid provisions applicable to Panchayats. However, it is necessary to make a specific reference to Art. 243-Z-D in Part IX-A which provides for the Constitution of the Committee for District Planning which is applicable both to the municipalities and Panchayats. It provides that there shall be constituted in every State at the district level a District Planning Committee to consolidate the plans prepared by the Panchayats and the municipalities in the district and to prepare a draft development plan for the district as a whole. The Legislature of a State is required to make provision by law with respect to the District Planning Committee and other details pertaining to the preparation of the draft development plan. Art. 243-Z-E requires the Constitution of a committee for Metropolitan Planning to prepare a draft development plan for a Metropolitan area as a whole, metropolitan area being an area having a population of 10 lakhs or more.

Schedule XII contains the subjects over which the municipalities can be given the power of administration.

Thus it is seen that the Constitutional amendments made by the 73rd and 74th Amendments ensure the setting up of Local Bodies, such as Panchayats and municipalities throughout India and to keep them going and for entrusting to them powers to administer matters which are of local interest. These institutions have thus acquired permanency and are considered as the third level of Government with responsibilities of decentralised governance and planning.

The rational underlying the Panchayat Raj Institutions is that since people's participation in them is ensured, planning for development will be consistent with people's needs and aspirations. Since, they use locally available resources men and material to the fullest extent, and produce goods and services which are locally required, the well-being of the people is promoted.

In the Panchayats as they are now constituted, what is however to be noticed is that there is lack of skills of governance and planning because of lower education levels of its members. Therefore there is need for capacity building in the case of members of Panchayats, by agencies such as State governments, non-governmental organizations and social workers, and for that purpose, these agencies have to work at three levels, namely at the level of citizens, at the level of members of Panchayats, and at the level of bureaucrats dealing with Panchayati Raj institutions.

The citizens should be enthused about self-government and self planning. Democratic atmosphere should pervade village life. Rural people should be motivated to participate in the political process and also in the process of governance, planning and implementation of rural development projects. The Gram Sabhas do give them opportunities to Articulate their needs and aspirations and also to review critically the progress of development projects. People must be motivated to pay their taxes and if possible to make voluntary contributions in the form of money, material and service so that the Panchayats have enough resources for sustaining themselves. The members of the Panchayats should be made knowledgeable about the basics of the Panchayati Raj institutions, the laws governing them, their powers, rights and privileges and limitations. They should be imparted planning skills — skills of identifying people's needs and their priorities and the resources available for executing the plan. The capacity of the bureaucracy working in the Panchayats for governing and planning should also be stepped up by providing necessary information, data and skills. This should be the agenda for the State government, Non-governmental organizations and social workers for the next five to ten years, so that Panchayati Raj institutions may be strengthened and that they may govern effectively and prepare sound plans at the grassroot level.

In view of the aforesaid Constitutional Amendments, it is no longer possible for the State governments to ignore these local bodies. These Panchayat Raj institutions are no longer at the mercy of the State governments. The provisions in the Constitution dealing with these Panchayati raj institutions, which have acquired permanency and Constitutional legitimacy have got to be implemented, the State government not having the choice any longer to brush them aside. The hopes expressed by the various committees constituted by the Central Government from time to time to go into the question of ensuring proper administration at the local level, have now become fully realised by the aforesaid amendments. It is for the people now to take appropriate action to ensure the Constitutional provisions and the laws made under them are properly implemented, for the benefit of the people—particularly in rural areas.

3

THE LOCAL PLANNING PROCESS
Evaluation and Transition to a New System

K.V. SUNDARAM

Introduction

1. The notion of a planning process cutting across several layers of governance in a multilevel hierarchy is a recent conception in the Indian Planning. Such a multilevel planning process has been enforced at the sub-national levels, after the passing of the recent Constitutional amendments in 1992. Planning is now conceived as a "people-driven" activity, in which each of the distinctive layers of governance who have been empowered with some limited autonomy and self-governance, has to negotiate successfully with its successive higher layers in order to obtain its share of benefits. If planning is deemed as an academic discipline, then like every other discipline, it has its own "norms" and "values". In this case, these are the qualities of planning as a technical and participatory exercise combined with the democratic values of "transparency" and "accountability", which lend to this activity its distinctive character i.e. the hallmarks that raise its quality, performance and credibility. The democratic and participatory approach to planning is really one of great challenges which involve techniques, institutions and performance. It should be noted that the term "Local Planning Process" implies the wider concept of "Planned development", which will include the three sets of

activities which include (a) data and analysis, (b) planning and programming, and (c) implementation/management of activities. Inevitably, there are numerous "actors" in this game; several "instrumentalities" through which the planning process has to be operated; a lot of "interlinked steps" to be gone through in a certain sequence; and a definite "time frame" to be adhered to in the whole process. Thus local planning process viewed in this light is a complex exercise. A lot of experimentation on planning has undoubtedly been made in India over the past eight decades of planned development. As assessment of this experience at sub-national levels will provide useful insights as to the achievements and shortcomings in our planning methodology and will enable us to charter our course of action for the new phase of multi level planning process envisaged in our current context. This chapter aims to make such an analysis and to outline the contours of the new process of planning that is yet to evolve in the country.

Decentralized Planning : Present State-of-Art

2. Undoubtedly, to grasp the present state-of-art in the decentralized planning, one must start with a brief account of the evolution of the planning process in the country. In order to make sense, we should distinguish two phases in our experience:-
Phase I – Reflecting the Pre-1993 Scenario[1] which will throw light on some important initiatives made in some States towards district and block level planning; and
Phase II – The emerging post–1993 Scenario, which shows that the new transformation is yet to crystallize and many things (including some essential pre-requisites) have not fallen into their places and the performance of the various States is uneven, lopsided, and in some cases halting, chaotic and even disappointing.

Phase I: Pre-1993 Scenario

3. Notwithstanding a Constitutional lacuna that existed before 1993 which did not specifically recognize the district as a third stratum of planning, there has been some substantial experiences

in decentralized planning in some States in the country during this phase. Since the commencement of planning in 1951, the Central Government has taken the following five major steps towards promoting decentralized planning:

- The Centre issued its first detailed guidelines for formulating District Plans in 1969 and for block level plans in 1979.
- The Centre has been providing special financial assistance to the States since 1972 for strengthening planning machinery at the State and district levels;
- In 1982, the Centre through a "Working Group on District Planning", provided updated and detailed guidelines covering all aspects of District Planning. The pre-requisites that must be fulfilled by the State governments for initiating decentralized planning on sound lines have been particularly stressed in these guidelines.
- In 1993, the Centre amended the Constitution, introducing Part-IX in it, which elaborates the structure, composition, elections to and scope of powers of Panchayats at the district, intermediate and village levels. The Eleventh Schedule added to the Constitution lists the subjects under which powers and functions could be given to Panchayats at District/ Intermediate/Village levels. The Constitutional status now accorded to the Panchayat bodies is expected to check the States from tampering with the life of these institutions, as has been the case so far. This will facilitate them to function as instruments of vibrant and viable rural Local Self Government and acquire the capacity to learn, to respond, to change and to mobilize better people's participation in managing their own affairs.

The task of training at three levels — officials at the sub-district level, officials at the district level, and non-officials and elected representatives at both district and sub-district levels, has received some awareness and attention (albeit inadequately) in the States. The training of trainers is being conducted at the national level, through institutions like the National Institute of Rural Development (NIRD).

4. The various initiatives made by the Centre were reinforced by experiments in District/Block level planning at the State level, which have thrown up specific methodologies on various aspects of planning from below. The 1970's is the age of methodologies. Maharashtra and Gujarat in the western part of India have been the forerunners in operationalizing district planning. Maharastra innovated, in the late' 60s, by devising a formula based on some managerial criteria for district allocations from the States "divisible pool", which was pegged at 40 per cent of the total development funds of the State. Gujarat refined this procedure, in the 70s, by providing a "modicum" of "un-tied funds" (along with an incentive grant) – placed at the sole discretion of the local bodies for meeting their perceived needs. In both these States, elected Local Self Government institutions (Panchayati Raj Institutions) existed and were performing "agency functions" for implementation of specific development activities devolved on them by the State government. But planning was deliberately kept out of their jurisdiction and placed with institutional structures called "District Planning and Development Councils" under a Minister of State as chairman. Initially,Maharastra and Gujarat experiments were considered innovative and pace-setting. But after some time, contrary pulls affected the process of decentralization. In Maharashtra, for instance, the State originally decided to allocate 40 per cent of the total plan funds at the State level to the district. Later, the State started making inroads into district outlays by introducing a component called "State sponsored District Sector Schemes" and diverting funds from the district outlays to the State. This resulted in a gradual shrinking of the proportion of the District Sector allocation. Arun Ghosh remarks, "Perhaps their (i.e., Maharashtra and Gujarat) success spelt their very demise. The MLAs and MPs, even the State Cabinet, felt disturbed and uneasy at the growing signs of a shift in the centre of power and authority in these two States. For, the fact remains that nobody really likes to shed powers; and the bureaucracy successfully played upon the fears and misgivings of the State government leaders. With time, therefore, the role and the

authority of the Panchayats receded into the background, and the role and the authority of the bureaucracy - backed by the Ministers, MLAs and MPs - increased. The planning process in Gujarat and Maharashtra, thus gradually came to be decentralized only in name, not in substance (Arun Ghosh, 1988).

5. Thus, it may be seen that the decentralization process never ran smooth. It oscillated back and forth (the "pendulum effect"). Sometimes, the forces of centralization asserted themselves and caused serious setbacks. For instance, even in the current Panchayat Raj renaissance phase, the Indian Government which took a bold initiative to push decentralization in the States, by amending the Constitution in 1993, came up with a scheme in 1994, of allocating a sum of Rupees one crore (10 million) to each Member of Parliament (MP) to be devoted to development project that will meet the needs of their constituencies, a patently retrograde step which threatens or dilutes the decentralization process. Similarly, in some States too, constituency funds are being provided to Members of Legislative Assembly (MLAs). Thus the funds available for the local authorities for planning have been seriously eroded.
6. In the 80's, some structural-functional and participatory aspects of local self government and the associated issues of planning and the integration of district plans with the State level planning process, received much attention in some States like Karnataka and West Bengal.The Southern State of Karnataka ushered in a new era of democratic decentralization in 1983 with an integrated set of Panchayati Raj Institutions (PRIs). All the development departments and agencies of the district were brought under the purview of the elected representatives and "organizational pluralism" was remarkably reduced, facilitating the integration and consolidation of the efforts and resources of development departments; also an element of accountability of bureaucrats to the elected representatives of the PRIs was introduced. A complete separation of the development and regulatory functions at the district level was made and both planning and implementation were brought under the purview

of the elected representatives at the grass-roots level. A time-bound planning process was introduced from village level upwards. Similarly in West Bengal, political Panchayats were constituted and land reforms were introduced by the Left Front Government in 1977 and since then, the Panchayats are performing a whole variety of functions like taking locational decisions on projects, implementation of land reforms and performing agency functions and extension activities. Over the years, the government have operationalised a local level planning process from village upwards. Each 'Panchayat prepares' its own plan, which are then combined, adjusted, planned and integrated into an overall plan for the whole district, including the urban areas.

7. In a well known planning experiment of the State of West Bengal, called "the Midnapore Experiment", each Gram Panchayat was asked to prepare a "needs statement" – or the most acutely felt problems of the Panchayat area (or anchal). Each Panchayat Samiti was to (a) prepare a series of maps of the block, outlining the existing facilities, resources and resource use; and (b) with the help of sub-assistant engineers available at block level, prepare schemes (within a total ceiling of Rs.10 million) to meet the most acute problems of each Gram Panchayat (based on the "needs statement" collected by them). Each Panchayat Samiti was also to prepare a statement of the on-going and proposed programme of plan outlay of different departments/authorities in each Block. These are then forwarded to the planning authorities at district headquarters. Then three sub-committees at the district level – a technical sub-committee, an economic committee, and a committee headed by the Sabhadhipati (elected chief of District Panchayat) – go into action. The technical sub-committee looked into the feasibility and estimated costs – benefits of each scheme. The economic sub-committee arranged all schemes in order of priorities, making sure of the required compatibility of and coordination between different schemes, as well as consistency with the "needs statements" prepared by the Gram Panchayats. The sub-committee headed by the Shabhadipati himself/herself

finally decided on the contours of the district plan. An academic institution, the Indian Institute of Technology (IIT), Kharagpur was closely associated with the project and assisted in the technical effort.

8. On the planning machinery aspect at the district level, considerable improvements in some States have been effected, thanks to a central assistance scheme providing for a 50% sharing of expenditure on planning staff at the district level. A number of States, however, have not availed of this scheme. Also where they availed of the benefits of this scheme, no consistent efforts have been made towards the capacitation of personnel. Thus the planning capabilities have not been built up to adequate levels to enable the State governments to face the new imperatives with confidence.
9. On the methodology front, over the last forty years or so, several methodologies of planning at the district and sub-district levels have also been evolved. Amitava and Yugandhar critically analyzed all the major methodologies, starting from the Gadgil's methodology down to the ones evolved by Misra and Sundaram in three published volumes (Amitava & Yugandhar, 1991). Each of these methodologies has their merits and demerits. Despite the existence of all these methodologies, the task of preparing a reasonably sound District Plan has not made much headway in the States. Before the commencement of the Eighth Plan (1992-97), the Planning Commission made attempts to have some pilot plans prepared, so that the methodology followed in them could be commenced for adoption by other districts as well. This involved the preparation of plans for five districts under the guidance provided by the National Institute of Rural Development (NIRD). In spite of a systematic effort aimed at, nothing worthwhile emerged from these exercises. There are several reasons why we have not been able to make much headway in the area of district planning (Sundaram, 1997). Some of these are:

* Even when it is not so obvious, there is some lurking reluctance on the part of Governments and their sectoral heads to devolve

sufficient authority – administrative and financial – to the planning bodies at the district level.

* Lack of effective coordination at the district level between various agencies involved in the planning exercise. Often, there is no arrangement for systematic integration of planning perspectives of different sectoral agencies operating at the field level. This applies even to the vertical integration between the responsible functionaries at different levels. The planning aspect tends to be neglected;
* Institutionalized arrangements, for seeking consultation with various participants in the planning processes, are either not well established or not sufficiently encouraged and developed. Hence, despite the use of planning techniques, a lot of subjectivity, even selfish arbitrariness, creeps in taking decisions. The planning aspect, thus, becomes a casualty;
* Lack of trained staff both, in terms of numbers and the adequacy of training. Training deficiencies are often noticed in the acquisition and mastering of necessary skills and techniques. The inculcation of right approach and attitude towards planning also requires attention. To promote planned way of thinking, it is necessary that a proper query system should be developed, analytical skills of the planning personnel sharpened and they should also be trained to assimilate and integrate seemingly different points of view, display responsiveness and cultivate a habit of exploring options. A planner must always be able to persuade others to his way of thinking. Above all, training must bring home the importance of the planning aspect of one's work;
* A very elaborate methodology may stifle whatever little initiative and efforts may be possible, by a limited number of staff. In some cases, non-availability of planning staff poses a serious problem. Complexities of methodology should not be allowed to become a pretence for not doing planning. In this context, reduced planning approaches need to be developed and promoted;
* While preparing the plan, sufficient attention is not given to the realities of resource constraints. The 'need' factor or the importance of a particular sector, in relation to other, motivates

the prescribing of higher and higher allocations. Financial constraints at this stage are relegated to a secondary position. However, by the time District level plans are firmed up and integrated with the State level plans, resources re-emerge as the overall constraint and quite often drastic re-adjustments have to be worked out. The deleterious side effect of this kind of re-adjustments is that the initial over-enthusiasm for planning turns to skepticism about its utility. This feeling, basically due to uninformed about the true character of the planning process, has in reality greatly impeded the effective operationalisation of district planning;

* At the district level more than at any other level, planning and implementation are almost visibly aligned. The planner is acutely aware of the realities of implementation. It is, therefore, necessary that the budgetary mechanism for the release of funds should be so devised that it supports the cause of planning rather than weakens it. Though not strictly a part of planning methodology, this is an important factor which should be sorted out if the cause of planning is to be advanced;
* The database presents its own problems. What may be termed as the "R & D dimension" in planning has not still received serious attention in the States. Thus we have now a surfeit of data at the local level thrown up to numerous agencies like the NIC, various technology missions, scientific natural resources data generated through sophisticated techniques like the satellite imagery and remote sensing and capabilities to quickly generate any missing data through rapid appraisal techniques etc. Yet, how to sieve the "critical minimum information" from this mass of data and use the same for some simple analysis for planning without going into highly sophisticated techniques, which are beyond the grasp and reach of the ordinary planning personnel managing the planning cells at various levels in the country is a highly relevant issue. Undoubtedly, more "reduced approaches" to planning should emerge to render local level planning into an easy and simple process; and
* Finally, district level planning is essentially a reflection of the belief that it is a step forward in the direction of bringing the

planning process tuned to the needs of the local people. If so, the people must be vitally involved in it. In this context, unless an enlightened pressure group develops or is developed, the success of the district planning exercise will always be at the mercy of people who may not be interested in it.

Phase II – Developments after the Constitutional Amendments

10. Since 1993, Decentralized Planning has assumed higher significance in the context of Constitutional backing provided to Panchayats, Municipalities, and Corporations. Article 243 (G) in the 73rd Constitutional Amendment Act, and Article 243 (W) in the 74th Constitutional Amendment Act specifically provide for Local Self Government institutions to take up the responsibility of preparation of plans for economic development and social justice and implementation of schemes. Article 243 (ZD) provides for Constitution of District Planning Committees, which will be responsible for consolidation of the plans prepared at the Panchayats and Municipalities in the district and preparation of a draft development plan for the district as a whole. Most State Governments have enacted conformity legislations, in which the above salient features of the Constitutional provisions have been incorporated.The modalities of operationalising the planning process and the performance in terms of real, devolution of powers and functions to elected local bodies, however, vary from State to State.
11. In the new phase of development, to enable the multilevel planning process to take off, the State has to take a number of preliminary actions in the nature of "pre-requisites". The most essential pre-requisites are:

* Familiarising the sub-State levels about the broad policies, goals, and objectives of the proposed State plan and its various sectoral strategies, priorities and targets,so that the local plans would be consistent with the framework of the State plan;
* Defining a devolution package with adequate administrative, technical and financial powers to the various levels covering the 29 subjects provided in the Eleventh Schedule of the

Constitution;

* Disaggregation and transfer of plan funds (Block Panchayats, Village Panchayats,and Urban Local bodies) on appropriate criteria.
* Establishing District Planning Committees (DPCs) and Metropolitan Planning Committees (MPCs), as mandated in the 74th Amendment of the Constitution;
* Establishing suitable supporting mechanisms for planning, coordination and participation, and operationalising the decentralised planning process according to a methodology;
* Making various administrative arrangements for:

  (a) Establishing a time-bound planning process
  (b) Integrating the District Plans into the State Plan
  (c) Organising the personnel in the local bodies for better performance and accountability
  (d) Budgetary control and other related matters
  (e) Review, monitoring and evaluation of plans;

* Making various administrative arrangements for the training of both officials and non-officials;

  The States are still struggling to establish these pre-requisites. Among the States, which have performed well, are West Bengal and Kerala. In both cases, planning from the grassroots (i.e., from village level upward) has definitely made some progress.

12. In these cases, the point of departure is the assessment of people's needs, as the people themselves saw them. Government field agents would concentrate on assisting the people to define their needs more accurately and supplying the technical support which the people needed to work out their own solutions to their development problems. Integration would arise from the locally concerned schemes for the family and village. Society as a whole, as a sheer necessity, rather than from attempts to coordinate disparate programmes that focussed on purely economic targets. It has been an exciting concept that hoped to draw THREE reactions from the people. First,

COMMITMENT. Now the people would be more deeply committed to projects that "they themselves had decided that they needed". Secondly, LOCAL CONTRIBUTIONS. It has been proved from these experiments that the people once committed, would contribute some local resources (e.g., labour, materials, information etc.), readily to the projects which they have chosen. And thirdly, INGENUITY. That is, allowing the people to select the projects needed and involving the people intellectually in the search for new means to improve their traditional economy. The great challenge has been to the administration, to the planning cells of the various technical departments, and to the State Planning Board, to support and guide these developments from below. A tradition of strongly centralized planning in the Departments and the Planning Boards has been broken and it has created psychological difficulties for those who are now obliged by this new concept, to withdraw from a dominant and paternalistic position, to one of support and technical guidance. Thus the temptation to plan from "top-down" has yielded place to a realistic "bottom-up" approach. The Departments and the Planning Boards have now to respond, by providing very strong and appropriate guidelines to enable the whole process to run smooth and function effectively.

13. Among the new experimentations, which emerged after 1993 Constitutional amendment, the decentralization programme of the State of Kerala, called the "Ninth Plan: the People's Plan", affords highly interesting example in micro level planning. This is an experiment in which three million people (10% of the total population of the State) took part in Gram Sabha meetings that articulated the local problems effectively and paved the way towards an objective and community specific local level planning. In the Kerala experiment, the planning exercise, starting from the grass-roots level, went through five stages, till the unfolding of the Ninth Plan. These five stages are:

* Stage I — Holding Ward/Gram Sabha assemblies to identify the local problems

* Stage II — Holding of development seminars to reach a consensus on the list of problems and the project ideas
* Stage III — The Constitution of task forces in 12 subject areas to distill the various project concepts into concrete proposals
* Stage IV — Finalising the "Panchayat Plans"
* Stage V — The integration of local plans into a wider district level plan

What makes the Kerala Experiment interesting is its intensive participatory approach through community based organizations (CBO's) and the various transparent and accountable procedures adopted in the planning process. The people really made "planning" into a vigorous "local movement" that drew forth people's energy and enthusiasm for local level planning. The allocation of a 40 per cent devolution of funds for local development acted as an incentive.

14. What has come out of these experiments is the role of village communities in grass-roots planning and the need to strengthen democracy as well as the planning process at this level. For this, we have to create the necessary instrumentalities, which are not there. Some of them, of course, have now been mandatorily provided for, through the Constitutional Amendment. The new instrumentalities that are visualized here are some essential structures at the village, block and district levels, to promote and facilitate effective planning, implementation and people's participation. While creating new structures, however it should be borne in mind that there can be no uniformity in the pattern. The diversity in culture and economic development would undoubtedly have a bearing on the systems that will be evolved.

The Instrumentalities

15. A village level plan need not be a highly sophisticated exercise: but it should be a practical programme of action, which will achieve the six-fold goals envisaged for sub-national level planning viz, growth, social justice, human welfare, sustainable

development, integration of programmes and projects, and participation of the local people. What is required in this context is:

(a) Identification of potentialities,
(b) Identification of felt needs,
(c) A rational way of deciding priorities and locating of schemes,
(d) Selecting some suitable projects that will benefit the community, particularly, the weaker sections,
(e) Selecting the beneficiaries of anti-poverty and other target group programmes, and
(f) Conserving and managing the Soil, Water, Vegetation and Common Property Resources of the Village for the economic well-being of the villagers.

If the procedures for doing the above can be improved, then the quality of the programme itself can be improved, and we can have a better plan of action. The programme itself should be responsive to the people who are supposed to benefit from it, and should be flexible, making it a learning process. The process must unfold in each village, through dialogue and consultations with the people. Thus it will be intensively participatory with the community, defining its own problems, setting its own goals, objectives and priorities, choosing the schemes which the community will undertake, and playing an active role in carrying out and monitoring them. The institutional mechanisms for village level planning are:

The Gram Sabha (mandatorily provided) which is entrusted with the functions of deciding the priorities and programmes for the village and approving the village plan, approving the village annual budget, and reviewing the progress of implementation of all schemes entrusted to the village Panchayat.

A Village Planning Forum (VPF), which should be a body of members of the Village Panchayat and representatives of the Village, like selected elders, teachers and youth as well as village government officials. The VPF will be the mechanism to plan and to bring about coordination in village programmes between the Village Panchayat and the local communities. It is expected to perform the task by dividing itself into smaller working groups. In the Kerala experiment, 12 Task Forces accomplished this job. These working groups or task groups should be richly complemented technically from above.

16. The Gram Sabha is intended to facilitate people's participation and resolve all conflicts and reach consensus on specific issues. Since such participation cannot be effective in a large forum, it has to be engineered through "group action". In this context what we need are "Polycentric (i.e., focussed on several interests) institutional arrangements" for binding, consolidating and unifying various "interest groups". They really constitute the "Social Capital". Some such "interest groups", already exist in our village societies in the form of "user groups", "resources management groups", "irrigation management groups", "forest interface groups", and various other types of collective self management groups. The role of these informal interest groups is immense in village development. They richly complement the functions of the local elected representatives, throw up relevant project ideas and keep track of developmental progress, and thus help in successful implementation of projects and programmes. In fact, if sustainable relationship between the village Panchayats and the "informal interest groups" can be established, it will be a major contribution to village development and provide the basis for success stories.
17. In fact, there are many "success stories" in rural development, scattered over all parts of the country. In these success stories, we find several types of participatory mechanisms and ingredients of transparent and accountable procedures in planning and implementation that have led to their signal success. The examples of Kundrakudi in the State of Tamil Nadu, Tilonia in the State of Rajasthan, "the Paani Panchayats" in the State of Maharashtra, and the Kalliaseri, Chapprapadavu and other recent experiments of the State of Kerala may be

cited. In all these success stories, it is a peculiar "mix" or "combination" of some catalyst forces at work (not always reproducible or replicable) which has been responsible for the success. In the Kundrakudi context, I have called this as a peculiar "technocratic, academic, and democratic mix" (T.A.D. mix). Since success stories cannot be replicated in their totality everywhere, relevant lessons from these experiments have to be drawn and appropriately put into place to render our village development throughout the country reasonably successful.

18. At the Block level, the instrumentalities will be, besides the Panchayat Samiti, which is a formal statutory body, there is a need for an institution to perform the planning tasks. This can be done by constituting a "Block Planning Committee (BPC)", which can function through a required number of task forces and working groups. In all these institutional mechanisms, the elected representatives of the Panchayats, selected nominated intellectuals, social activists from the area, and the concerned officials from the government departments will constitute the planning team. After the plan itself emerges from this team work, it can be further whetted by transparently discussing it with the larger public of the area, by arranging a series of seminars/meetings and obtaining their feedback. These procedures apply to planning at all levels (Village, Block and District) and they help to increasingly align the planning effort to the field realities.

19. The instrumentalities at the District level, where coordination and integration become the cardinal issues, are of a different kind. They will consist of the Zilla Parishad (statutory) and District Planning Committee (statutory), besides a number of functional committees which may be (i) an executive committee for day-to-day administration and monitoring. (ii) a few subject matter committees to screen all plan proposals coming from below and adding many "linkage programmes/schemes to them, and (iii) a joint coordination committee to put together all plan proposals from the rural areas into the contours of a district plan, within financial and other parameters. a District Planning Committee (statutory) has been deliberately provided to bring

about rural-urban integration and an element of "inter-local planning" as complementary and adjunct to the local area plans emerging from the different local bodies [Sundaram, (1997), (1)].

20. In the context of the emergence of the new organizational structures for planning, as outlined above, there will arise a need for restructuring the "Orgware" at the local level, weeding out those organizations that are no longer relevant. One of them could be the "District Rural Development Agency (DRDA)", established as a nodal agency for the implementation of anti-poverty programmes. One of the considerations while setting up this agency,was that, being an organization outside the main stream of government, it will have a certain flexible manner of functioning, would not allow funds to lapse and thus would lead to better utilisation of funds. In the new scenario, it is a pertinent issue for consideration whether it should be retained. Some committees set up by State governments have already recommended its dissolution and thus avoid the "Organizational Pluralism" at the district level.

21. The Planning process for local level planning, envisioned here, seeks to provide a "normative" or "ideal" construct and begs for many "conditions" or "pre-requisites" to be fulfilled before it may be opreationalised. These were cited earlier in Para 10. They constitute a wide of range of pro-active measures. The States are yet to operationalise this dream and are progressing along these directions with many "aberrations" and defaults committed on the way. Some enlightened States (e.g. Kerala, Karnataka and now Tamil Nadu and Andhra Pradesh) have gone about it somewhat systematically. In the States of Kerala, Karnataka and Tamil Nadu, Expert Committees have been set up under eminent individuals to put 'thinking into right channels". We also hear echoes of planning movements on the Kerala model in some of these States e.g. "Namakku Naame" (by ourselves for ourselves) in Tamil Nadu and the "Janma Bhoomi" movement in Andhra Pradesh. In most other States, there are no "think-tanks" to guide and directionless efforts are going on with decisions being arbitrary and progress desultory,

disappointing and sometimes counter-productive to the very tenets of decentralization.

22. The planning process in decentralised planning, to be successful, needs five essential things:

* Committed and enlightened key actors,
* The right instrumentalities,
* Constant capacitation and re-orientation to the key actors,
* Clearly envisioned steps as decentralization should be conceived as an "incremental strategy" for our country (I do not elaborate here); and
* Time scheduled activities with a planning calendar of operations to ensure that the planning endeavours at various levels, ultimately mesh into the State Plan and the State Budget.

These are colossal tasks and there are many issues here to which we have to address ourselves more seriously now than ever.

The Transparency and Accountability Factor in the Planning Process

23. The functioning of the new Panchayati Raj System should be characterized by total transparency in deeds and accountability for expenditures by both officials and non-officials. Transparency in planning stems from the following measures:

* Through changing the "STYLE", "STANCE" and "SUBSTANCE" of planning. The "STYLE" refers to the democratic and participatory character of planning "STANCE" refers to "People doing and Government supporting" a two-way planning process, in a greater transparent and accountable manner and "SUBSTANCE" refers to the programmes and project components informed by the goals of growth, equity, stability, and sustainability and greater relevance to the community;

* By making the planning process intensively participatory. This is achieved by establishing the various "instrumentalities" at all levels, as discussed in this chapter.
* By strengthening and enhancing the involvement of the democratic institutions (i.e. the PRIs) in the planning process.
* By actively involving and associating all grass-roots level institutions and voluntary autonomous groups in the area with varying interests, giving them a role to play, defining their tasks functions and equipping them for these tasks (organising them for planning) by capacitating them through training and education workshops (the idea of a "planning extension" activity).
* Bringing in the national and international Non-governmental Organizations (NGOs) engaged in specific activities into "planning" and defining their complementary roles and functions.
* Encouraging "popular movements" in planning in order to sustain and strengthen people's involvement in planning.
* By extending transparency into implementation and monitoring and evaluation of projects by setting up, for each important project, citizen groups consisting of elected representatives and other prominent citizens, to act as "watchdogs" of performance.
* By giving the "right to information" to the Public both in the Public and the Private Sectors.
* By establishing a Development Support Communication system for effectively communicating all details about the plan and the planning process to the local people from time to time. This is achieved through multi mass media like newspaper, radio and television and through theatrical techniques of entertainers performing in the folk tradition. This is to be seen not merely as an information provision activity or publicity but as a step rendering the whole planning process totally transparent and visible to the public, generating a genuine public opinion on the plan, inviting healthy criticism and making interaction with the public, a continuous activity during the plan formulation stage and after.

24. In the Public Sector, information on funds received and allocated to different schemes, selection of beneficiaries and expenditure incurred by break-up of costs etc., must be made available to anyone who is interested. For this purpose, a "Review Room" should be maintained by each Panchayat. The Review Room should be accessible to all citizens and should contain maps and charts visually depicting the area plan of the particular Panchayat,statistical particulars about the Panchayat and information about the various schemes being implemented on an up-to-date basis.By providing all basic development information, the Review Room would enable the citizens to think and analyze their area problems and would stimulate them towards greater participatory endeavours.
25. From the point of responsive administration, developmental projects and service delivery agencies should be directed to have simple mechanisms that will provide all details of the government activities to interested groups or individuals. In this way, it will be possible to put in place, effective preventive mechanisms that will ensure transparency in dealings by the government. It is understood that a draft bill, in this regard, is under consideration of the Central Government, which among the other things, seeks an Amendment to the Officials Secret Act 1923 and the Civil Services Conduct Rules 1964, which contain some negative provisions. It should be noted that the Tamil Nadu State Government has already enacted such a legislation (Act No. 24 of 1997 – the Tamil Nadu Right to Information Act, 1997). Another State, the Madhya Pradesh State Government, has allowed access to records of Public Distribution system (PDS) in the State. An NGO in the State of Rajasthan, the Mazdoor Kisan Shakti Sangathan (MKSS) is campaigning in a big way for transparency in public dealings. It need not be over emphasized that the "right to information" and "transparency" in government dealings would go a long way in curtailing corruption in public life.The argument for "transparency" applies equally to the Private Sector. In this context, it is interesting to mention that one of the NGOs in the country – SWRC Tilonia (also called Barefoot College) in

Ajmer district of the State of Rajasthan made public, the details of its income and expenditure and thus sent a strong message to all voluntary agencies that it is possible for them to be transparent and accountable. This incident has served to silence the critics in political and administrative circles.

26. While rules, regulations and punishments have been conceived as the usual government measures to ensure accountability, experience shows that they are not quite effective systems of control. Particularly, their mode of functioning leaves much to be desired. For instance, the present Local Fund Audit System has proved to be quite unsatisfactory for taking timely remedial measures. Further for paucity of adequate audit staff and other reasons the audit is said to be "in arrears" in most States. In this context, the alternatives suggested are: an empowered "Audit Commission" and a well designed "Query System" in the PRI meetings and face communication with senior officers. The media can also serve as successful "alternate devices" to unearth any scams or scandals. Thus, both organizational strengthening and enlightened community action are needed to improve accountability.
27. In a democratic decentralized system of governance, the autonomous self-governing institutions are accountable to the local people through their appropriate institutional forums like the Gram Sabha, the Panchayat Samiti and the Zilla Parishad. This aspect of accountability seems to have been missed in the conforming legislations by the State Governments.Most of the State acts have provided for a system of supervision and control of Panchayats through the Bureaucracy, which goes against the very principles of democracy. In this context, the West Bengal model is a departure. It provides for supervision of Gram Panchayats by the Panchayat Samitis and of the Panchayat Samitis by Zilla Parishad (Rajiv Gandhi Foundation, 1997).
28. The accountability question is also related to the degree of local autonomy is fiscal and financial management enjoyed by the local bodies. A system of funding the Panchayats through tied grants (as happens now) automatically encourages accountability only to a bureaucratic system rather than to the

local people. In this context, the question of devising suitable forums for making Panchayats accountable to the local people, is an important issue that must be addressed in State Legislations.

29. Accountability can be effectively ensured only when Panchayats have control over the administrative and technical staff working for them. In the new Panchayat Raj System, the planning task is expected to be done by the PRI's, assuming that the official planning machinery will be in their complete control; but the execution of the plan will be performed by staff working in various State Government Departments. This results in a dual control. Until such time till the PRI's are able to hire their own staff and have an entirely decentralized staff structure, the technical staff needed by them for implementation have to be assigned from the other State Technical Departments. During their services under Panchayats, the implementing staff should be deemed on deputation to the PRIs and be totally under their administrative control. The PRIs should have certain disciplinary powers over them. The State legislation for PRI's should explicitly provide for such powers. But this is suggested only as an interim measure. In the long run, the PRIs should develop their own cadres (i.e. a unified personnel system). There could be other patterns of staff control as well. In any case, the establishment of an accountable personnel system in the PRIs needs to be discussed at length in a State-specific context, taking note of the various problems to be countered in their situations.

Some Shortcomings and Issues for Consideration

30. Against this background account, some major pertinent issues may be raised. As a prelude to this discussion, some operational as well as conceptual issues may be clarified. So far as decentralization is concerned,we are at the cross roads, with a future yet to be born for a systematic process of decentralised planning. In most States, the elected representatives are in place and they are performing varyingly under severe constraints of different kinds. A review of studies on performance conducted

by various researches (Aziz 1997, Palanidurai 1997, Prashant *et al.*, 1996, Mishra *et al.*, 1996, Singh 1995, Mahipal 1998, Sudha Pai 1998) shows that the elected members of Panchayati Raj institutions are woefully lacking in their knowledge about their roles and responsibilities, particularly in regard to matters relating to planning.

31. My close observation in some States shows that a big vacuum exists in regard to official machinery for planning at all the three levels. Without the existence of a capable "technical secretariat" to assist the elected representatives, how can we expect "participatory planning" to make any headway? Recently, some field studies conducted in the State of Haryana, revealed that the elected Sarpanches lacked total understanding about their roles and responsibilities and had no skills in conducting the meetings of Gram Sabhas, with the result that they were hardly conducted. Even if conducted, the Gram Sabha meetings were poorly attended and without any discussion really taking place, the Minutes of the proceedings were written and signatures obtained by the Village Secretary going from door to door (Renu Paruthi, 1998). One of the informants told us that it was the traditional method. (Is It?). The lack of attendance of women in the meetings and lack of participation by the Poor and Scheduled Castes in these meetings were particularly striking. The planning process was going on as a bureaucratic procedure, with no change.

32. If these deficiencies are considered as "teething" and "transition" problems, then on what basis should we plan for a "transition development strategy" at least on an incremental basis? This is an issue that we must seriously consider. Any how all the findings from various case studies, project very clearly the need for a massive capacitation approach through training of both officials and non-officials. I saw some one-day and one-time training programmes conducted in a State on a "crash basis" covering 150 to 200 trainees at one go in a big cinema hall. I wondered what contribution and impact such training could make and what degree of capacitation was achieved by such training festivals. These are serious issues which we must

consider. NIRD has drawn up some meaningful outline modules for training; but these should now be translated into State specific manual with appropriate readings and case studies. This is a big and demanding operation. Can the States take up the challenge?

33. Although we insist on saying that "people should plan" (and rightly so in our present context), we should also recognize that the full range of "actors" in this game are many and consist of the officials and the elected representatives as well as the 'Public" at large acting in groups.They have their respective roles in planning, each according to their expertise as well as limitations. In this context, a distinction may be drawn between "development from below" and "development from within" (Sundaram,`1997).

The distinction is subtle. "Development from within" refers to "people-initiated-people-directed" and "people-managed-projects" that spring from "capillary effect" or "trickle-up-effect" from the village community itself, conforming to the German concept of "auto centric development". "Development from below", on the other hand, refers to those bigger projects with a higher technical component, which require feasibility studies and technical design in their formulation. These can be handled better by technical officials in Government Departments with such people's participation as possible. If these ideas are clearly understood in project formulation, and related to the nature and intensity of people's participation, then all planning tasks in micro level planning could be handled as complementary tasks and accomplished in a harmonious manner.

34. Planning at any level includes a heavy backlog of past schemes with their lingering maintenance aspects, on-going programmes with some doubts about their continued relevance, and new programmes chalked out with great expectations. How do we introduce the principles of "zero-based" budgeting to weed out irrelevant Programmes? Also keeping Plan and Non-plan expenditure separate, creates a bias against consolidation, maintenance and upkeep. In one Five Year Plan Period, the

investment in new school buildings and new primary health centres will be plan expenditure. In the very next plan period, the money to run these will be non-plan. Once it is put in non-plan category, it gets starved of funds. No wonder that health centres without medicines or doctors are common all over the country. How do we allocate the total development funds among new, on-going as well as past schemes?

35. In this context, an important question is: How to bring in people's participation into maintenance aspects? In Nepal, the process of planning and implementation with 'Users' groups has been perfected by legally providing for the establishment of these groups and spelling out their composition, functions. responsibilities and rights in the Decentralization Act itself. This has revitalised the whole planning process by encouraging a greater degree of spontaneous participation by the people. We should consider the relevance of such procedures in our context, so that the maintenance of assets created through planning are properly cared for.

36. Creating proper inter-linkages between the State planning machinery and the local planning machinery is a vital issue. Some State Governments have established a "State Development Council" for this purpose, with the State Chief Minister as Chairman, and Presidents of Zilla Parishads, Mayors of Municipal Corporations, Cabinet Ministers, Senior Administrators, and members of the State Planning Board, as Members.

37. The question of rendering Gram Sabhas to function effectively as "peer decision-making forums" is another important issue. The Gram Sabhas should be able to facilitate peoples' participation, without becoming battle grounds for competing interests. Much depends on how its technical secretariat, the Village Planning Forum (VPF), prepares the ground for conducting the Gram Sabha meetings. For instance, one of the important functions of the Gram Sabha is to prioritise the various needs, activities and projects for the village. This could be done reasonably effectively, if the VPF does its homework

and presents the proposals by suitably classifying them on the basis of two principles —

* On the basis of priority
* Projects that are essential
* Projects that are important
* Projects that are desirable
* On the basis of the resource of funds needed to implement the projects and their range of influence
* Projects whose effects are limited to the village area, and all resources needed come from the village itself (e.g. proposals to improve the village temple religious activities)
* Projects and activities whose effects are limited to village area and its inhabitants, but which require besides a considerable amount of resources from the village, some external resources, expertise and assistance (e.g. proposals to improve economic conditions such as requests for planting material, or drainage and refuse disposal).
* Projects whose effects exceed the village boundaries and which require a considerable amount of external resources (e.g. construction of a high school, hospital, roads, and electrification)

A classified approach, suggested as above, will enable the people to discuss the merits and de-merits of the proposals openly and arrive at decisions collectively.

38. Accountability is a major issue and already some points have been made in this chapter. How to deal with non-performance of responsibilities by the officials (staff) of the PRIs and the elected leaders, if they do not function in an accountable manner, is a vexed issue. In a village context, how can the Gram Sabha be used to enhance the element of accountability?
39. The objective of social equity and how to ensure it in the micro level plans is yet another important issue. While finalising the area plans at each level, it is necessary to look into this aspect carefully in regard to each project proposed in the plan. The

proportion of beneficiaries in each project and to which social stratum they belong, should be quantified and for the plan as a whole. This should be portrayed in terms of both numbers benefited and investments made. Imparting sufficient visibility on such matters itself will help to correct matters at the appropriate stage of formulating plan proposals. Transparency and Accountability thus become the cornerstones for judging the merits (including credibility, acceptability and implementability) as well as the efficient performance of micro level plans.

Conclusion

40. The emphasis of this chapter is on the micro level planning process and its related issues, which are inextricably bound with the decentralized governance process. Developing countries like India, who are in this transition go through some vital stages of transformation. These are:

(a) Enfranchisement, with positive discrimination in reservation of seats in favour of the weaker sections of the society.
(b) Empowerment, with some degree of political and financial autonomy, and
(c) Enlightened and effective participatory planning, coupled with the ethical functioning of the system, with a moral code of conduct enshrining the qualities of transparency and accountability

According to Robert Dahl, a well known political scientist, the last among these stages relating to the functioning and performance of the system is the "third democratic transformation". This is a process of consolidating the democratic Institutions, materialising the multi-level planning process and ensuring their effective functioning with a good deal of work ethics and managerial efficiency. Decentralized governance is not just a matter of putting an organizational framework in place and appointing some individuals. It is going beyond mere infrastructure provision. The new Panchayat Raj System is a *fait accompli*. But the transformation of what was previously a bureaucratically controlled and State funded delivery arm of the government into a people controlled institution of self government, functioning in style and efficiency, is still a far cry. Even as we are groping with the intricacies, complexities and inherent paradoxes in these changes, time is running out for the State governments in the country to consolidate their thinking and efforts and move towards a swift and successful democratic transformation in a committed and constructive manner.

NOTE

1. 1993 is considered the Cut-off point because the Constitution (73rd Amendment) Act 1992 came into effect from 24th April, 1993. It is deemed historic legislation.

REFERENCES

Amitava Mukherjee and Yugandhar, B.N. (1991), "Methodology and Database for Decentralized Planning", *Studies in Multilevel Planning*: Vol.III, Heritage Publishers, New Delhi.

Arun Ghosh (1988) "Decentralized Planning: West Bengal Experience", *Economic and Political Weekly*, March 26, 1988.

Aziz Abdul and Shenoy, P.V. (1997), "District Planning: Principles and their operationalisation", *Journal of Rural Development,* Vol 16(4)

Dahl Robert A. (1988), *Democracy and its Critics*, Yale, USA.

Mahipal (1989), "Women in Panchayats: Experiences of a Training Camp", *Economic and Political Weekly*, January 24.

Mishra,S.N., Kumar Lokesh, Pal Chaitali (1996), *New Panchayati Raj in Action*, Mittal Publications, New Delhi.

Palanithurai, G.(1997), "Capacity Building exercise for Elected Representatives in Tamil Nadu", *Journal of Rural Development* Vol. 16(4)

Prashant Prem, Mishra Suresh, Singh Charanjeev (1996), "Popular Participation in Rural development", (Emerging Dynamics of Panchayati Raj Institutes in Haryana), *HIPA*, Gurgaon

Rajiv Gandhi Foundation, New Delhi (1997) : Report of the Task Force on Panchayati Raj.

Renu Paruthi (1998): A Study on Training Needs Assessment of Panchayat Raj members in context of "Local Decentralised Development Planning including Health", (Unpublished thesis submitted to the Faculty of Medical

Associations, New Delhi).

Singh, Hargian (1985), *Panchayati Raj Administration in Haryana*, Indira Publications, Gurgaon, pp.6-7, 127-139.

Sundaram (1997) (1), District Planning Committee: Its implications, *Journal of Rural Development,* Vol.16, No.4 October -December 1997 (Special issue on Panchayati Raj), National Institute of Rural Development, Hyderabad (India)

Sundaram (1997) (2), *Decentralised Multilevel Planning: Principles and Practice Asian and African Experiences*, Concept, New Delhi).

Sudha Pai (1998), "Pradhans in the New Panchayats – Field Notes from Meerut", *Economic and Political Weekly*, Vol. 33 (18).

4

THE PANCHAYATS OF THE SCHEDULED AREAS

B.R. PUROHIT

I. HISTORICAL BACKGROUND

India is truly a land of diversities; it is, indeed, a community of communities. One of such communities is of the tribals who have their own ways of life, customs, cultural identities, customary models of living together as well as their customary modes of resolution of disputes. For centuries they lived in isolation, far away from the national main stream, worshipped their gods whom they identified with their hills, mountains, lands, rivers, forests and nature. Such an isolation kept them socially, economically and politically backward with its attendant handicaps of poverty, ignorance, disease, malnutrition and exploitation. The colonial rulers looked to these social groups from the point of views of maintenance of law and order, or as objects of social antiquities to be preserved in isolation. However, after independence the tribal communities received the attention of the Central and State governments which started undertaking measures for their socio-economic welfare and upliftment.

But when it came to be integrating or associating the tribal communities with the democratic processes of the country, a major hiatus was felt. For instance, when the Right to Equality was granted to the citizens of free India or when the system of Panchayati Raj was introduced in the States of India for the sake of establishment of self-government at the grassroots level, the socio-cultural values and life styles of the ribal communities presented some insurmountable difficulties to the Constitution makers of the country: neither it was possible to implement right to equality of opportunity in such a society nor was it possible to introduce the principle of democratic mode of decision-making in a society where decisions were arrived at by traditional methods of community consensus.

It was under these conditions of socio-economic and cultural diversities and distinctive characteristics of the tribal communities that the framers of the Constitution assigned special Constitutional status to them. Therefore, the architects of the Constitution, along with the principle of non-discrimination, made some exceptions for the Scheduled Tribes, Scheduled Castes and other backward classes.

Thus, under Part X, entitled the Scheduled and Tribal areas, it was provided that the administrative set-up for the tribal people would be different from other State or Union Territory administrations. The areas, where tribal people clustered in majority, were designated as Scheduled Areas and for such Scheduled Areas, special provisions were made for their 'administration and control' under Article 244(i) of the Indian Constitution.

Administration and Control of Scheduled Areas under Article 244 (i)

Article 244(i) maintains the distinctive identity of the Scheduled areas. It requires that Governor of such State, which has Scheduled Areas therein, shall annually, or whenever so required by the President of India, shall report to the President regarding the administration of the Scheduled Areas in the State. Also, the executive power of the Union Government extends to the giving of direction to the State about the administration of such areas. As we know, such executive directions are not given to other States under normal conditions.

Another significant feature incorporated in the Fifth Schedule was the institution of "Tribal Advisory Council" [Article 244(i)(4)] for the administration and control of the Scheduled Areas. The

Constitution required that these TACs should be in each State, which has Scheduled areas therein. A Tribal Advisory Council shall consist of not more that 20 members, of whom nearly three-fourths should be representatives of the Scheduled Tribes in the State Assembly. The primary duty/function of the TAC was to advise on such matters pertaining to the welfare and advancement of the Scheduled Tribes, as referred to the Council by the Governor. Such were the special provisions under the Fifth Schedule in the Indian Constitution before 1992-93 to protect the distinctive character of the tribal communities in various States of India.

To the question of determination as to which were the Scheduled Tribes, Art.342(1) lays down that the President, after consultation with the Governor of the concerned State, shall specify the tribes and the tribal communities, or groups within them, to be deemed as Scheduled Tribes. Thus, before the enactment and enforcement of the 73rd Constitutional Amendment Act, such were the special provisions related to the administration and control of the Scheduled Areas.

II. SCHEDULED AREAS IN MADHYA PRADESH

Madhya Pradesh is a rich treasure house of tribal communities. Within the State boundaries we find representation of nearly all the principal tribal groups of Central India; they inhibit all the four corners of the State. According to 1991 census, the tribal population of the State was 15,339,034 (one crore fifty three lac ninety-nine thousand and thirty four) which is nearly 25 per cent of the total tribal population of India. So far as the tribal population of Madhya Pradesh of 425 scheduled tribes of India, Madhya Pradesh alone has a share of 46 tribes, divided into nearly 161 ethnic groups, and out of the 46 tribes, seven tribes of the State have the status of "primitive tribes".

Anthropologists and sociologists are of the view that tribal population is not evenly distributed in all the districts of the State. They are spread over "Five tribal zones" of Madhya Pradesh. The Eastern Zone comprises of the districts of Sarguja, Shahdol, Raigarh, Bilaspur and Sidhi. In the hills of Sarguja we come across the Pahari Korwas, who are recognized as the most backward of the primitive tribes of the State. In the Central Zone are the districts of Mandla, Betul, Chhindwara, Seoni and Balaghat where in Gond, Korku, Kol and Baiga are the principal tribes. The Southern Zone comprises of Bastar district and parts of Raipur, Durg and Rajnandgaon fall under this Zone. Maria, Muria, Sawara, Halba and Bhatra are the tribal groups of the area. The Western Zone, comprises of Jhabua, Dhar, Khargone, Ratlam and Khandwa districts wherein the Bhils, Bhilas, Patalias and Barelas are the principal tribal communities. Finally, in the North-Western Zone, there are Saharia tribal people/ communities that inhabit districts of Shivpuri, Morena and Guna.

Scheduled Areas of Madhya Pradesh

A deeper look into tribal habitation of the State would show that there are four districts which may be described as wholly "tribal districts". Those districts are Jhabua, Mandla, Sarguja and Bastar. However, there are some districts which may be described as "Partially tribal districts" and where people of these communities are found in certain areas.

According to the notification issued by Government of India, there are four wholly Scheduled Areas while in another 17 district we find "Partially tribal" areas. Details of these two categories of areas are given here :

(A) Scheduled Areas : Four in number

The four declared Scheduled Areas of the State are :

(i) Jhabua district
(ii) Mandla district
(iii) Sarguja district and
(iv) Bastar district

(B) Such Tehsil Areas within a District which have Preponderance of Tribal Population:

	Name of District	*Tahsils/within the District*
(i)	Dhar	Sardarpur, Dhar, Kukshi and Manawar
(ii)	Khargone	Badwani, Rajpur, Sendwha, Bhikangaon, Khargone and Maheswar

(iii)	Khandwa	Khalwa tribal development block and Khaknar Tribal Block (TDB)
(iv)	Ratlam	Saliana
(v)	Betul	Bhainsdehi and Betul
(vi)	Seoni	Lakhnadon and Kurrai Tribal Development Block
(vii)	Balaghat	Baihar
(viii)	Hoshangabad	Kesla TDB
(ix)	Shahdol	PushpRajgarh, Sohagpur and Jaisinghpur
(x)	Sidhi	Kusmi TDB
(xi)	Raigarh	Jashpur Nagar, Udaipur, Ghargoda and Khawasia TDB
(xii)	Bilaspur	Kathghoda, Marwathi TDB, Gorailla TDB, Goorailla Community D.B. & Kota revenue Circle
(xiii)	Durg	Dondi TDB of Balod Tehsil
(xiv)	Rajnandgaon	Bhanpur and Mohla TDB and Chowki Community TDB
(xv)	Raipur	Gariyaband, Manipur and Churu TDB of Bindranavgarth Tehsil, Sinhawa Community TDB of Dhamtari Tehsil
(xvi)	Morena	Karahal TDB of Sheopur Tehsil
(xvii)	Chhindwara	Tamia and Jamai TDBs of Chhindwara Tehsil and nearly 15 villages and TDBs of various Patwari Circles

Thus there are seventeen such districts in Madhya Pradesh that have tribal majority populations spread over various villages, Tribal Development Blocks and Community Development Blocks of various Tehsils of these districts.

Before 1996, these Scheduled Areas of the four aforesaid districts and of the various Tehsils of Madhya Pradesh had distinct modes of administration and control under Art. 244(i) of the Indian Constitution.

So far as the pattern of Panchayati Raj System in the Scheduled Areas of the State is concerned, it was not very different from other areas of the State, except, of course, that the special provisions under para 5, sections (1), (2) and (3) of Part B of the Fifth Schedule were also applicable to them. Thus with the implementation of Panchayati Raj System in Madhya Pradesh for the 1962, when PR system was introduced in Madhya Pradesh for the first time, the three-tier Panchayats of the Scheduled Areas had similar powers and functions as exercised by other PRIs of the State.

The 73rd Constitutional Amendment Act, 1992 was another significant milestone in the journey of Panchayati Raj Institutions in Madhya Pradesh. Madhya Pradesh was the first State in the country which enacted and implemented PR system in the true spirit of the 73rd Amendment Act. The major gain from M.P. Panchayat Raj Adhiniyam, 1993, accruing to the tribal people, was in the field of reservation of seats for their representatives in the three-tiers of the Panchayats as well as for the positions of Panch/Sarpanch etc. The quota of reserved seats for the Scheduled tribe people was to be in proportion to their strength in the population of the areas of Gram Panchayats, Janpads and Zilla Panchayats.

Though the 73rd Constitutional Amendment Act and the Madhya Pradesh Panchayati Raj Adhiniyam, 1993, which was modeled on the lines suggested by the 73rd Amendment Act, provided respectable spaces to the tribal people in the working of the PR system, such legislations could not make the tribal communities the sole masters of their socio-political destinies in their homelands. The need was always felt that the institutional structures within the Scheduled Areas were to be in consonance with the tribal needs, ethos and tribal institutions with which these people were familiar for ages. Also, many of such areas which were once freely managed by the tribal people themselves, for example, the management of their forests, lands, water resources etc., were now out of their purview and were under the authority of external institutions/agencies. Added to such disgruntlements were the voices of the friends of Panchayati Raj system as well as of the tribal people themselves who pleaded for more powers to the Panchayats under Scheduled Areas in a way that their institutions while enjoying decentralised status and functioning as units of self-government, could at the same time preserve and safeguard the traditions, customs and cultural identities of their people.

As a result of such demands and felt needs of the tribal communities a Committee of Parliamentarians and Experts (22 members in all) was appointed in June 1994 by Government of India under the chairmanship of Shri D.S. Bhuria. The purpose of the high level committee was "to discuss and examine the issues relating to extension of the provisions of Part IX of the Constitution of the scheduled areas and to make recommendations on the salient features of the laws for extending the provisions of this Part of the Constitution to the Scheduled Areas. "When adopted, many of the principal recommendations of the Bhuria Committee were accepted by the Union Government and legislation was passed to be known as Panchayat (Extension to the Scheduled Areas) Act, 1996. The Panchayat (Extension to the Scheduled Areas) Act, 1996 received the assent of the President and was forwarded to the States to enact similar legislations so as to extend those provisions to the Scheduled Areas. accordingly, 1997 was enacted by State Assembly. The Adhiniyam received Governor's assent on December 2, 1997 and was promulgated on December 5, 1997.

III. SPECIAL PROVISIONS FOR PANCHAYATS IN THE SCHEDULED AREAS

While redefining the powers of the PRIs the Madhya Pradesh Panchayat Raj (Dwitiya Sanshodhan) Adhiniyam, 1997, adds Chapter XIV-A which delineates the Constitution of Gram Sabhas, Gram Panchayats, prescribes the mode of reservation of seats for them along with the powers and functions of these bodies/institutions of the Scheduled Areas. A perusal of the powers and functions of the PRIs of Scheduled Areas and those of the general functions of the PRIs of Scheduled Areas, particularly the Gram Sabhas, have their distinctive characteristics. Suffice it to say at this stage that the Panchayats of the scheduled areas have been assigned some special powers and functions. Details of the nature/mode of Constitution of the PRIs of the Scheduled Areas and their powers and functions are given hereunder:

(A) The Institutional Structure and Functions

The Gram Sabha

Though the Panchayat Raj Institutions under the Scheduled Areas bear the same nomenclatures as those of the general districts, their mode of composition and their powers vary from Panchayats of the general districts. At the foundational level is the "Gram Sabha". It is a body consisting of persons whose names are included in the electoral rolls relating to the area of a Panchayat at the village level. As the tribal people live in a scattered manner in the *phalias* or hamlets/group of hamlets, the Act defines a village in the Scheduled Areas as "which shall ordinarily consist of a habitation or a group of habitations or a hamlet or a group of hamlets comprising a community and managing its affairs in accordance with (its) traditions and customs". Ordinarily, every village shall have a Gram Sabha, but if the members of the Gram Sabha so desired, more than one Gram Sabha may be constituted in the village, keeping in view the habitation pattern of the tribals under a hamlet or group of hamlets. Not less than 1/3rd of the total number of members of the Gram Sabha shall constitute quorum for a meeting, and out of this number not less than 1/3rd of them should be women members. The meeting of the Gram Sabha shall be presided over by a Scheduled Tribe member who will be elected for the purpose by the majority of the members present in the meeting. Reservation of seats for Scheduled Tribes (as also for Scheduled Castes) in every Panchayat of the Scheduled Areas shall be in proportion to their respective population in that Panchayat area. But the reservation of STs shall not be less than 1/2 of the total number of Panchayat seats. Also, all seats of Sarpanch-President of Panchayats at all levels in the Scheduled Areas are reserved for members of the Scheduled Tribes. In case if there is no representation of Scheduled areas at the Janpad or Zilla Panchayat level, State Government may nominate shall not exceed one-tenth of the total number of the elected members of that Panchayat.

There is also provision for reservation for Scheduled Castes in Scheduled Areas (Sec.129-E3) where such number of seats shall be reserved for other backward classes but such reservation shall not exceed three-fourths of all the seats in that Panchayat.

Special Powers and Functions of Panchayats of Scheduled Areas

Gram Sabha

In addition to the powers and functions, as enumerated under Section– 7 of M.P. Panchayat Raj (Dwitiya Sanshodhan) Act, 1997, the following are the special powers and functions of the Gram Sabha of a Scheduled Area:

(i) To safeguard and preserve the traditions and customs of the people, their cultural identity and community resources and the customary mode of dispute resolution;

(ii) To exercise control over institutions and functionaries in all social sectors transferred to the Gram Panchayat through that Panchayat;

(iii) To manage natural resources including land, water and forests within the area and in harmony with the provisions of the Constitution and with due regard to the spirit of other relevant law for the time being in force;

(iv) To advise the Gram Panchayat in the regulation and use of water bodies

(v) To manage village markets and *melas* including cattle fair, by whatever name called , through the Gram Panchayat;

(vi) To control local plans, resources and expenditure for such plans including tribal sub-plans, and

(vii) To perform and exercise such other powers and functions as the State Government may confer on or entrust under any law for the time being in force.

This catalogue of powers of scheduled area Panchayats must convince any reader that they have been equipped with special powers for the preservation of tribal identities.

Gram Panchayat

The Gram Panchayat in Scheduled Areas shall work under the general superintendence, control and direction of the Gram Sabha. In addition to the powers conferred on the Gram Panchayats under the 1993 Act, the Gram Panchayat shall also have the following powers and functions:

- (i) To carry out the recommendations and decisions made by the Gram Sabhas
- (ii) To manage village markets and *melas*, including cattle fairs;
- (iii) To plan, own and manage minor water bodies up to a specified area situated within its territorial jurisdiction,
- (iv) To lease out any minor water body up to a specified area for the purpose of fishing and other commercial purposes;
- (vii) To exercise control over institutions and functionaries in all social sectors transferred to the Gram Panchayats
- (viii) To exercise and perform such other powers and functions as the State Government may entrust to it.

Janpad Panchayat and Zilla Panchayat

The M.P. Panchayat (Dwitiya Sanshodhan) Act, 1997 brackets together the powers of Janpad and Zilla Panchayat in the Scheduled areas. The Act entrusts these bodies with some additional powers viz.,

- (i) To plan, own and manage minor water bodies upto a specified water area;
- (ii) To exercise control over institutions and functionaries in all social sectors transferred to them;
- (iii) To exercise control over local plans, resources and expenditures for such plans, including tribal sub-plans; and
- (iv) To exercise and perform such other powers and functions as the State Government may confer or entrust under any law for the time being in force.

A look at the powers and functions of the Panchayats as presented above would show that the real beneficiary of special powers is the Gram Sabha and the Gram Panchayat, though Janpad and Zilla Panchayats too have some share from the lion's share received by Gram Sabha and Gram Panchayat. Suffice to say at this stage that the powers and functions specially assigned to the Gram Sabha make the institution the hub of democratic governance at the grassroots level.

IV. SIGNIFICANCE OF THE POWERS AND FUNCTIONS ASSIGNED TO THE PANCHAYATS IN SCHEDULED AREAS

So far a descriptive account of the composition, powers and functions of the Panchayats under the Scheduled Areas has been presented. Now is the need to interpret the significance of the special provisions introduced for the Panchayats in the Scheduled areas, particularly the special powers conferred on the Gram Sabha and the Gram Panchayats. This exercise has been undertaken in the following pages.

The foremost and significant aspect of the amendment package is the recognition of the need of safeguarding and preserving the traditions and customs of the tribal people/communities, their cultural identities as well as their customary modes of resolution of personal/community disputes. One of the primary reasons of keeping separately the Panchayats in Scheduled areas and non-application of Union and State laws related to these Panchayats before 1996 was to safeguard and protect the distinctiveness of the tribal communities. Such needs and requirements of the Panchayats of Scheduled areas of Madhya Pradesh, including Jhabua, stand to be fulfilled by the Madhya Pradesh Panchayat Raj (Dwitiya Sanshodhan) Act, 1997, which in fact has been modelled on the guidelines provided by the Panchayat (extension to the Scheduled Areas) Act, 1996, legislated by Union Parliament. Thus, the Panchayats of Scheduled areas in Madhya Pradesh, on one hand, will have the first taste of democratic decentralization, and, on the other hand, will be able to protect and safeguard their cultural identity, cultural traditions and customs. What a surprise! The tribal people will eat their cake and yet have it!

Secondly, history of tribal societies during the last-forty-five years in India would show that people of Scheduled Tribes lost their rights over forests and other resources. The resource bases of the tribal people were snatched away from them by the 'outsiders' and the tribals societies were disposed by such laws as Land Alienation Act, Mining laws, Forest Act and Wildlife Act. Tribal societies after the passing of the Madhya Pradesh Panchayati Raj (Dwitiya Sanshodhan) Act, 1997, should now feel compensated as section 129-C(iii) empowers the Gram Sabha in Scheduled Areas "to manage natural resources, including land, water and forests within the area of the village with its traditions". This would be like regaining "the lost horizon" for the tribal people.

A perusal of the mode of composition of the Panchayats of Scheduled Areas as well as the powers and functions entrusted to them would show that such arrangements pave the way for participatory democracy. More than this, the special provisions give the Panchayats the opportunity to work for achieving the goals of socio-economic development and realisation of social justice. They have been authorized to undertake measures for removal of poverty, illiteracy and the conditions of ill-health. As the list of powers and functions to the Gram Sabhas and Gram Panchayat would make it clear, these institutions have been assigned power to promote education, child welfare, sanitation and take care of public health sectors and women's development. These are the very facilities that the tribal people lacked for ages.

One of the burning problems of Panchayati Raj System ever since its inception has been that of the right relationship between the PR representatives and the government servants and functionaries associated with the Panchayat administration. Complaints from both the sides were often heard that the other side was responsible for the failures of the Panchayat system; bureaucracy raising the accusing finger at the ignorance of people's representatives and their political ambitions while elected representatives accused the civil servants for their non-cooperation with the new system for fear of loss of authority which they enjoyed before the advent of the Panchayat regime. Practically every seminar/

workshop that discussed the relationship between these two operators of Panchayat Raj System came to the conclusion that for the successful working of the PR system there was need to put a bridle on the obstinacy of the civil servants as also on the political ambitions and feelings of mistrust of the people's representatives. The Dwitiya Sanshodhan Adhiniyam, 1997, resolves this crisis situation by conferring on Gram Sabha and Gram Panchayat in Scheduled Areas the "powers of general superintendence, control and direction". Sections 129-(C) (ii) and 129-(d) (vi) of the Act (1997) authorise Gram Sabha and Gram Panchayat of Scheduled Areas respectively "to exercise control over functionaries" in all social sectors transferred to them. Such provisions do rein the spirit of non-cooperation of State officials for the sake of smooth working of the Panchayat system.

The new distension opens also ample opportunities to such NGOs in the Scheduled Areas who have interest in the welfare of the Panchayats and the tribal people living in these areas. The NGOs can positively help the Panchayats and the people living under these areas in many ways: such areas are training of Panchayat representatives, particularly women representatives; project formulation and implementation awareness generation among the tribal people about various Government Programmes; literacy programmes; agriculture and extension and development; watershed schemes; utilization of common property resources; planning and resource mobilization etc. More items of the kind can be added to this list. But what is to be remembered is that NGOs have to swim with , but not against the currents of the welfare of the tribal people and their Panchayats. This kind of NGO-PRI partnership at the grassroots level will surely open up new vistas of rural democracy and development.

V. POSSIBLE HURDLES AND HINDRANCES

Before we conclude, we may pause here to ponder over the possible hurdles and hindrances that may come up with the operationalization of the Dwitiya Sanshodhan Act. One such possible problem may arise when we look at the task before the Gram Sabha of Scheduled Areas, namely that of reconciling of the forces of modernity with its function of "safeguarding and preserving the traditions and customs of the people, their cultural identity.....and the customary mode of dispute resolution". We can easily foresee that the powers and functions conferred on the three tier Panchayats of Scheduled Areas, for example, those of management of public land, removal of social evil like dowry, promotion of education, removal of untouchability, implementation of schemes for economic development and social justice and administration of the functions which were formerly performed by DRDA and now merged with Zilla Panchayat, etc., would act in due course of time as catalyst agencies of social, economic and cultural changes in society, throwing up force and values of modernity which may come into conflict with the traditional value system of the tribal communities of the Scheduled Areas. This would revive the old controversy of tradition versus modernity in the Scheduled Areas to the detriment of development and welfare of the tribal people particularly tribal women and children.

No one knows for certain as to what sort of new social forces would be unleashed by the administrative, economic and social welfare inputs under the PR system, but one can imagine that such inputs should generate values of individualism; in fact, such a behaviour is easily discernible among such tribals who outmigrate seasonally to nearby cities and come back home imbibed with a different value system after an interlude of some months. But it is one of the salient characteristics of a tribal areas society acts like one unit and that society prevails over individual views. This is to surmise that the train of social change would follow such individualistic values/forces that would challenge the customary practices and values of tribal society of the Tribal Areas. Friends of tribal societies/people have to take care of this possibility.

Another possible factor/institution likely to influence the ways, the values and social life of tribal people of the Panchayats of Scheduled Areas is the party system and its politics. India is a democracy based on the working of political parties. Unfortunately, there is a plethora of political parties in the country, many of them standing polar opposite to the aims, methods and programmes of contending parties. It is feared that the generation of such contending parties into the area of Panchayats would politicize tribal people with all its attendant evils and further vitiate the unity of tribal society which already has its fragmenting sub-societies. The danger of breakdown of tribal harmony as a result entrance of devise politics of national/regional parties in Panchayats of Scheduled areas is a real one and has to be guarded against. The hitherto maintained social and cultural unity of the tribal communities should not be allowed to be broken by the inroads of political parties into the Panchayats of the Scheduled Areas.

Finally, the lingering and evergrowing problems of tribal indebtedness, and alienation, deforestation, entry of multinational into the tribal areas for mining, industrialization, outmigrations of tribals to far away cities and industrial centres which thereby shatter their family life, seasonal unemployment, displacement of tribals as a result of construction of big dams and problems like poverty, illiteracy, poor health and some issues related to sustainable development in tribal areas are some of the major burning problems of the tribal communities. Outside world would watch with their fingers crossed at the Panchayats of the Scheduled Areas that they grapple with such problems with foresight, and establish a system that provides them the fruits of economic-political development, social harmony, enlightenment and social justice, but all in consonance with tribal systems, traditions and methods. These are some of the challenges before the Panchayats of Scheduled Areas for which they should be prepared to face them from the very first day.

ANNEXURE

FUNCTIONS OF PANCHAYATS

Functions of Gram Panchayat

It shall be the duty of a Gram Panchayat insofar as the Gram Panchayat funds allow, to perform within its areas the following functions.

1. Sanitation, conservancy and prevention and abatement of nuisance;
2. Construction, repair and maintenance of public wells, ponds and tanks and supply of water for domestic use;
3. Construction and maintenance of sources of water for bathing and washing and supply of water for domestic animal;
4. Construction and maintenance of village roads, culverts, bridges, bunds and other works and buildings of public utility;
5. Construction,maintenance and clearing of public streets, latrines, drains, tanks, wells and other public places;
6. Filling in of disused wells, insanitary ponds, pools, ditches and pits and conversion of step wells into sanitary wells;
7. Lighting of village streets and other public places;
8. Removing of obstructions and projections in public streets or places and in sites not being properly or which are open to use of public, whether such sites are vested in the Panchayat or belong to the State Government;
9. Regulating and control over entertainment shows, shops, eating houses and vendors of drinks, sweetmeats, fruits, milk and of other similar articles;
10. Regulating the construction of house, latrines, urinals, drains and water closets;
11. Management of public land and management, extension and development of village site;

12.(a) Regulating places for disposal of dead bodies, carcasses and other offensive matters;

(b) disposal of unclaimed corpses and carcasses;

13. Earmarking places for dumping refuse;
14. Regulation of sale and preservation of meat;
15. Maintenance of Gram Panchayat property;
16. Establishment and management of cattle ponds and maintenance of records relating to cattle;
17. Maintenance of ancient and historical monuments other than those declared by or under law made by Parliament to be of national importance, grazing lands and other lands vesting in or under the control of the Gram Panchayat;
18. Establishment, management and regulation of markets and *melas* other than public markets and public *melas*;
19. Maintenance of records of births, deaths and marriages;
20. Rendering assistance in the census operation and in the surveys conducted by the State Government or Central Government or any other local authority lawfully constituted;
21. Rendering assistance in prevention of contagious diseases;
22. Rendering assistance in inoculation and small pox vaccination and enforcement of other preventive measures for safety of human beings and cattle prescribed by Government department concerned;
23. Rendering assistance to the disabled and destitute;
24. Promotion of youth welfare, family welfare and sports;
25. Establishment of Raksha Samiti for :

(a) Safety of life and property;

(b) Prevention of fire and extinguishing fire and safety of property during outbreak of such fires;

26. Plantation and Preservation of Panchayat forests;
27. Removal of social evils like dowry;
28. Granting loan for purposes of:

(a) Providing medical assistance

(b) Disposal of dead body of an indigent person or

any member of his family; or

c) Any other purpose for the benefit of an indigent person as may be notified by the State Government from time to time subject to such terms and conditions as may be described.

29.(a)Carrying out the directions or orders given or issued by the State Government, the Collector of any other officer authorized by the State Government in this behalf with respect to the measures for amelioration of the conditions of the Scheduled Castes and Scheduled Tribes and other backward classes and in particular in regard to the removal of untouchability.

(b) Perform such functions as may be entrusted to it by the State Government. Zilla Panchayats or Janpad Panchayat by general or special orders;

(c)With prior approval of Janpad Panchayat, it may also perform other functions as it may desire to perform.

Provided that where any such functions are entrusted to the Gram Panchayats it shall act as an agent of the State Government, Zilla Panchayat or Janpad Panchayat, as the case may be and necessary funds and other assistance for the purpose shall be provided to it by the State Government, Zilla Panchayat or Janpad Panchayat, as the case may be.

Functions of Janpad Panchayat

(1) Subject to the provisions of this Act and the rules made thereunder, and subject to general or special orders, as may be issued by the State government, from time to time, it shall be the duty of a Janpad Panchayat, so far as the Janpad Panchayat funds allow to make reasonable provision in the block for the following matters :

(a) Integrated Rural Development Programme, Agriculture, Social Forestry, Animal Husbandry and Fisheries, Health and Sanitation, Adult Education, Communication and Public Works, Co-operation, Cottege Industries, Welfare of Women, Youth and

Children, Welfare of Disabled and the Destitute and Welfare of Backward Classes, Family Planning and Sports and Rural Employment Programmes;

(b) Provision of emergency relief in cases of distress caused by fires, floods, drought, earthquake, scarcity, locust swarms, epidemics and other natural calamities;

(c) Arrangement in connection with local pilgrimage and festivals;

(d) Management of public ferries;

(e) Management of public markets, public *melas* and exhibitions; and

(f) Any other function with the approval of the State Government or Zilla Panchayat.

(2) The Janpad Panchayat shall control and supervise the administration of the community development block or tribal block within its jurisdiction, as the case may be, and functions and schemes assigned to such block by the State Government shall be implemented under the superintendence, directions and control of the Janpad Panchayat in accordance with the Instructions issued by the Government from time to time.

Functions of Zilla Panchayat

1. Subject to the provisions of this Act and rules made thereunder, it shall be the duty of the Zilla Panchayat to:

(i) Control, coordinate and guide the Janpad Panchayat and Gram Panchayat within the district;

(ii) Coordinate and consolidate the Janpad Panchayat plans;

(iii) Coordinate the demands for grants for special purpose received from the Janpad Panchayats and forward them to the State Government.

(iv) Secure the execution of the plans, projects, schemes or other works common to two or more Janpad Panchayats in the district;

Panchayats in the district;

(v) Advise the State Government in the development activities, social forestry, family welfare, welfare of the disabled, destitute, women, youth and children and sports;

(vi) Exercise and perform such other powers and functions as the Sate Government may confer on or entrust to it.

2. The Zilla Panchayat shall control and supervise administration of District Rural Development Agency within its jurisdiction and all functions and schemes assigned to the District Rural Development Agency by the State Government shall be implemented under the Superintendence, direction and control of the Zilla Panchayat in accordance with the instructions issued by the State Government from time to time.

5

GOVERNANCE FROM THE GRASSROOTS

M.P. Boraian

People and Government

While evolving rural welfare policies, formulating development plans and executing programmes, should the government listen to the people or the people listen to the government? Ideally the government should listen to people but practically it is the reverse in many a country irrespective of the political system. Wherever the government is people-friendly, the people benefit largely. On the contrary, wherever the government is indifferent to people's needs and problems the people suffer greatly.

When the people are conscious of their rights and responsibilities and are well organised, they demand their share from the government, and keep the government conscious if not people conscious. But where the government is not people friendly, it would not wish to be people conscious too! Hence, such a government would not keep people's welfare as their primary agenda. Instead, it might like to keep people at a distance, and function autonomously because, involving the community always means inviting botheration to the government, endangering its autonomy and dwindling its domination over people.

Despite being the largest democracy in the world, and having passed 50 years of independence, India is no exception to this phenomenon. We find the people depending more on the government than the government depending more on the people. Planning for the rural poor, Dalits, the downtrodden and a galaxy of other neglected segments always begins from above. This 'top down' approach has to give way to the 'bottom up' approach gradually. In order to reach this stage, there should be a transition from the present situation of 'people listening to government' to that of 'each one listening to the other' and finally to the government listening to people.

At present the government evolves a policy, formulates a programme, works out the modalities and implements the programme directly or thrusts it on the local bodies for the implementation without any room for flexibilities or deviation. This is indeed an 'enforced development' and not a 'participatory development'. People should express their needs and problems and the government should formulate policies and programmes accordingly. However, current reality unfolds totally the reverse. We have experimented with this 'reverse approach' for over 50 years, starting from Community Development Programme during 1952 and Panchayat Raj System in 1959.

Panchayat and NGOs

Even after 73rd Amendment, Village Panchayat and Gram Sabhas, which are the micro level mechanisms for rural welfare and development, grapple with their own issues, most of which elude early solution. The Panchayat and Gram Sabhas invariably tread on the lines toed by the government and hence they are less autonomous and self reliant.

At this juncture, where the people and Panchayat are not in a position to galvanize the government, the Non-government Organizations (NGOs) can play a vital role by activating the government to involve the community in planning, implementation, monitoring and evaluation, thereby listen to people in the process of ushering in participatory development system. Undoubtedly, the NGOs often struggle with the government in order to obtain people's share. But in the process, some have enmitized the government while others have befriended. A small segment, of course, remains neutral, but they would not prefer to annoy the government at the cost of their relationship.

Development Distance

Since recent years, the Government of India has a huge share of money to be channelised to the NGOs for execution of community based activities in order to promote participatory development at the grassroots level. Many NGOs therefore prefer to toe the line of the government and tame themselves to be 'government friendly'. under these circumstances, not many NGOs could be expected to initiate the process of bridging the distance between people and the government effectively.

Consequently, the distance between the Government and people remain neither bridged nor reduced. For obvious reasons, the Government may not take up the thread. Nor do the people seem to bother about this 'development distance' between the government policies and people's problems. Instead, the people are more concerned about their immediate and personal problems rather than the long term, societal problems.

Even while doing so, they yearn for loans, subsidies, loan waives etc., as solution to their problems, rather than locate their root causes and trace out the real sources of these problems for thrashing out suitable solutions. Such a dependent attitude among people has systematically been developed by the government through a series of strategies and schemes which made the people more as 'beneficiaries' and objects but rarely as 'partners'. People would therefore not bother about the basic causes of their problems but look at political parties and politicians as the primary solution to all their pressing problems. Under these circumstances, people may not emerge as a source of distress to the government.

With the government unwilling to be responsive and people unable to be sensitized, the process of participatory rural development requires to be redefined and fortified. In order to accomplish this task, it would be ideal to establish a Forum for review and analysis of all Rural Policies formulated by the Central and State governments as well as those policies of bilateral and multilateral organizations which have implications for rural life. Such a forum may be named as 'Rural Policy Forum' and based at

Gandhigram, which has cordial relation with all segments of the population viz., village people, Panchayat leaders, NGOs, Donors and Government officials.

Aim

Towards achieving this end, a new forum at the micro level viz., Rural Policy Forum is considered as an alternative. This forum would serve as a platform for the rural people to share their experience with welfare and development programmes of the Panchayat, government, donors and NGOs. Equally, the government, Panchayats, donors, NGOs as well as other change agents can air their views on their experiments with rural development and programme implementation experience with people. In sum, this would serve as an enduring ground for critical analysis and review of the formulation, reformulation or revision of rural policies.

Objectives

The proposed Forum may have the following major objectives:

1. To harvest the experience of rural people and Panchayat leaders regarding the implementation of welfare and development programmes and the difficulties encountered.
2. To invite the government officials and political dignitaries to share their development experiences with the rural people and leaders.
3. To enable the NGOs and Donor agencies to reflect their views on the government's rural policies and their experience with the people.
4. To provide a common platform for analysis and review of the rural policies and programmes between and among the various change agents.
5. To disseminate the outcome of all discussions and dialogues to the concerned institutions and individuals for follow up.
6. To undertake rapid policy research at micro level on the previous, current and proposed rural policies of government and NGOs.

7. To document the policies, programmes and the policy review exercises and serve as a clearing house for rural policies.

Programmes

This Forum can undertake the following programmes:

Grassroot Dialogue

People from various segments of the rural communities will coverage at Gandhigram for sharing their experience on a select theme i.e., a programme, a problem or an issue. The theme of dialogue will be focussed and on a select issue currently bothering them intensely. Strategies for poverty eradication, loopholes in the process of utilization of development programmes, elimination of child labour, empowerment of women etc., may constitute as some of the issues.

The duration will be suited to the convenience of the participants, in any case, not more than two days. The area for selection of participants will be based on the preponderance of the problem proposed as the theme of discussion and review.

Selection of participants from villagers will be `need based' and restricted to those pertinent to the prime theme of the proposed discussion. Beneficiaries of programmes, representatives of select groups such as women's Sangam, and youth club, traditional leaders,members of community organizations and the like will constitute the audience.

Panchayat Leaders

In addition to the people, elected leaders of village, block and district Panchayats will also be invited to deliberate on their development transactions with the people and the government - the process, procedures and problems. Their views on various policies and programmes of the government as well as NGOs will be identified for suggesting necessary policy changes particularly in the structure and functions of Panchayats. They will also share their experience with the people in utilising the benefits of various Panchayat programmes. On the other hand, they will provide insights about the functioning of officials on the one hand and NGOs on the other hand.

The duration will be for one or two days. Those themes which emerged during discussion with the people, government and NGOs, particularly relevant to their interest will be discussed.

Government Officials

Under this programme, officials at the field level as well as block and district level drawn from various development departments—such as Extension Officers, Block Development Officers from Rural Development Department, Social Welfare Department as also officials from other allied departments will meet for short interactions and experience sharing on select themes. The themes will be identified based on the discussions held earlier with the people and Panchayat leaders.

Donors and NGOs

Representative of Donor agencies from different thrust areas will be invited to share their experience with the government, NGOs, and the community. The theme will emerge from the discussions held with the people and officials. Selection of Donor agencies will depend upon the theme, problem or policy being currently debated by the forum. Donor agencies which have their regional offices in the south or in the union capital will be invited for such discussions.

Further, head of Non-Government Organizations will be invited to share their experience in problems identification, project formulation and implementation besides monitoring and evaluation. Their impressions and actual experience with the community on the one hand and the Government on the other hand will be brought out. In particular, their perception about the policies and programmes of the Donor agencies and the government of Donor countries will be studied closely.

Expert Consultations

Experts drawn from educational institutions, training and research centres, and consultancy organizations too will be invited to share their views and ideas in the various themes deliberated by a cross section of people, leaders, officials, donors and NGOs.

In addition, statesmen, select government officials and dignitaries and charismatic political leaders from above and below, who were or are directly involved in the formulation of policies under review or execution of programmes under debate will be invited as and when warranted.

The experts and dignitaries will also deliberate on the policies and programmes of bilateral and multilateral funding and development agencies such as the various UN bodies, World Bank, Ford Foundation, DANIDA, NORAD, CIDA etc. which have supported various on-going programmes in India. However, their role will be confined to reflect on the policies, programmes and the processes besides giving suggestions for future course of action. They will share their vision and wisdom on the various facets of rural development. This will be a one day meet.

Collective Meet

Besides meeting by the above category of individuals/officials separately, there will be collective meets too, depending upon the nature of the theme and type of participants required for deliberations. Equal importance will be given to meeting by specific category of participants such as people, officials, leaders or NGOs as well as meeting between two or more categories depending upon the need for such a collective meet. The duration of such meets will also be restricted to not more than two or maximum of three days.

Policy Research

The Forum will undertake policy research in a rapid manner using Participatory Rural Appraisal (PRA) techniques, focussed group discussion method and case studies. The topics of study will be those which emerge during the discussions and dialogues. The approach is to collect the most essential data from the most appropriate persons at the minimum possible time and cost. The findings of the study will be discussed in the relevant forums and suitable recommendations will be made to the government and other institutions for action.

Documentation

Equal priority will be given to documentation and dissemination.

The Forum, besides documenting the deliberations of the various meets, will also obtain vital documents on various policies, Acts or programmes available with the Government and other for enlightening the target groups.

Importance will be given to various forms of documentation such as video, audio cassettes and printed literatures.

Dissemination

The proceedings of every forum will be neatly compiled and transmitted to those Governments, Ministries or Departments which are directly concerned. In addition, such matters will also be shared with other institutions or experts who are working on such issues.

Important matters which have news value will be relayed through the electronic and print media for a wider reach to the masses.

Clearing House

The Forum would collect all the relevant documents, reports and reading materials regarding the plans, programmes and copy of legislations which form the subject matter of the theme.

In every forum, information regarding these programmes or provision of Acts will be shared with the participants in order to apprise them with the latest facts and thus enhance their awareness. The outcome of all such deliberations will be documented and distributed to the user group. In addition, such documents would serve as reference materials for future discussions on the same or related themes. Every forum, therefore, not only will serve the purpose of sharing but also empower people with information and knowledge.

The Process

1. Hotly debated issues of utmost relevance to ordinary people's lives and work will be taken up for discussion at the first instance. Upon selection of the themes, the participants and guest speakers will be decided and invited.
2. Equal importance will be given to keep the participants enlightened about the provisions of the new Act, policies or programmes which constitute the focus of discussion.
3. Every hour will be spent directly in discussing and debating the issues under focus, after a general enlightenment session.
4. Topmost priority will be accorded to the views and ideas of the participants. The participants will be the resource persons. The resource persons, wherever invited, will only be considered as participants. There will thus be a 'reversal of roles' in the deliberations of the proposed Forum.
5. Meticulous documentation of the proceedings of all the sessions will be made. Actual views and opinions of the people or leaders of officials will be disseminated without filtering or editing.

The Method

1. Participants will take part in both plenary sessions and group discussions. Resourceful persons among the participants will also be assigned 'lead roles' in the appropriate sessions.
2. Besides, the above, other methods proposed by the participants will also be followed in order to make the sessions lively and rewarding.
3. Publicity oriented ceremonial talks by popular personalities who have no relevance to the theme of discussion will be avoided.

Probable Outcome

1. People from rural areas including elected leaders will be empowered with relevant information on recent policies or programmes.

2. People will be able to reflect on the prospects and problems of every new policy or programmes of the Government or NGO or Donor.
3. Government will get a feedback about its policies directly from the actual beneficiaries which can be used for policy review exercises.
4. The community will come out with its own set of policies or programmes for consideration by the government.
5. Democratic governance will get cemented by such a healthy dialogue in the rural sector.

6

THE PANCHAYAT SYSTEM IN WEST BENGAL

PRABHAT DATTA AND
CHANDAN DATTA

The monograph — eighth in the series of PRIA Information Pack— seeks to present an overview of the structures and processes of the third generation Panchayats in West Bengal against a brief backdrop of colonial past and post-colonial experience before the advent of the present Left Front Government in the State. An attempt has been made to identify the characteristic features of the present Panchayat system coupled with innovative institution building initiatives in West Bengal and to assess the performance of the Panchayats , particularly Gram Panchayats, in the light of empirical research studies. The bibliographical references at the end of the monograph will be useful to those who would like to learn more about the West Bengal model of Panchayats.

We hope that the study based on secondary source material, would be a helpful guide to those who are engaged and involved in promoting and strengthening village self-governing institutions in different parts of the country.

The British rulers had started taking interest in local self government in India after the Seopy Mutiny. The colonial interest was largely motivated by the specific concern for replenishing colonial coffer which had suffered losses because of the Sepoy

Mutiny, unleasing initiative to facilitate increase in productivity, co-opting nationalist leaders into the fold of political institutions to contain their anti-Imperialist ideology and the general concern for the maintenance, entrenchment, consolidation and legitimization of the British regime.

Lord Ripon, however, struck a slightly different note in 1982. He conceived local self governing institutions in terms of instruments not only for effecting improvement in administration but also for political education of the people. Having been influenced by the ideas of J.S. Mill, Hume and other liberal thinkers, he proposed the establishment of a large network of rural local boards in India. He suggested that two-thirds of the members of the boards would be non-official representatives, elected wherever possible. He pleaded for giving them adequate powers, functions and resources. He was not successful in translating his ideas into reality for a number of reasons, e.g., lack of genuine political support of the colonial rulers, reluctance of the landed aristocracy to share power with people, resistance of the colonial bureaucracy, inequitable social structure dominated by the zamindars, lack of participative culture of the people etc.

Panchayats in Colonial Bengal

During the days of the colonial rule rural Bengal had witnessed a short spell of a type of Panchayat called the Chowkidari Panchayat introduced in 1870. It had nothing to do with normal municipal functions, and was principally concerned with the maintenance of the village watch and ward. The Chowkidari Panchayat became very unpopular shortly after its introduction and went into disuse soon.

The Bengal Local Self Government Act was passed in 1885 as a sequel to the famous Ripon Resolution of 1882. The Act provided for two tiers of local government, one at the district level and the other, at the sub-divisional level. It had also provided for Union Committees for groups of villages. Because of its wide jurisdiction the district tier failed to live upto the expectations. They became rapidly redundant because of their complete reliance upon limited grants and subsidies. The Union Committees had even fewer responsibilities and insignificant role outside the context of village politics. The Local Boards at the sub-divisional level had no autonomy, and were abolished shortly. Despite there being a provision for the extensive use of democratic principles and non-official chairman under the Act the Bengal Administration Report of 1891-92 had shown that the elected members were in minority. At the close of 1891-92 of the total 790 members in 38 districts of Bengal 168 were ex-officio members, 313 were nominated by the government and 309 were elected by the Local Boards. In the Local Boards of 1248 members, 40 were ex-officio members, 739 were nominated by the Government and only 469 were elected. Of 790 members in the District Boards, 31.5 per cent were government servants, 26 per cent were Zamindars and landlords and 26.6 per cent were legal practitioners. In the Local Boards 47.7 per cent were landlords or their servants, 23.8 per cent were legal practitioners and 12.8 per cent were government servants.

The District Boards had surrendered their responsibilities to functional boards like the District School Boards and turned into appendages of the colonial State in the districts. The primary purpose was to appease the nationalist leaders and to co-opt them into the fold of the colonial rule.

The Bengal partition agitation of 1905 heralded a new era in the nationalist movement making administrative reforms inevitable. The imperial Government had no other alternative but to decentralise administrative powers. In 1914 the District Administrative Reforms Commission appointed by the Government of Bengal pleaded for a unified system of rural local government and favoured the establishment of a network of unified rural local authorities combining the functions of the Chowkidari Panchayat and the Union Committee. This led to the birth of the Union Board under the Bengal Village Self Government Act, 1919.

Each Union Board covered on an average 8 to 10 villages with a total population of 10,000. They functioned under District Boards. Thus the traditional institutions of village Panchayat were incorporated into the administrative and revenue structure of the colonial rule and the emerging middle class was accommodated into the fold of colonial rule to enable them to fulfil their political aspirations. But the institutions did not have effective powers and resources. The Union Board was elected on a limited franchise and continued till 1956 when the West Bengal Panchayat Act 1957 was passed. It gave birth to the first generation Panchayats in West Bengal broadly in line with the Balwant Rai Mehta Committee Report.

Village Panchayats after Independence

Of the part 'A' States West Bengal was the only State which did not have any legislation on the subject till 1952. Part of the complexity lay in the peculiar character of the village in West Bengal. With homestead lands scattered all over West Bengal the concept of residential village does not make much sense in the State as residential alignments keep on changing periodically. The Zamindari system tended to choke one of the channels of modernization. It has been argued that because of the interposition of the zamindari system administrative and political linkages of rural West Bengal with Calcutta were also weak.

The West Bengal Panchayat Bill was passed in 1957 although it was introduced in 1956. The Union Boards gave place to two-tier structure at the lowest level—Gram Panchayats and the Anchal Panchayat. The implementation of the Act was however phased. By 1963 only 50 per cent of the villages and 60 per cent of the rural population were covered by the Panchayat system. The Anchal Panchayats were based on the earlier Union Board, and were located above Gram Panchayats in legal and administrative hierarchy. They became the main focus of formal political power. As the members were indirectly elected, it nullified the call for popular participation at the lower level.

The next step in completing the structure of the first generation Panchayat system was taken during the Third Five Year Plan Period. The West Bengal Zilla Parishad Act was passed in 1963 to provide for re-modelling of rural local government with a view to associating the local authorities with development activities and bringing about democratic decentralization and people's participation in planning and development. The two Acts provided for a four-tier structure consisting of Zilla Parishad, Anchalik Parishad, Anchal Panchayat and Gram Panchayat. The Zilla Parishads and Anchalik Parishads died prematurely. The other two bodies did not play effective role as institutions of local government. They had some involvement in the disbursement of relief, collection of tax, fees and rates of very limited amount and in respect of payment of chowkidars and dafadars. Elections were not held for years and members remained in office without resource to local opinion.

Clearly, West Bengal started its journey at a time when the phase of decline of the Panchayat institutions in other States of the country had begun primarily because of the lack of political support, bureaucratic neglect and inadequate statute to make Panchayat bodies representative, responsive and strong. According to one observer the Zilla Parishads and Anchalik Parishads faced their inglorious death as soon as they were born. The Gram Panchayats and Anchal Panchayats continued at the local level. But they had no effective role.

The delayed birth of Panchayats in West Bengal received a further setback because of series of political developments in the State after its ceremonial inauguration on October 2, 1964. The State witnessed an unprecedented food crisis in 1965. The law and order situation in the State became alarming as a result of bandhs, demonstrations and the strikes. The Congress was defeated in the fourth general election held in March, 1967. The United Front (UF) Government which was installed, proposed a completely new scheme for overhauling the Panchayat system but the Government was dismissed. The next coalition ministry of the Progressive Democratic Front and the Congress rejected the proposal of the predecessor Government and considered some modification in the Acts.

But it met with the same fate very soon. The State was brought under the rule of the President in early 1968. In the next elections the United Front was again voted to power. And quite obviously it proceeded with its earlier scheme. All the Zilla Parishads were superseded in 1969 followed by the suppression of other bodies. The annual report of 1967-68 observed that there was doubt about the effective functioning of even 10 out of 19 Gram Panchayats. A comprehensive bill was introduced in the Assembly. But the second UF ministry fell in March 1970 and the State was again brought under the President's rule. The Congress which captured power in March 1972, took up the matter. This effort bore fruit. A consolidated piece of legislation called the West Bengal Panchayat Act was enacted in 1973. The Act provided for a three-tier Panchayat system—Gram Panchayat at the village level for a group of villages, Panchayat Samiti at the Block level and Zilla Parishad at the district level. Thus came the skeleton of the second generation Panchayat the flesh and blood to which was provided by the Left Front Government in 1978.

Pressure for the reform of the Panchayat system emerged in West Bengal on the basis of two forms of criticism, as Webster has argued, one of implementation failure and the other of political naivety. The first point to the failure of the State government because Panchayats were not given adequate powers to play an important role in the field of rural development. They were also not used by the various departments to aid the implementation of their programmes. Care was not taken to develop effective channels of communication between the State government and the people through these bodies.

The failure was aggravated by the grinding rural poverty and the growing call for new initiatives in rural development policies based upon reorganization in the form of State intervention at the local level. The Left parties had criticized the Panchayat system because it was not possible to ensure genuine participation of the people in the countryside without altering rural class structure through land reforms. As long as it is not done, it is argued, they will continue to be undemocratic institutions in the hands of the landed gentry.

While the 1973 Act was based for the most part on the original Acts of 1957 and 1963, the aim of the new legislation was to reorganise Panchayats and to have them playing a major role in the implementation of development programmes. The legislation however remained unimplemented for some time. The national political scenario was not conducive for effective decentralization of powers. Growing centralization of powers was the most dominant phenomenon in national politics. Added to it was the infighting and internal bickerings within the Congress in the State. Rampant factionalism had further damaged the party organization. The Congress party in the State did not have effective, efficient and acceptable leadership. The central leadership started intervening in many issues and the factional leadership began to depend on them for strengthening their respective positions.

The Approach of Left Front Government to Panchayats

The Left Front Government was installed in 1977 after a period of political upheaval in the State for about a decade. The Left Front Government was faced with three major tasks on the rural front. In the first place, it was required to regenerate stagnant rural economy and to promote distributive justice. Secondly, it was necessary to set the democratic processes in rural West Bengal in motion. Thirdly, it had to undermine 'rock departmentalism' rooted in deep elitism and conservatism permeating the bureaucratic structures. It is ideologically committed to Marxism-Leninism and thus to radical social change. It is however a 'Marxist Government' with a difference because it was not born out of socialist revolution. It has to operate within the framework of a base and superstructure, of the capitalist State, highly centralised Constitutional and political structure backward feudal culture etc. The character and commitment of the regime and constraints on the regime determine the approach of the Government to Panchayats.

The second generation Panchayats under this phase are political Panchayats. West Bengal was the first State in the country to hold election to the Panchayat institutions on the basis of open participation of political parties and at regular intervals. Panchayats are not merely instruments of rural development but those of mobilization of the masses. The biggest partner of the Left Front, CPI(M), has participated in the Government to use it as an instrument of mobilization of masses and struggle for the cause of people's democracy.

Panchayats in West Bengal are instruments of pro-poor socio economic change. They have played significant role in the implementation of land reform programmes in the State and thus to create objective conditions for the successful working of Panchayat bodies.

The Gram Panchayat

As instruments of rural development and social change the Panchayats are required to play an important role in respect of implementation of land reforms programme. Land reforms are considered the core of rural development — a programme for changing the correlation of class forces in the countryside.

During the regime of Left Front, West Bengal has experienced two generations of Panchayats — the second generation and the third generation. While there are many commonalities between these two generation of Panchayats, the third generation phase lays stress on the development of Panchayats not only as instruments of rural development but also as units of self Government. Thus it combines the instrumentalist and institutionist — perspectives on Panchayats.

There is a Gram Panchayat for every gram. A gram may be a mouza or a part of a mouza or group of contiguous mouzas or parts thereof.

A Gram Panchayat consists of the following members:

(a) members elected by the people, and
(b) the members of the Panchayat Samiti, not being Sabhapati or Sahakari Sabhapati, elected thereto from the constituency comprising any part of the gram.

The Application of Anti-Defection Law to Members

The anti-defection law applies to the members of the G.P. It is laid down that a members of the GP will be disqualified for being a member if he is an elected member set up by a recognised political party, and has voluntarily given up his membership of such party or exercised the voting right contrary to the manner of voting of the party members set up by the recognised party, or if he is an elected member not set up by any recognised party and he has joined a recognised party on the expiry of six months from the date of election.

The elected members set up by the recognised political parties have to select one member from amongst themselves to be the leader with in one month from the date of the first meeting of the GP. The leader has to furnish to the Block Development Officer (BDO) the following :

(a) a copy of the Constitution;
(b) signed statement containing the names, addresses and constituencies of himself and other members; and
(c) a copy of the rules and regulations of his party.

Where there is only one elected member set up by a recognised political party, he is required to furnish the documents as mentioned earlier also in relation to himself.

A member not belonging to any recognised political party has also to inform the BDO about his status within one month from the date of the first meeting of the GP.

The process of disqualification of membership and removal from Panchayat need to be intimated by the leader of the party who will file a petition to the prescribed authority in this regard. The petition will State that one or more members of their party have voluntarily given up his or their membership or have exercised the voting right contrary to the manner of voting of the majority members set up by the party.

The only elected member of a party or an elected member who does not belong to any party, is also liable to be disqualified following the same procedure.

After having received the petition the prescribed authority examines the validity of the petition within six weeks from the date of the receipt of the petition. He is required to take a decision within eight weeks.

Meeting

Every Gram Panchayat is required to hold meeting at least once in every month on such date and at such hour as the GP may fix at the immediately preceding meeting. In case this is not done, the matter is left to the Pradhan (the political head of the Gram Panchayat)

At least seven day's notice of the list of business to be transacted in the meeting except an emergency meeting, is sent to each member.

A notice is also put up in the notice board.

Functions, Duties and Powers

As the units of self-government, the third generation Gram Panchayats in West Bengal born out of the amendments of the West Bengal Panchayats Act in line with the requirement of the 73rd Amendment of the Constitution perform, *inter alia*, the following general functions.

(a) preparation of development plan at the village level;
(b) development of infrastructural facilities for overall economic development; and
(c) implementation of anti-poverty programmes, literacy programmes, family and child welfare programmes and programmes meant for ensuring social justice.

The GPs have three different types of other functions, obligatory, delegated and discretionary, while the obligatory functions are civic functions, the other two are concerned with development and reconstruction. Subject to the availability of funds, the GPs are responsible for providing sanitation, conservancy and drainage, prevention of public nuisance, taking curative and preventive measures in respect of malaria or an epidemic, vaccination, maintenance and repair of public streets etc.

The GPs have to perform some other functions as may be assigned to it by the State government in respect of primary, social, technical or vocational education, rural dispensaries, maternity and child welfare centres. The ZP or the PS may also delegate some of these functions to the GPs in which case they have to obtain the consent of the concerned GP and to make available to it necessary funds and technical assistance.

The discretionary functions of the GPs include lighting of public streets, construction and regulation of markets, promotion of cottage industries, co-operatives etc.

It is also the duty of the GP to prepare in October and April every year half yearly report showing the amount received by it during the previous year from different sources including the opening balance and the amount actually spent on different items of work and a list of beneficiaries.

The list along with the report to be prepared in October needs to be approved by the GP. They are then placed before the Gram Sansad meetings held in November for approval and necessary action. A copy of the report and that of the list are put up in the notice board. The Gram Panchayat has also to get approved in the December meeting of the Gram Sabha a report on the expected income and expenditure along with the proposed activities.

A copy of the revised report to be adopted in the Gram Sansad meetings in May and November have to be sent to the BDO and the PS.

It is the duty of the GP to prepare a report showing the work done during the previous year under different heads, the receipts from different sources and the expenditure incurred for each type of work. The report has to indicate the amount of money placed at the disposal of the GP and the amount spent for the performance of functions.

The GP is also required to prepare a report in the prescribed form on the work proposed to be done during the following year, indicating the anticipated receipts from different sources and the nature of work proposed to be executed.

These reports are brought before a meeting of the GP and need to be adopted by a resolution. They are then sent to the PS by May 31 of every year.

It is also the duty of the GP to submit inspection report on audit of accounts or record required by the District Council.

The Gram Panchayat is empowered to regulate building operations within its area, control public sectors and waterways, prevent pollution of water supply, improve sanitation and fight epidemics. For performing any of these functions two or more Gram Panchayats may form joint committees, subject to the previous approval of the PS or PS concerned, consisting of representatives of the constituent Gram Panchayats. The Gram Panchayats which combine to form the joint committee, have to subscribe to a written instrument to be drawn up for this purpose. The instrument spells out, *inter alia*, the purpose for which the joint committee is formed, the period for which the committee is to function financial and administrative powers of the joint committee and the like.

The committee has to make such report of progress of work to the constituent Gram Panchayats as may be required by them.

In case of any difference between the constituent Gram Panchayats, the matter is decided by the officer appointed by the State government for this purpose.

A Gram Panchayat may also appoint work scheme committees to which it can delegate particular responsibilities. Such a committee might be set up to manage a particular piece of work within a locality under GPs jurisdiction. It exists for the duration of the work only. An example would be a road scheme committee established in an area to undertake road improvement under JRY. Such a committee will have one Gram Panchayat member, with the other members being the local residents from amongst whom the committee's chair and secretary are appointed. The Gram Panchayat member will be responsible for funds and their accounts.

The Gram Panchayats have also been empowered to make bye-laws in conformity with the provisions of the West Bengal Panchayats Act and rules made thereunder.

Gram Sansad and Gram Sabha

The Gram Sabha has been incorporated by all the States in their amended laws on Panchayats although there are variations in respect of number of meetings to be held, the issues to be discussed in the meeting and the like. West Bengal has however taken a step forward by making provision for a Gram Sansad apart from Gram Sabha. All the voters of each of the electoral constituencies of a Gram Panchayat constitute a Gram Sansad and all voters of a Gram Panchayat area constitute a Gram Sabha.

A Gram Sansad is required to guide and advise the Gram Panchayat in regard to the schemes for economic development and social justice undertaken or proposed to be undertaken in its area and may:

(a) Identify or lay down principles for identification of the schemes which are required to be taken up on priority basis for economic development of the village;

(b) Identify or lay down principles for identification of the beneficiaries for various poverty alleviation programmes;

(c) constitute one or more beneficiary committees consisting of not more than five persons who are not members of the Gram Panchayats;

(d) mobilise mass participation for community welfare programmes and programmes for adult education, family welfare and child welfare;

(e) promote solidatory and harmony among all sections of the people irrespective of religion, faith caste, creed or race; and

(f) record its objection to any action of the Pradhan or any other member of the Gram Panchayat for failure to implement any other development scheme properly or without active participation of the people of the area.

The Gram Sansad meets twice in a year. The half yearly meeting to be held in November considers the budget for the coming year and the written opinion of the members on the budget and the last audit report. The annual meeting of the Sansad to be held ordinarily in May considers the revised budget of the previous year, the accounts of the last six months, the activities undertaken during the last year and proposed to be undertaken in the coming year. The resolutions adopted at the meeting have to read out at the meeting itself. The meetings of the Gram Sabha and the Gram Sansad are to be convened by the Pradhan, in his absence, by the Upa-Pradhan. The inability on their part to convene the meeting empowers the State Government to remove them. If the Panchayat is held responsible, the State Government can dissolve the Gram Panchayat concerned.

The Gram Sabha meets ordinarily in December every year after the completion of the half yearly meeting of the Sansads in November. The agenda items of the Sansad are included in the Gram Sabha meeting. It is the duty of the Gram Panchayat to place before the meeting of the Sabha the budget of the Gram Panchayat, annual plan, the last audit report, the income and expenditure of the last year. The Gram Panchayat has also to place before the meeting of the Sabha the decisions of the Gram Sansads along with the observations of the Gram Panchayat. The opinions of the Sabha have to be recorded in the resolution book. The resolutions of the Sansad and the Sabha are considered by the Panchayat concerned the failure of which is recorded in the audit report as a case of gross irregularity.

I

THE FUNCTIONARIES

Gram Panchayat Level

The Pradhan

The executive powers of a GP are vested in the Pradhan (chairperson) and in his or her absence, in the Upa-Pradhan (vice-chairperson). They are elected at the first meeting of the Gram Panchayat after an election. This meeting is convened by the Block Development Officer.

The Pradhan who is a whole -time functionary, is responsible for the custody of the seal of the GP. Subject to the approval of the GP he has power to enter into any contract relating to work and expenditure of the GP. He can suspend any office employee appointed by the GP for misconduct or negligence of duty. He is required to report the same for approval at the next meeting of the GP. He is therefore the repository of all executive powers.

He may delegate some of his powers to the Upa-Pradhan. He cannot delegate his financial power without approval of the Gram Panchayat.

A GP may, at a meeting specially convened for this purpose, by a resolution, delegate to Upa-Pradhan such duties or powers as it may think of.

The West Bengal Panchayat Act requires the Panchayats to delegate to two or more of its members severally or jointly such powers or duties as they may think fit. This is done by adopting a resolution in a meeting convened for this purpose, which can be withdrawn or modified. No financial power can however be delegated. In fact, all the Gram Panchayats have formed standing committees on different matters largely in line with the standing committees at the Samiti level.

Government Functionaries

The Secretary

The Secretary is appointed by the District Magistrate. He acts under the direct supervision of the Pradhan or Upa-Pradhan, and is responsible to the Gram Panchayat through them.

He prepares the list of business to be transacted at every meeting of the GP under instructions from the Pradhan or in his absence, Upa-Pradhan. He has to send to each of the members the notice of the list of business. He has to maintain the attendance register in the prescribed form. It is his duty to record the proceedings of the meeting.

He is responsible for the preparation of the list of tax prayers and rates of taxes, formation of the draft budget within the stipulated time period, writing of cash books and other ledgers. He has also to frame a draft budget under instructions from the Pradhan. He is the custodian of all papers of the Gram Panchayat.

The Job Assistant

He is appointed by the Pradhan and is responsible for making plan and estimate of all programmes administered by the GP. His other functions include regular supervision of different programmes, preparation of report on the progress of different work etc.

Financial Resources

The sources of income of a GP include the following

(a) contributions and grants if any, made by the central and the State Government;
(b) contributions and grants made by the ZP, PS or any other local body;
(c) loans, if any, granted by the Central Government or State Government;
(d) loans from the financial institutions;

(e) all receipts on account of taxes, rates and fees levied by it;
(f) all receipts in respect of any schools, hospitals, dispensaries, buildings, institutions or works vested in, constructed by or placed under the control and management of the GP. The State government has transferred all *khas* lands and Government tanks to the GP.
(g) all sums received as gift or contribution and all from any trust or endowment made in favour of the GP;
(h) fines and penalties realised by the GP in terms of the provisions of the Act; and
(i) all other sums received by or on behalf of the GP.

The GP is authorized to create remunerative assets of its own, for example, converting waste land into converting bamboo plantations which can yield a return.

Subject to the general control as the GP may exercise from time to time, all orders for payment from the GP fund are signed by the Pradhan, or in his absence, by the Upa-Pradhan. All cheques are signed jointly by the Pradhan and the Upa-Pradhan and in the absence of the Pradhan or the Upa-Pradhan, as the case may be, by the Upa-Pradhan or the Pradhan and another member authorised by the GP at a meeting in their behalf.

Budget

The GP has to frame its budget for the next year by October 1 of every year. This is done by the Secretary under instructions from the Pradhan. The draft budget is considered in a meeting held before October 15. The modified budget has to be placed before the Gram Panchayat in a meeting to be held by November 1.

It is then sent to the PS by November 5. Copies of the budget are also put up at the public places. The voters are free to inform their reactions to the Pradhan within November 15.

The draft budget is then placed before the Gram Sansad in a meeting to be held in November. The opinions of the Sansad and the draft budget then go to the Gram Sabha. The Gram Sabha considers the observations of the PS and Gram Sansads and may suggest modifications. Now comes the turn of the GP to finalise the budget.

The Planning Process

Immediately after the first meeting, a GP has to initiate the process for drawing up plan for five years. It has to identify the work to be undertaken during the five years. It has to depend primarily on its own sources for implementing development plan. It will however take into account the money expected from the State Government, ZP and PS.

The annual plan has to be drawn up by October of every year. This has to be finalised in the meeting of the GP. The activities under the annual plan have to be integrated with the Five Year Plan. In case any new programme beyond the Five Year Plan has to be included, it has to be done by taking a resolution at the GP meeting.

The plan to be drawn up by October for the next year has to be placed before the Gram Sansad meeting in November. The annual plan along with the decision of the Sansad needs to be approved by the Gram Sabha in its meeting held in December. The annual plan has to be finalised in a meeting of the GP to be held before January 31.

Audit

There is an internal auditor of the GP known as the Panchayat Audit and Accounts Officer (PAAO) posted at the PS level. He is required to do this work at least once in every month. The PAAO has to regard himself as a part of the management system of the Gram Panchayat. He is to identify the errors, irregularities, illegalities, if any, in the manner of maintenance of the accounts and to make notes of the same.

Three copies of the monthly report are to be prepared. One copy will be handed over to the Pradhan for follow-up action and the second copy is to be submitted to the BDO through the Extension Officer for Panchayats, while third copy is retained by the officer.

In case the GP keeps on making persistent defaults he is authorised to make a special report to the BDO through EOP stating the defaults and the corrective steps suggested.

The PAAO has to prepare internal audit report every three months in the prescribed form in triplicate. One of the copies is forwarded to the Pradhan, and the other one, to the BDO through the EOP.The statutory audit of the GP is done by the EOP.

All audit inspection reports may be required by the District Council which may also call for any record from the Gram Panchayats.

The Panchayat Samiti

The Panchayat Samiti is the intermediate tier at the Block level. It consists of four categories of members:

(a) Pradhans of the Gram Panchayats within the Block;

(b) not more than three persons to be elected directly by the voters of each 'gram ;' Gram refers to a mouza or part of a mouza or group of categories of mouzas or parts thereof.

(c) MPs and MLAs elected from the Block (not being ministers);

(d) members of the Zilla Parishad, not being Sabhadhipati or Sahakari Sabhadhipati; elected from a constituency comprising any part of the Block.

The Samiti elects it own chairperson, Sabhapati and vice-chairperson, Sahakari Sabhapati. It has to meet at least once in every three months.

Powers and Functions

The PS is entrusted with a lot of powers and functions. It has power to:

(a) undertake schemes or adopt measures including giving financial assistance with regard to a wide range of matters such as agriculture, livestock, cottage industries;

(b) undertake execution of any scheme, performance of any act or management of any institution entrusted to it by the State government;

(c) manage or maintain any work of public utility or any institution vested in it or under its control or management;

(d) make grants-in-aid to schools, public institutions or public welfare organization within the Block;

(e) contribute, with the approval of the State government such sum or sums, as it may decide, towards the cost of water supply or anti-epidemic measures undertaken by a Municipality within the Block;

(f) adopt measures for the relief of distress; and
(g) co-ordinate and integrate the development plans prepared by the GPs in the Block as and when necessary.

Like the GPs it can also implement schemes assigned to it by the State government. Some of such schemes implemented by the PS are Rural Water Supply, Rural Housing.

The Samiti has been given power to regulate construction of building if the State government, by notification, declares its intention to prepare and publish a developmental plan for a specific area.

The Samiti has been empowered to prohibit such trades and business as may be declared offensive and dangerous by the State government. For this purpose the power of issuing licenses has been vested in the PS.

The owner or the lessee of a *hat* or market or an owner or lessee of a land intending to establish a *hat* or market, is required to obtain a license from the PS.

The Functionaries

The Sabhapati

The Sabhapati who is a whole-time functionary, is elected at the first meeting of the PS. He presides over the meeting of the Samiti. He is responsible for the financial and executive administration of the PS, the transaction of business connected with the West Bengal Panchayat Act, 1973 and for the maintenance of the records of the PS. He is authorised to exercise administrative supervision and control over the work of the staff of the PS and the officers and employees whose services are placed at the disposal of the PS.

The Executive Officer

The Block Development Officer is the Executive Officer of Panchayat Samiti. He attends the meetings of the PS and Standing Committees. The EO is responsible for taking necessary action on the decisions arrived at the meetings of the PS. He has to keep the Sabhapati posted with the progress of various development activities in the blocks as also with the problems and difficulties, if any, experienced in the working of the PS from time to time.

He is required to obtain orders from the Sabhapati in writing on important issues arising out of the sanction and decisions of the PS and its standing committees and on matters falling within the powers of the Sabhapati.

He is responsible to the PS and the Standing Committee through the Sabhapati in many matters such as

(a) budget,
(b) contributions and grants by the Central or by the State government or by any local authority,
(c) loans,
(d) custody of the PS fund in treasury/bank.

He has to submit a quarterly statement of accounts to the Artha-O-Sthayee Samiti, which is ultimately laid before the PS.

The EO signs the cheque for money to be drawn from personal ledger account. Before doing that he has to make sure that the expenditure has been approved by the Sabhapati and Kamadhakshya and that the Artha-O-Unnayan-O-Parikalpana Sthayee Samiti has also consented to incur this expenditure.

He may however delegate his power of signing the cash books and verification of treasury pass book with the cash book to the Secretary.

He plays a significant role in the preparation of the budget. He is responsible for drawing up a budget in the prescribed form and for circulating the copies of the same to the members of the Artha-O-Sthayee Samiti. He scrutinises the budget of the GP and places the same before the Artha-O-Sthayee Samiti. He has to place the budget before the PS for approval after having obtained recommendations from the Artha-O-Sthayee Samiti.

The EO's administrative responsibility extends to, for example, co-ordination among the Block level officers in all matters relating to the execution of schemes and works approved by the PS and standing committees, issuing of necessary instructions to the Block level officers for the execution of schemes and works. He is responsible to the Sabhadhipati and through him to the PS, for the management of the office of the PS. He is empowered to inspect institutions under the management of the PS and any work undertaken by the PS or Standing Committee.

The Secretary

The Secretary of the PS who is the Extension Officer of Panchayats, works under the overall control of the EO and is responsible to the PS for his work. He calls meetings of the Samiti and prepares, under the guidance of the EO and the Sabhapati or the Sahakari Sabhapati, the list of business to be transacted at every meeting of the Samiti. He is required to attend the meetings also.

Standing Committees

The PS performs its functions through 10 functional standing committees. Each of the committees consist of (a) chairman of the Samiti (Sabhapati) and the vice chairman of the Samiti (Sahakari Sabhapati), ex-officio; (b) 3-5 members elected by the Samiti from amongst themselves; (c) Such number of persons being officers of the State government or of any statutory body on corporation or being eminent persons having specialised knowledge, appointed by the State government.

Some functions of some of the Standing Committees are given below:

(1)	(i) Finance, (ii)Budget, (iii) Accounts, (iv) Audit, (v) Taxation,(vi) Mobilization of resources,(vii) Administration and Establishment, (viii) Co-ordination and supervision including the scheme assigned by different departments of Government	Artha-O-Sanstha Sthayee Samiti (Finance)
(2)	(i) Public Health, (ii) Sanitation, (iii) Rural Water Supply, (iv) Nutrition, (v) Dispensaries, Health Centres and Clinics, (vi) Family Welfare	Janasathya Sthayee Samiti (Public Health)
(3)	(i) Roads including bridges, Sthayee	Purta, Karya

	culverts and drains, Works) (ii) Public Buildings, (iii) Works and Properties,(iv) Rural Housing	Samiti (Public
(4)	(i) Agriculture, (ii) Agro-Industries (iii) Irrigation including small irrigation, (iv) Social Forestry, (Agriculture (v) Soil Conservation, (vi) Horticulture, (vii) Marketing, (viii) Co-operative movement.	Krishi, Sech-O-Samabaya Sthayee Samiti irrigation and Co-operation
(5)	(i) Primary Education, (ii) Social Education, (iii) Adult Literacy, (iv) Recreation, (v) Information and mass communication (vi) Games and Sports, (vii) Youth Services	Shiksha Sthayee Samiti (Education)
(6)	(i) Cottage and Small Scale O- Industries, (ii) Handlooms, Sthayee (iii) Village industries, and (iv) Industrial Estates,(v) Relief, (vi) Unemployment assistance and pension, (vii) Social Welfare Welfare) including welfare of women and children, (viii) Tribal welfare and welfare of weaker communities and handicapped groups.	Khudra Silpa,Tran- Janakalyan Samiti (Cottage Small Scale Industries, Relief and Social
(7)	(i) Preparation and implementation, Parikalpana- monitoring and evaluation of Panchayat Samiti, Plans, (ii) Integrated Rural Development Programme,(iii) Assisting in the implementation of land reform programme, (iv) Small Savings, (v) Preparation of resource inventory and data base of Panchayat Samiti Planning, (vi) Management of *Hat*, bazar ferry assigned by Government to Panchayat Samiti.	Unnayan O-Bhumi Sanskar Sthayee Samiti (Development Planning and Land Reforms)

(8) (i) Fisheries, (ii) Animal Husbandry, (iii) Poultry, (iv) Veterinary Services	Mastya-O-Pasupalan Sthayee Samiti (Fisheries and Animal Husbandry)

There are two other standing committees styled as Food and Civil Supplies and Electricity and Non-conventional Energy.

The members are elected in a meeting of the PS convened by the Sub-Divisional Officer or by an officer, not below the rank of the gazetted officer. The names are proposed and seconded in the meeting. The election takes place through ballot, if necessary.

The head of each of the Standing Committees is the Karmadhyaksha who is elected in a meeting of the Standing Committee to be held generally within one week from the date of the election of the Standing Committees. This meeting is convened by the SDO.

The meeting of the Standing Committees is generally convened by the Karmadhyaksha at least once in a month. He presides over the meeting. The proceedings of the meetings are recorded by the Secretary. The Secretary provides the copies of every meeting of the Standing Committees to the Sabhapati.

The Karmadhyakshas are responsible for financial administration in all matters within the purview of the Standing Committees. He is required to approve each and every payment made for implementation of any scheme.

Before taking up any scheme assigned by the Government, the Samiti is to forward the contents of the assigned schemes to the appropriate Standing Committee for drawing up detailed plan for its execution.The latter gets the plan and estimate of the scheme prepared by the appropriate Block level officer of the concerned department. Then follows the execution of the scheme by the Standing Committee.

Each Standing Committee exercises the powers and performs the functions of the Panchayat Samiti in relation to the subjects allotted to it within their financial limits subject to any direction of the PS. It is responsible for the implementation of the works and schemes of the PS and those assigned to it by the different departments of the Government.

It is required to obtain the views of the Artha-O-Sanstha Sthayee Samiti before according approval and financial sanction to it. In case of disagreement the matter is disposed of by the PS.

Every Standing Committee has to submit quarterly report to the PS about the progress of works and schemes.

The most powerful standing committee is the Artha, Sanstha Unnayan and Parikalapana Committee. It is responsible inter alia for preparation of budget of the Samiti and annual administration report. It is authorised to take decision regarding the issue of license for dangerous and offensive trades, transfer of property of the Samiti etc. It has to submit to the meeting of the Samiti a quarterly report on the general financial condition of the Samiti including monthly income and expenditure statement.

Each standing committee has a Secretary who helps the Kharmadhyaksha in the discharge of his administrative responsibility. He prepares agenda items in consultation with the Kamadhyaksha and under the direction of latter. He takes down the dicisions taken at the meeting of the standing committee. His other important functions include preparation of quarterly progress report for submission at the meeting of the committee, transmission of copies of the resolutions of the standing committees to the Sabhapati etc.

Samanvaya (Co-ordination) Committee

There is a Co-ordination committee for every PS consisting of the Sabhapati, Sahakari Sabhapati, the Kamadhyakshas of the Standing Committee and the Executive Officer of the PS.

It is responsible for co-ordinating the functions between a standing committee and PS and among different standing committees. The Standing Committee may modify their decisions in the light of the decisions taken by the co-ordination committee. It monitors the activities of the Gram Panchayats in respect of schemes for which funds are allotted by the PS. Apart from discussing important items like budget, planning before they are placed before the PS, it also discusses agenda items to be considered in the meeting of the PS. It meets at least once in a month

The Secretary, PS has been empowered to act as the Secretary (Samanvaya) Co-ordination Committee.

Relationship with the Gram Panchayats

The Sabhapati has the general power of supervision in respect of financial and administrative matters relating to schemes assigned to Gram Panchayats. He is empowered to call from a Gram Panchayat such information, report, register or records as may be necessary in respect of schemes assigned to Gram Panchayat. The latter is bound to furnish such details. The Sabhapati is required to place in a meeting of the PS action taken on the material. The Sabhapati can also with the approval of the PS withhold release of grant to a Gram Panchayat which fails to carry out his directions in the matter of execution of the assigned schemes.

The Sabhapati has to collect or get collected from Gram Panchayats monthly progress report of work in respect of schemes assigned to Gram Panchayats and to keep the concerned standing committee informed about the progress of work. He is also required to submit or cause to be submitted each month a consolidated report of progress received from the Gram Panchayats with its comments thereon to the Zilla Parishad.

The Sabhapati exercises his administrative power through the executive officer, P.S. i.e., through the BDO.

The EO, PS has also some control over theGram Panchayat. He is empowered to inspect the office and works of the Gram Panchayats and the institutions managed by them. He has to submit reports of his inspection to the Sabhapati.

Funds

The PS may, subject to the rates prescribed by the State government, levy tolls on persons vehicles or animals or any class of them at any toll bar established by it or under its management on any road and on ferries established by it or under its management. The rates and fees it can impose, include:

(a) a fee for providing sanitary arrangements at such places of workshop or pilgrimage, fairs, *melas* within its jurisdiction, as may be specified by the State government;

(b) a fee for license on items specified in the Act;

(c) a fee for license for *hat* or market;

(d) water rate where arrangement for the supply of water for drinking, irrigation or other purposes is made by the PS within its jurisdiction; and

(e) a lighting rate for lighting public streets.

The PS is empowered to make bye-laws for ensuring the income as mentioned above.

Apart from the grants from the State and Central Governments the PS may raise, with the approval of the State government, loans and borrow money from banks or other financial institutions.

Audit

The Samiti Audit and Accounts Officers organise accounts and internal audit of the PS. The Parishad Audit and Accounts Officers are required to supervise internal audit of the accounts of the PS. The SAAO is a part of the management system of the PS. He examines accounts of the PS every month and reports to the EO, PS for follow-up action, to a PAAO and to the SDO. He makes an assessment of the work done by the PAAO in the matter of organization of accounts and internal audit of the GPs.

Apart from examining relevant books Parishad Audit and Accounts officer has to process the statement giving particulars of action taken by the PSs on the annual report of the examiner of Local Accounts as received from the SDO before the same is forwarded by the DM to the Accountant General, West Bengal. He also processes the statement giving particulars of action taken by the ZP on the annual audit report of the Examiner of Local Accounts before the same is forwarded by the DM to the Accountant General, West Bengal.

The Planning Process

After the election of the office bearers, the PS has to frame Five Year Plans for which its has to carefully consider the sources of funds and the felt needs of the people.

The annual plan is prepared in the month of January of every year. It incorporates the programmes formulated for five years on the basis of priorities.

There is a Planning Committee at the Samiti level with the Sabhapati as the Chairman. Its other members include the Sahakari Sabhapati, Kamadhyakshas, Pradhans and the Block level officials of the State Government. It meets twice in a month.

The five year and annual plans are drafted by the Artha, Sanstha, Unnayan, Parikalpana Sthayee Samiti. The Sabhapati places it in the meeting of the co-ordination committee. The Sthayee Samiti has to modify the draft, if necessary, in line with the suggestions from the co-ordination committee.

The draft modified, if necessary, by the Sthayee Samiti, goes to the planning committee for approval.

THE ZILLA PARISHAD

For every district, except the district of Darjeeling, there is a Zilla Parishad bearing the name of the district. It consists of (a) directly elected members, not more than three from each Block, (b) Lok Sabha members and MLAs elected from the district (excluding ministers) and Rajya Sabha members having a place of residence in the district (excluding ministers), and (c) the Sabhapati of the PS in the district, ex-officio.

The ZP is the unit of self government at the district level for the attainment of economic development and establishment of social justice. It prepares and submits annually in the prescribed manner a report on the work done during the previous year and proposed to be done during the following year. It is expected to set the pace of development activities in the district. Generally, it undertakes any scheme which extends more than one Block. It can take up programmes which need big investment or which the Samiti are not capable of implementing because of some other reasons. The ZPs of two or more adjacent districts may jointly undertake at common cost any development scheme or may jointly establish a common ferry on such terms and condition as may be agreed upon. As in other tiers some assigned programmes of the Central or the State government are implemented by the ZP.

The ZP has powers to advise the State government on all matters relating to the development work among the lower tiers of Panchayats in the district. It is ultimately accountable to the State government with its budget and accounts submitted annually for auditing and assessment.

It exercises general supervision and control over PSs and GPs in the district. It is the duty of these bodies to give effect to these directions. The ZP or its standing committee has right to ask for papers, information from any PS or GP. The latter are bound to furnish such things. The ZP may also send its officers to them for inspections. The PS and ZP are required to do the needful. It has to co-ordinate development plans and programmes undertaken by the Samitis.

The ZP or its standing committees can entrust the Gram Panchayats or Panchayats Samiti the Work of implementation of any scheme in which case the concerned body has to submit progress report to the ZP, and is bound to act on the directions from the former in this regard. The ZP may undertake or execute any scheme if the same is beyond the competence of the PS concerned financially or otherwise. In such a case it has the option to entrust the work to the PS by rendering necessary assistance.

The ZP may also delegate with the concurrence of the GP, many of its functions to the GP in which case the GP acts as the agent of the ZP. It has to co-ordinate the development plans and programmes undertaken by the Samitis.

As in the case of PS, a ZP functions through 10 functional committees. The composition and functions of the committees are similar to those of the Panchayat Samitis as outlined above.

There is also a co-ordination committee consisting of the office bearers of ZP and Kamadhyakshas. The functions are similar to those of the same at the PS level.

The Functionaries

The Sabhapati

The ZP meets once in every three months. Every ZP at its first meeting elects one of its members to be the Sabhapati and the another members to be the Sahakari Sabhapati. The Sabhapati has recently been conferred the status of a minister of State.

The Sabhapati who is a whole-time functionary, is responsible for the maintenance of the records of the Parishad. He has general control over the financial and executive administration of the ZP. He exercises administrative control over all the officers and employees of the ZP and those officers and employees whose services are placed at the dispersal of the ZP.

The EO of a ZP is the District Magistrate. There is also an Additional Executive Officer who is the Additional District Magistrate. The functions of the EO, ZP are similar to those of the EO, PS. The EO is to assist the ZP in formulating policies and programmes and in seeing to their implementation. Secondly, he exercises control over the officers transferred to the ZP. Thirdly, he assists the ZP in the exercise of its general powers to supervise the PSs and GPs in the district. The AEO exercises such powers, performs such functions and discharges such duties of the EO, as the State government may from time to time direct.

There is also a Secretary for every ZP. He is to assist the EO in the discharge of his responsibilities. For the purpose of exercising technical supervision over the development schemes, the State government has placed at the disposal of the ZP an Executive Engineer.The Regional Audit and accounts Officer under the administrative control the Divisional Commissioner conducts internal audit of the accounts of the ZP. His role is similar to that of the internal auditor of the PS. The statutory audit of the ZP is conducted by the Examiner of Local Accounts, West Bengal.

As in the case of PS, the statutory audit report is placed in the meeting of the Artha-O-Sthayee Samiti of the ZP. The recommendations of the Sthayee Samiti on the actions to be taken by the ZP to remedy the defects or the irregularities or failing any remedial action, reasons for such failure, should be clearly recorded.

This is followed by a special meeting of the Parishad for considering the observations made by the Auditor and the recommendations of the Artha-O-Sthayee Samiti. The Auditor is kept informed about the action taken.

District Council

There is a District Council for each district on the model of the Public Accounts Committee in the legislature. The chairman is the leader of the opposition. One vice chairman and five other members are elected by the members of the Parishad from amongst themselves. The State government nominates three Government officers as members. The AEO is the Member-Secretary.

The District Council is empowered to examine the accounts of the Panchayats within its territorial jurisdiction in relation to the budget approved by the Panchayats concerned for the expenditure to be incurred by such Panchayats, the annual report of such Panchayats as the DC thinks. While scrutinizing the accounts of the Panchayats, the DC has to satisfy itself that the amount of money spent was legally available for the purpose for which it was spent. It has also to satisfy itself that the expenditure incurred conforms to the rules and that every appropriation has been made in accordance with the relevant rules.

It considers inspection report on the annual audit of accounts of the Panchayats conducted by the auditors including the replies furnished by the respective Panchayats. It can pursue the matters relating to the unsettled objections raised in the inspection report on audit of accounts and refer such matters to the authorities concerned suggesting corrective actions.

It is also authorised to examine the accounts of stores and stocks maintained by the Panchayats within the area of their jurisdiction.

It is required to suggest ways and means to remove the difficulties, if any experienced by the Panchayats in giving effects to the provision of the Act and rules made thereunder.

The DC has the right to obtain a copy of every inspection report on audit of account of any Panchayats and may call for any record of any Panchayats to be produced for inspection.

II

THE WORKING OF PANCHAYATS IN WEST BENGAL

The Approach of the Left Front Government to Panchayats

In its election manifesto the Left Front promised to hold election to the Panchayat institutions. It was further emphasised that all development activities of the government in rural areas in the State would be handed over to the Panchayat bodies. The elections were held in 1978 with the active participation of the political parties. An eminent journalist and scholar, Bhawani Sengupta comments, "For the first time in this republic's history there was a keen contest for roots of power. In an open democratic and peaceful context.... never in the history of India's politics did a political party penetrate so deeply and methodologically the ancient fairness of the village"[1].

The electoral slogan of the Left Front in 1978 election was 'destroy the centres of vested interests'. The Left Front spelt out its intention to use Panchayats as platforms for fighting against rural vested interests and raising the hopes of the rural people thereby. The then Left Front chairman characterised the election as a struggle for establishing the rights of the poor peasants, agricultural labourers, village craftsmen etc. against the vested interests and exploiting classes in the village'[2]. It was further held that through Panchayat elections the power will be decentralised and only with the organised force of the village poor and middle class the task of establishing the power of the people curbing that of the administrative officers, could be carried out.

It was an election in which the parties for the first time in history of Panchayat elections in India participated with their flags, banners and festoons. The idea of political Panchayats is in tune with the leftist approach to Panchayats, Arguing the case for it E.M.S. Namboodiripad, a veteran leader of the CPI(M), says that in the name of non-partnership the Sarvodaya approach seeks to disarm the poor in their fight against local gentry who are interested in transforming the Panchayats into their instruments.[3]

Clearly, this perspective on Panchayats is substantively different from the mainstream perspectives in which emphasis is primarily placed on non-political Panchayats as instruments of rural development. In approach of the Left Front government the Panchayats are also instruments of struggle for fighting against the vested interests and launching battle for implementation of an alternative development model. The minister-in-charge of Panchayats and rural development, Government of West Bengal, observes, "while extending maximum possible relief to the people increasingly forced to bear the burden of the economic crisis in the country, utmost restraint is considered necessary to see that people do not suffer from any illusion that their basic needs could be achieved without a radical structural change of the existing production relations .... People learn from their experience of participation in an organised manner about the limitations inherent in the existing socio-economic structure and thereafter they can unleash struggles for implementation of an alternative development strategy in a nation-wide scale to overcome these limitations.[4]

New Rural Leadership

The elections brought in a completely new type of rural leadership in West Bengal unheard of in modern India's Panchayat tradition. The ground was however prepared in 1969-70 during the days of United Front Government when a massive drive had been undertaken to detect and vest lands that had been clandestinely retained by landowners beyond their legal entitlement. This had weakened the hold of the big landlords on village society. The Panchayats in West Bengal or in most parts of India, as Kohli writes, "have seldom been free of domination by landlords or rich peasants. This is beginning to change in West Bengal. The CPM is carving out a pattern of political organization in rural West Bengal rare in India, namely, that of involving a penetration in the countryside without depending on the larger landowners".[5]

A large number of macro and micro studies suggest that Panchayats are free from the domination of the big landlords. Several studies suggest that the Panchayats at the village level are controlled mainly by the middle farmers who already have significant resources under their control with a large percentage being teachers and other professionals.[6]

The representation of the rural poor on village Panchayats has been fair, and that there has been an increasing representation of Scheduled Tribe and Caste members. The significant presence of poor peasants, bargadars, agricultural labourers, school teachers etc. in Panchayats has been proved in many research studies.[7] All these have brought about a change in the balance of class forces in the countryside.

The social background of the members of the Gram Panchayats proves that the Left Front has been reasonably successful in mobilising different sections of rural people. The new leaders now carry on the task of mobilization of masses in rural areas. The rural development policy of the government helps them extend political penetration among the majority of the rural people. The main electoral base of the Left Front coalition, as Dreze and Sen observe, "consists of landless labourers, sharecroppers, slum dwellers and other disadvantaged groups. This change in the balance of power has made it possible to implement a number of far reaching social programmes that are often considered 'politically infeasible' in many other States.[8]

The transformational potential by Panchayats has been documented by Echeverri Gent's study, the State and the Poor. This study views Panchayats as an institutional system that allows for the possibility that subaltern groups may exercise their agency to accumulate political and economic resources and reduce social inequities.

Rural Development Policy

Rural Development Policy of the Left Front Government is guided by the philosophy of what may be called redistribution before growth to ensure growth with social justice. In his letter to the Prime Minister in 1986, the Chief Minister observed, "We recognize on the basis of hard evidence the superior production potentiality in the poorer farmers and producers and, therefore, that rural development process primarily through the rural poor will mean a progress towards the desired goals of both productivity and equity at the same time. In the rural development programmes in our State we have, therefore, given special emphasis on land reforms and then on helping the beneficiaries".[9]

The policy has three broad objectives. In the first place, it aims at involving the people not only in the process of implementation of development programmes but also in the process of preparation and monitoring of development plans by building up decentralised structures at the grassroots level. Secondly, it seeks to being about a change in the correlation of class forces in favour of the poor and working people by involving them in an organised manner in the process of development. Thirdly, it attempts to raise class consciousness of the people through radicalization of political processes and politicization of development.

Two important features characterise the rural development process in West Bengal, barely, curbing the power of the bureaucracy as far as possible within the framework of Indian Constitution and horizontal mobilization of the masses.

The three-tiered Panchayats constitute the foundation on which stands the entire edifice of rural development in West Bengal. The GPs which function at the grassroots level and are in direct touch with the people, carry the responsibility of implementing various development programmes, projects and schemes at the village level in terms of identification of beneficiaries, location of project sites etc. They are informally, though significantly, associated with the peasant organizations. The PSs and ZPs are responsible for adoption and implementation of schemes and measures for development of agriculture, cottage industries, water supply, irrigation , execution of any function assigned by the State government, and coordination and implementation of development plans, schemes, projects and programmes relating to the development policy of the State government at the Block and districts respectively and through various standing committees.

Land Reforms

The core of rural development policy is land reforms. The government lays stress on two aspects of land reforms, namely, recording of names of share croppers and redistribution of surplus lands among the landless. Added to it is the policy of the government to extend institutional credit cover to the land reforms beneficiaries.

In the field of land reforms numerous studies have documented that the bureaucracy has colluded with the land-holding classes to stall the implementation of the programmes. The Government of India's report of the Task Force on Agrarian relations in India for example, has cited bureaucracy as an important factor responsible for the failure of the land reform. It has indicated that the members of the civil service are closely aligned with the landed gentry in the rural areas who want to stifle the reforms. At the lowest levels, the bureaucratic functionaries are petty landlords and cannot otherwise survive without the support of the richer peasants.[10]

Thus the successful implementation of land reforms class for clipping the wings of the bureaucracy and political mobilization of the respective beneficiaries. In fact, at one point of time it was felt by the Task Force on Agrarian Relations and quite rightly that a certain degree of politicization of the peasantry was the *sine quo non* of implementation of land reforms programme. And the Committee on Tenancy Reforms recommended that the Panchayats be associated with the task of implementation of land reforms as the official agencies would require more experience.

The Panchayats and peasant organizations play the most effective roles ın implementing these programmes. In fact, "West Bengal", as Baruah argues, "provides one of the rare instances of land reform programmes initiated in radical rural political mobilization with significant participation by the agrarian underclass".[11] The programme of recording of names of sharecroppers popularly known as the Operation Barga (OB) programme was formerly undertaken by the bureaucracy. The traditional method has been supplemented by the establishment of functional linkages between the bureaucracy and the Panchayats while the Gram Panchayats play the most crucial role on the OB programme.

The programme was implemented through two innovative strategies :

(a) There were legal changes supportive of sharecropper's claims. Among the changes in the land laws onus of proving that he does not have sharecropping rights, was placed on the landowners. The eviction of sharecroppers for the ostensible purpose of self cultivation was made more difficult by defining self cultivation more rigorously to mean participation by the land owners/and or his family as manual labour related to cultivation.

(b) The Left Front utilised the mobilization of the rural poor in this task. The strategy was to rely on "the group action on the part of the beneficiaries to enable them to overcome the fear psychosis by creating mutual support system,".

Meetings were held in the villages attended by the sharecroppers and the officials. While doing a study on the processes of implementation the author had noticed that the OB camp started with an address by the Panchayat Pradhan. He promised all sorts of support to the beneficiaries. While interviewing the sharecroppers we had gathered that his was preceded by a meeting in every locality organised under the auspices of the Krishak Samiti[12].

It should be mentioned here that the State government had organised earlier what was called conscientization camps which helped the bureaucracy to think afresh of their role as change agents. "It sets in a process of change of mind at least among a few functionaries at the cutting edge of administration".[13]

However, after such meetings a tentative list is prepared. The landowners were allowed objections which were also heard and verified in public. This was followed by the issue of certificates.

The recorded Bargadars are not afraid of confronting their landowners for getting their dues. The study by this author had shown that in case of disputes regarding the share of crops between them and their landowners they would not submit to the former. They would like to take the matter up with the Gram Panchayats and peasant organizations.[14] While Gram Panchayats provide them support from within the political sub-system, the peasant organizations, from outside.

The Panchayat Samitis are entrusted with the task of carrying out the land redistribution programme. At the Panchayat Samiti level there is a standing committee on land reforms which perform this task. It is this committee which, with the help of the Gram

Panchayats, prepares the list of persons to whom the vested lands would be redistributed. The success has been commendable. It is claimed that with the association of Gram Panchayats the average rate of recording increased by about 300 per cent. Of the total agricultural land re-distributed through land reforms in India nearly 20 per cent has been contributed by West Bengal though in the total agricultural land in our country the State's share is less than 4 per cent.

Land redistribution has affected more than 21 per cent of the rural families and 8 per cent of the total cultivated area in the State. There has been a shrinkage at the top categories of the land owning classes in the State. A report prepared by the Centre for study of Social Sciences, Calcutta for International Labour Organization (ILO) revealed that landholders with more than 10 acres owned a mere 14.3 per cent of the agricultural lands, while the small and marginal farmers owned 29 per cent of the agricultural land in India, in West Bengal the figure is 60 per cent. Adding the land recorded under cultivation of share this figure may exceed 75 per cent. The two measures together have resulted in a structural situation considerably different from that in most other States in India. These steps have tilted the power balance in rural areas in favour of the small and poor producers and have thus created conditions conducive to the empowerment of the poor.

Non-Land Input Support

In order to make land reforms measures effective it is essential to support these measures with the provision of non-land inputs, such as irrigation, agricultural implements, manures, and fertilisers and infrastructural facilities, particularly credit and marketing. Otherwise, the beneficiaries would be left to the mercy of the market. In the provision of all these non-land inputs there is again the question of choice of technology. In West Bengal this has been done keeping in view the interests of the poor farmers. To quote a government document, "The working farmers are endowed with labour power and there is in rural areas often a relative abundance of local resources. The socially appropriate choice of technology regarding the non-land inputs in this alternative approach should therefore be one which should be modern and at the same time, make efficient and improved use of labour and local resources. This philosophy has prompted the State government to extend minor irrigation facilities.[15]

This support has far reaching consequence on the beneficiaries. It has instilled in them a 'sense of self-confidence and dignity'. More than 70 per cent respondents for the study done by the author on land reforms had reported their ability to cultivate land without any support from the landowners. The International Labour Organization commented favourably on the government's decisive action for peasants, share croppers and agricultural labourers against landlords and big farmers and on the direct communication in a way that instilled confidence in the poor.[16]

Centrally Sponsored Schemes

The Panchayats in West Bengal have done remarkably well in respect of implementation of the centrally sponsored beneficiary-oriented and employment generating anti-poverty programmes like national rural employment programme (NREP), rural landless employment guarantee programme (RLEGP), integrated rural development programme (IRDP), Jawahar Rozgar Yojana (JRY) etc. For the implementation of IRDP there is a sub-committee at the Block level with the Sabhapati as the chairman. The list of beneficiaries is prepared by the Gram Panchayats. Although the concurrent evaluation had brought out that all the beneficiaries were selected by the Gram Panchayats, the actual work was done by the peasant organizations and branch committees of the party at the village level.

The findings of the concurrent evaluation of 1987-88 shows that in terms felt needs, maintenance and after-care of assets in generating additional income for the beneficiaries as well as crossing over the poverty line, West Bengal performed relatively better. The evaluation done in 1989 found that West Bengal performed better than the average in terms of proportion of people crossing the poverty line of Rs. 3500; maintenance and quality of assets created, inclusion of working capital in costs and sufficiency of help. And the selection process is 100 per cent controlled by the Gram Panchayat compared with 65.41 per cent average for the country as a whole.[17]

Westergaard's study suggested that NREP had considerable success in providing employment of the rural poor[18]. Chaudhuri's and Kohli's studies of food for work programme accorded the programme some success.[19] Dreze also found that IRDP overwhelmingly benefited landless labourers.[20] Swaminathan has also noticed similar success while comparing the State's performance in implementing IRDP in West Bengal and the Southern State of Tamil Nadu.[21] Webstar found that the benefits under the employment generation programme and IRDP had gone to the poor and improved their living conditions.[22]

In the pre-Left Front era, rural development activities fell under the absolute charge of the bureaucracy in line with the tradition of our country. The bureaucratic dominance could have partly been justified if it would have provided some superior technical or economic expertise in the formulation of development schemes/ projects, if it could add speed to efficiency, economy and honesty in implementation. India had experimented with rural development through bureaucracy for over three decades and every programme had revealed a familiar pattern of bureaucratic neglect, defaults and distortions. The bureaucratic domination in administration of development programmes also alienated the people who became passive recipients.

The Left Front Government established the precedence of the people's elected representatives over the bureaucracy (the chairman of the Zilla Parishad over the district magistrate, the chairman of the Panchayat Samiti over the Block development officer). West Bengal is one of the two States in India where DRDA started getting headed by the elected head of the district level Panchayat. The chairman of the Zilla Parishad has recently been accorded the status of the minister of State.

This decision has both merits and demerits. It will improve the status of the ZP and clip the wings of the bureaucracy further. But it may make the district administration look like the State headquarters. One wonders if it will lead to alienation of the people from the ZP the effects of which will be disastrous.

The implementation of rural development programmes through Panchayats and land reforms constituting the core, have produced desired results. During 1980s production of foodgrains in West Bengal grew more rapidly than in any other Indian State. Food-grain production in West Bengal averaged 6.5 per cent during the period 1983-84 to 1991-92 compared with 2.7 per cent for the country as a whole.[23] West Bengal became the highest foodgrains producing States leaving Punjab and Haryana behind. The State also registered highest rate of growth of per capita cereal consumption while the same had declined for the country as a whole.

The employment generation programmes have benefited the local people by creating some useful assets and tackling poverty. The State governments' commitment to decentralization through Panchayats meant that the Gram Panchayats have been able to play an important role in planning and execution of programmes. The study suggests that funds allotted to JRY should be made available to the Panchayats well in advance as late disbursement has led in the past underutilization of resources. It has been observed that in order to make more qualitative improvement in the programme attention should be concentrated on fewer projects in any particular year with more emphasis on long term asset durability.[24]

Rural economic scenario has undergone remarkable change. Rural employment has increased by about 63 per cent from 22.24 lakh in 1980 to 36.47 lakh in 1991. The total number of enterprises has increased over by 71 per cent from 10.44 lakh to 18.88 lakh during the second period. As a result the share of agricultural labourers in the total main workers in the State declined from 25.2 per cent in 1981 to 24.5 per cent in 1991. During the same period the share of the agricultural labourers in the total work force in the country has increased from 24.9 per cent to 26.2 per cent. The average daily rate of the agricultural labourers in the State has increased by more than 71 per cent from Rs. 14.78 in 1986-87 to 1990-91.[25]

Compared to other States West Bengal has a significantly low rate of debt to private money lenders in rural areas. Admitting this in a report the Union Labour Ministry attributes this to land reforms. Private money lenders exist in a much reduced number in the State.

While in 1977-78 less than 26 per cent of the total outstanding rural debt was with the private money lending system, the same source can be accounted for about 12 per cent of the total outstanding rural debt in 1993.[26]

The National Sample Survey (NSS) data show that poverty rate declined more rapidly in West Bengal during 1980s than in any other India's 18 largest States. According to Planning Commission estimates based on NSS data the percentage of West Bengal's population below the poverty line declined from 39.2 per cent in 1983 to 27.6 per cent in 1987-88. The all-India figures are 37.4 per cent and 29.9 per cent. Abhijit Sen and C.P. Chandrasekhar have shown that, among the 15 most populous States of India, the decline in the proportion of rural population under poverty line between 1977-78 and 1993-94 was the highest in West Bengal.[27]

Incidentally, between 1983 and 1993-94 the average calorie intake in rural areas rose in only 3 States — Kerala, West Bengal and Orissa. The largest absolute increase in calorie intake consumption per person per day had taken place in Kerala followed by West Bengal.[28]

Grassroots Participation

The Left Front Government has also taken participative institutions to the doorsteps of the people to establish direct contact between the leaders and the people as an effective method of interacting with the people not only at the time of election but at regular intervals at least twice in a year. A comprehensive amendment of the West Bengal Panchayat Act in 1992 provided for a new tier called Gram Sabha to be constituted at each electoral constituency. The Gram Sabha was to meet at least twice a year. It was required to hold discussion on the report to be submitted to it by the Gram Panchayat. The Gram Panchayats were required to carefully consider the comments, observations and recommendations of the members in the meeting. The steps taken were to be reported in the next meeting.

The West Bengal Panchayat Act, 1973 has now been amended again to make it conform to the requirements of the 73rd amendment of the Constitution. The institution called Gram Sabha has been substituted by Gram Sansad. This is an institutional innovation for ensuring participation of the people in matters pertaining to their interests.

This will act as a double edged sword. It will not only ensure people's participation in the administration of their affairs but also enhance transparency of Gram Panchayats' activities.

It is clearly laid down in the legislation that inability on the part of the Gram Panchayat to hold the meetings of the Gram Sansad empowers the State government either to remove the Pradhan or Upa-Pradhan, if they are found guilty or to dissolve the Gram Panchayat if the latter is responsible for it. It speaks of the seriousness and desire of the government to strengthen grassroots participation.

There are some studies of the previous gram sabha meetings where issues discussed were almost down-to-earth. Lieten observes, " In the Gram Sabha meetings . . . . . . although the Boktrita culture is not altogether absent, participation takes place. Around one-fourth of the males state that they take active part and occasionally speak up at the meetings".[29]

Webster's findings differ from those of Lieten in terms of participation in the meeting. But the notes, "these meetings do take place, that the attendance is high and that the subsequent hotly discussions amongst households in the poorer *paras* serve as a secondary forum for expressing views which later can come back to the Gram Panchayat via members or, as is more often the case, via local Krishak Samiti members".[30]

The meetings of the gram Sansad's have started gaining momentum. In 1995, 63 per cent of the November meetings were held. The figure rose to 88 per cent in 1996 and 96 per cent in 1997.

The Gram Sansad meetings are being held in many places keeping the local tradition in mind. For example, the meetings are preceded by folk songs, dances, dramas etc., in which the local people take part. This is an innovative method of encouraging the people to be present.

It seems relevant to mention here that there are different kinds of natural assemblies in the villages like *hats* (village markets) fairs, religious, festivals which bring in spontaneous participation of the people. The holding of Gram Sansad meetings along with them synchronises the modern institutional assemblies with the natural rhythm of the rural life adding a great significance to the meeting.

The authors had the opportunity to be present in some of the Gram Sansad meetings held in the north and south Bengal. In two of such meetings in Birbhum some people had referred to their local problems, namely, poor road conditions, waterlogging, the need for resinking tubewells. A group of people had walked out of the meeting when the Panchayat Pradhan expressed his inability to give positive assurance. In one of such meetings it was noticed that the Pradhan was not fully aware of what he was supposed to do. He seemed to have considered it a as kind of an election meeting.[31]

Resource Mobilization

The average resource mobilization per GP (1994-95) has been about Rs.12,000 which is only a small fraction of the grants-in-aid inflow even though a few enterprising GPs earned as much as Rs.1 lakh, mostly from various remunerative ventures, rather than their tax base.

The taxation power of GPs in West Bengal are derived from Section 46 of West Bengal Panchayat act, 1973. Section 46(1)(a) of the Act lays down the provisions of a Tax on Lands and Buildings which is the mainstay of the GPs 'own resources'. Section 46(1)(b) of the Act had made provisions for a parallel tax on profession and employment but this was deleted during the 1992 amendment in line with the decisions of the State government to levy a 'single point' Profession Tax.

Even allowing for the loss of the Tax on Profession and employment, there is according to the assessment of the Finance Commission, considerable scope for enhancing collection of tax on lands and buildings. Further, Section 46(5) makes provisions for levy of an additional stamp duty on ten per cent on all admissions to entertainments. These provisions have not been utilised over the last seventeen years and it is for the State government to frame appropriate rules and enforce the legal provisions.

Many GPs have adopted building rules under which building plans are to be approved on payment of small fee and, in semi-urban GPs, this can also be a good source of income. Such building fees, trade license fees, fees on registration of non-motorised vehicles, fees of sanitary arrangements at fairs and tolls on roads/bridges/ferries maintained by the GP are also sources of income that could be better utilised. Section 47(1) also provides for rates for water, sanitation and electricity where such services are extended by GPs but these provisions have seldom been utilised. Cattle pounds, markets, fisheries etc. have been other sources of income from remunerative assets which have been used by some GPs.

Though GPs in West Bengal have by and large not taken their fiscal powers too seriously, the Commission noted an innovation adopted by many of the GPs. While trying to match allocated resources to local needs, the GPs often called for local mobilization of resources and such local voluntary contributions in cash, kind, technical support or labour inputs have been significant. This enterprise needs to be encouraged particularly as the local people tend to regard such assets for which they have contributed personally, as their own, rather than as government assets and take care of their maintenance.

PSs, in general, are even more dependent on Government grants. PSs in West Bengal have no taxation powers but Section 133 empowers them to lay tolls on roads/bridges, ferries maintained by them, rates on water and lighting where such services are rendered by them and fees for registration of vehicles, sanitary arrangements at fairs and license fees for markets. Some PSs have been able to earn a good income from their remunerative assets including social forestry plantations but their performance has not been uniform.

Likewise, ZPs in West Bengal, have remained largely dependent on Government grants. The ISS study refers to the micro-situation of Murshidabad ZP where internal resource mobilization has been only 1.28 per cent of the annual income in 1992-93. In terms of section 181 of the West Bengal Panchayat Act, the financial powers of the ZPs are more or less in conformity with those of PSs. Traditionally, Land Revenue collections were shared with ZPs but Land Revenue is no longer a significant revenue source. Section 180 of the Act assigns net cess collections under the Cess Act, 1880 to ZPs but, though the income of certain ZPs (such as the

Burdwan ZP) is significant on this count, Cess collections are very unevenly distributed amongst the districts.

Involvement of PRIs with State resources mobilization has been on the increase. An incentive scheme has been in operation relating to Small Savings collection where 37.5 per cent of net small savings collections above the district targets are ploughed back into the district as Districts Plan additionality. In actual terms, this implied a net additional resource inflow of Rs. 29.87 crores as District Plan additionality to sixteen districts in 1994-95. Likewise, under the decentralised Resource Mobilization Scheme launched on December 1, 1992, 50 per cent of collections in excess of district targets in respect of some items such as Entertainment Tax, Motor Vehicles Tax, Stamp Duty/Registration Fee and Royalty/Cess from major and minor minerals are also ploughed back to the districts. Greater involvement of PRIs in resource mobilization is expected to yield good returns, as there will be a built-in incentive to maximise State revenues if devolutions are pegged to a share of the tax base. Certain minor irrigation schemes are being operated by beneficiary committees under Panchayats who are able to meet maintenance costs from collection of water rates. On the other hand, collection of irrigation rates in major irrigation schemes was extremely poor. It was felt that collection of irrigation rates would revive a boost if responsibilities for water management and collection of irrigation rates in respect of major irrigation scheme could be handed over to ZPs.[32]

The Commission has suggested setting up of a State Panchayat Finance Corporation if entitlements turned out to be insufficient in comparison to the needs of the local bodies. This will meet a part of the capital needs as suggested by the Santhanam Committee (1963) and as established in Uttar Pradesh and Bihar. The Government is yet to take a decision on that.

Training and Capacity Building

The Government of West Bengal has paid special attention to training of the Panchayats functionaries, particularly the elected ones. The task has been assigned to State Institute of Panchayats and Rural Development which *inter alia* offers centralised and decentralised training, both being week-long residential courses and prepares training materials in Bangali. It has published separate training material meant for functionaries at different tiers and members of the different Standing Committees. While Zilla Parishad members are imparted training through interactive sessions with the resource persons drawn from government departments and academic institutions, the Panchayat Samiti and Gram Panchayat members are trained locally by the duly trained personnel drawn from the different spheres of public life and NGOs. SIPRD has prepared huge volume of focused material on watershed management, DWCRA, the role of Panchayats in the development of women and children for generation and enhancement of awareness of the members about development and gender issues.

NOTES AND REFERENCES

1. B. Sengupta (1979), *CPI(M) Promises, Prospects and Problems,* New Delhi: Young Asia Publication, p.118. See in this connection P.Datta (1996) Revitalization of Panchayats: The West Bengal Experience, Calcutta: State Institute of Panchayats, Government of West Bengal. P. Datta, The Second Generation Panchayats in India (1996), Calcutta, Calcutta Book House.
2. P. Dasgupta (1978), Calcutta: *Desh Hitaishi* (in Bengali), April 7
3. E.M.S. Namboodripad (1962), "Political Parties and Panchayati Raj", *Indian Journal of Public Administration*, October-December, p. 621. For an elaborate discussion, see P. Datta 'Political Panchayats in West Bengal', Madras: *The Frontline*, June 28, 1996.
4. S.K. Mishra (1991), *An Alternative Approach to Development: Land Reforms and Panchayats*, Calcutta: Department of Information and Cultural Affairs, Government of West Bengal, p. 10.
5. A. Kohli (1989), *The State and Poverty in India: Politics of Reform*, New York: Cambridge University Press, pp. 112-113
6. T. Beck (1994), *The Experience of Poverty*, U.K.: International Technology Publication, T. Nossiter (1988) *Marxist State governments in India*, London and New York: Printer Publishers, A. Kohli (1986), op.cit.
7. G.K. Lieten (1988), 'Panchayat Leaders in a West Bengal District, *EPW*, October 1. S.Pramanick and P. Datta, (1994) *Panchayats and People*, Calcutta: Sarat Book House, For a review of the studies see P. Datta (1993) *The Second Generation Panchayats in India*, Calcutta: Calcutta Book House, pp. 42-67
8. J. Dreeze and A. Sen (1995), *India Economic Development and Social Opportunity*, New Delhi: Oxford University Press, p.56.

9. Department of information and Cultural Affairs, Government of West Bengal (1985), Anti Poverty Programmes: The Role of Panchayats Correspondence Between Shri Rajiv Gandhi, P.M. of India and Shri Jyoti Basu, C.M. of West Bengal
10. *Report of the Task Force on Agrarian Relations (1973)*, New Delhi: Planning Commission, p.25
11. S. Baruah (1990), 'The End of the Road in Land Reform' Limits to Redistribution in West Bengal', *Development and Change*, vol. 21., p. 122.
12. P. Datta (1998), *Land Reforms Administration in West Bengal*, New Delhi: Daya Publishing House, p.48.
13. D. Bandyopadhyaya (1978), *Land Reforms in West Bengal*, Calcutta, Government of West Bengal, p.11
14. P. Datta (1988,) Land Reforms Administration in West Bengal, *op. cit.* p. 102.
15. Department of Information and Cultural Affairs, Government of West Bengal: *Jyoti Basu Speaks* (1991), p. 79.
16. Overcoming Rural Underdevelopment (1979) Geneva: International Labour Organization.
17. Cited by B. Desgupta (1995), Institutional Reforms and Poverty Alleviation in West Bengal, *EPW* October 14-21, p. 2700. See in this connection, P. Datta (1996) 'Rural Development Through Panchayats: The West Bengal Experience', *Kurukshetra*, April.
18. K. Westergaard (1986), Copenhagen: Centre for Development Research. People's Participation, Local Government and Rural Development - The Case of West Bengal.
19. S, Chaudhury (1980), Study on Food For Work in West Bengal (mimeo) Santiniketan: Agro-Economic Research Centre, A. Kohli (1987), *op. cit.*, p.137.
20. J. Dreeze (1990), 'Poverty in India and IRDP Delusion' *Economic and Political Weekly*, September 29.
21. M. Swaminathan, (1990) "Village Level Implementation of IRDP: Comparison of West Bengal and Tamil Nadu, *Economic and Political Weekly*, March 31.
22. N. Webster (1992), *Panchayati Raj and Decentralization of Development Planning in West Bengal*, Calcutta K.P. Bagchi, pp. 78-90.
23. Centre for Monitoring Indian Economy (1993), Performance of Agriculture in Major States, Cited by B. Desgupta (1995) 'Institutional Reforms and Poverty Alleviation in West Bengal' October 14-21, *EPW*, p. 2092.
24. R.P. Slater, *et al* (ed.) (1991), *Participation and Development*, Hyderabad: National Institute of Rural Development, p.63.
25. Tushar Mohanti (1994), 'Bengal Farm Labour Gains Little, Calcutta, *Economic Times*, July 12.
26. Calcutta: *The Statesmen* 1994, November 5.
27. A. Sen and C.P. Chandrasekhar (1996), *Frontline*, February 23.

28. M. Swaminathan and V.K. Ramachandran (1999), *Frontline*, March 12.
29. G.k. Lieten (1994), 'Rural Development in West Bengal: Views from Below', *Journal of Contemporary Asia*, Vol. 24, No.4, p. 528.
30. N. Webster (1992), Panchayati Raj and Decentralization of Development Planning in West Bengal, *op. cit.*, p.99.
31. P. Datta (1999), The Gram Sabha Experience, *Frontline*, July 30.
32. *Report of the State Finance Commission* (1996), Calcutta: Government of West Bengal.

7

PANCHAYATI RAJ, DECENTRALIZED PLANNING AND DEVELOPMENT IN KERALA

SUNNY GEORGE AND
K.N. LELITHABHAI

"Kerala's decentralization programme is probably the largest of its kind in the World"

– World Bank

I

INTRODUCTION

Kerala has made historical achievements by entering into a new phase in its democratic decentralization by experimenting decentralized planning with people's participation. The Local Self-Government Institutions (LSGIs) have been strengthened by means of devolving powers and functions based on the Kerala Panchayat Raj Act, 1994 [hereafter KPR Act], on the one hand, and introducing the People's Campaign for the Ninth Plan (hereafter, Campaign), on the other. The recommendations of the Committee on Decentralization[1] have been accepted by the Government and on the basis of its Report the Kerala Panchayat Raj (Amendment) Act, 1999 [hereafter KPR (A) Act] has been introduced. Notable features of the KPR (A) Act are : (1) strengthening of Gram Sabha; (2) changes in the structure of Panchayats both in terms of number of constituencies and in terms of committees; (3) emphasis on transparency; (4) new institutions such as Ombudsman and Appellate Tribunals; (5) new system of auditing; (6) more decision making powers to elected functionaries; and (7) provisions for wide people's participation. The overall capacity building has been undertaken by various measures including training, seminars, discussions, workshops, etc. Since there exists no model elsewhere in the world, the entire process is based on 'learning by doing' approach. In fact, the cynicism that existed in the State regarding Government intervention in development activities has been disappeared and a new enthusiasm found expressed by the people. About 35-40 per cent of the Plan Grant has been earmarked for the LSGIs and they are now making all out effort to utilise the money. An important aspect of people's participation is resource mobilization by them. In fact, the total development works by local bodies would be much higher than what has been anticipated because of people's contribution. However, the entire process has not been stabilised yet. The rules based on the KPR(A) Act have to be formulated and the planning process has to be standardised and institutionalised. The decentralization process of Kerala has been widely acclaimed by people from all over the world. Indeed, a new methodology in decentralized planning has been coined. Other States in India, and even economies elsewhere in the world, may emulate the model of Kerala. However, while attempting to adopt this model, one has to bear in mind the background — geographical, social, cultural, political, development experiences — of the regional economy. In order to understand and digest the process, it is desirable to have a brief look at the historical background in which the experiment has been introduced. Such an evaluation would definitely help those who attempt for adoption of the methodology of Kerala elsewhere. This chapter is divided into seven sections. Following this introduction section, in section II, a brief account of development history of Kerala is given. It gives an overview of the forces/ developments that have moulded the background for the present experiment in participatory decentralized planning. The philosophy behind the process of decentralization is given in section III. In section IV, the concept of decentralized planning is given. The overall expectation from the system also is included in this section. A detailed account of the Panchayati Raj System in Kerala, including the historical background, is given in section V. In section VI, the process of decentralized planning is discussed. Finally, in section VII a quick evaluation of the entire process is made.

II

KERALA ECONOMY

Kerala's achievements in development are legendary, particularly in quality of life measured in terms of human development index. The index of human development of Kerala is found to be comparable to that of the middle income countries in the world whereas its per capita income is as low as $100, which is lower than that of the average per capita income of the low income countries. Thus, the Kerala model[2] shows how an economy can achieve high quality of life with low per capita income. Many of the development trends/features in Kerala have been tending towards the capacity building of local level planning, and since independence these centrifugal forces have gained momentum and resulted in sustained improvement in the quality of life, despite very low per capita income. The following are, among others, important features of the regional economy, which have tended towards moulding a background for such an experiment in the Participative Decentralized Planning (PDP).

Geography and Ecology

Kerala is the Southern most State in India having geographical area of about 39,000 sq. km. with population of 29,098,518 as recorded by the 1991 Census. It is one of the densely populated States with population of 749 per sq. km. There are four major geographical zones in the State: the Highlands, the Middle zone, the Lowland plain, and the Coastal plain. Kerala is a region of relatively heavy monsoon rain. There are 44 streams/rivers in Kerala.[3] The even availability of water rendered possible an even settlement pattern, as distinct from the cluster villages in the rest of the sub-continent, and it helped reducing the chances of rapid spread of epidemics in the region.

Rural-Urban Continuum

An idiosyncratic feature of the development trends in Kerala is the absence of rural-urban polarization. The public policy has been so targeted that the disparity between the rural and urban area reduced to the minimum. These developments in Kerala — 'rural-urban continuum' — have resulted in the coinage of a new term 'rurban'.[4] Woodcock, during the late sixties, described the situation very beautifully in the following way.

> Kerala villages bear little resemblance to the tight, squalid settlements of North India which huddle along a single street or in a knot of houses for mutual protection. In spite of their unorganised appearance, the Malayali villages have quite elaborate social structures. Each will have at least one school and a public library; it will have a public health service, trade union branches and political party groups, places of worship (often a temple, a church and a mosque) and always a few tea shops which serve as meeting places for the various communities. Many Malayali intellectuals and officials return to their native villages in middle age and take an active part in local activities, so that there is a cultural sophistication about rural life in Kerala. In many respects, it is urban.
>
> (Woodcock, 1967, pp. 44-45).

Public Action

Kerala's accomplishments shows that the well-being of the people can be improved, and social, political and cultural conditions be transformed, even at low levels of income, if there is appropriate public action. In Kerala, the action of mass organizations and mass movements against social, political, and economic oppression and the policy actions of governments have been the most important constituencies of public action.[5] In these activities, people's participation has been quite considerable. In fact, these movements have been, one way or other, turned out to be citizens' education programmes. With this historical background Kerala had been able to 'take off', during the sixties and seventies, in terms of social infrastructure and quality of life.

Development of Social Infrastructure

The social activism of the people have been reflected in the political economy in terms of policy decisions in favour of mass literacy, Public Distribution System (PDS), and development of social infrastructure. A study of the Central Statistical Organization, of 22 basic facilities in Indian villages, shows that Kerala ranks first in 17 out of 22 indicators. Most of the basic facilities are available in Kerala villages within 2 to 5 kilometers (see Table 7.1).

Universal Education for Children and Total Literacy

Kerala is the only State in India having total literacy. Because of the dense and fairly even distribution of population, it is simply easier and more cost effective to provide health and educational services in Kerala than in other parts of India. Kerala's physical and geological characteristics help account, in part, for the State's unique ability to deliver public services.

Early Demographic Transition

Kerala has experienced one of the sharpest fertility declines in the South Asia region. With very low level of per capita income this Indian State has achieved results in controlling population growth comparable to those in the most successful middle-income countries. In 1987 itself the State had crossed the restating rate of birth. In 1996 Kerala observed a birth rate as low as 17.8 with a death rate of 6.3 and infant mortality rate 13. The comparable rates for India were 29.5 (birth), 9.8 (death) and 80 (infant mortality). And Kerala is the only State in India with a sex ratio favourable to women. In 1991, for every1000 men in the State there were 1036 women corresponding to the all-India sex ratio of 927.

TABLE 7.1 : Distribution of Social Infrastructure in Kerala and India

Features	Rank of Kerala among all Indian States	% of villages covered (Kerala)	% of villages covered (All India)
Within 2 kilometers			
All-weather roads	1	98	46
Bus stops	1	98	40
Post Offices	1	100	53
Primary Schools	1	100	90
Middle Schools	1	99	44
Secondary Schools	1	99	21
Fair Price (ration) shops	1	99	35
Health dispensaries	1	91	25
Health centres	1	47	12
Daily Market	1	56	15
Within 5 kilometers			
Higher education facilities	1	97	21
Hospitals	1	78	35
Fertilizer Depots	1	93	44
Agricultural pump repair shops	1	65	19
Veterinary Dispensaries	1	82	40
Credit Cooperatives	1	96	61
Banks	1	96	40
Seed Stores	2	63	40
Storage and Warehouses	4	34	21
Railway Station	8	23	18
In the Village			
Drinking water	5	96	93
Electricity	3	97	33

Source: Based on First Economic Census, CSO, GOI, Monthly Abstract of Statistics, quoted from M.A. Oommen: 'Development Experience, Development Priorities and Fiscal Resources of Kerala', in People and Development, Centre of Science and Technology for Rural Development, Thrissur.

Absence of Gender Discrimination

One of the peculiarities of the Kerala's development experience is that there is not much gender difference in social development unlike elsewhere in India. We have noted that the sex ratio in Kerala is in favour of women as against the all India picture. While this ratio has been increasing in Kerala, the same in India as a whole has been decreasing. Moreover, life expectancy of women is more than that of men, unlike in India. In some aspects of educational attainments, girls in Kerala are in fact ahead of boys. Though the girls enrolled in lower classes are fewer than boys, their number exceeds that of boys by the time they reach the tenth standard in schools. Teaching profession has come to be dominated by women who form 61.5 per cent of teachers in schools.

Land Reforms

Redistribution of wealth is considered to be one of the important prerequisites of development. Kerala is the foremost State in implementing land reforms effectively. Amin (1991) commends Kerala for its land reforms and the success attained in providing basic services to the people, "in itself a policy of redistribution of wealth and income".

Public Distribution System

Kerala has the best Public Distribution System in India. All households in Kerala possess ration cards. The scheme for supply of rice at concession rates to families below poverty line to the extent of 25 per cent of population, launched by Government of India had been extended to 42 per cent of the total population, in Kerala. There are 14,262 ration retail shops in Kerala, of which 12,325 are in rural areas. Apart from the PDS, the government promotes fair price shops for groceries and medicines.

Remittances from Abroad and its Impact

Malayalees (people of Kerala) are found all over the world. Looking for higher earning avenues, they go to elsewhere in the world, particularly to Gulf countries. One of the unique features of Malayalees is that they are keeping their contact with their homeland,

Kerala. Most of the migrants come back to the homeland after working 15-20 years abroad. Others support their relatives by sending money. The economic aspect of this culture is that, Kerala has a good opportunity for loanable funds for development. It stands to reason that an international airport, the Nedumbassery Airport, has been financed mostly by Malayalees abroad.

III

DECENTRALIZATION : THE PHILOSOPHY

Decentralization becomes meaningful only when there is democratic decentralization, which is characterised by flow of power through the elected bodies and its members to the people. By power we mean the power to augment capabilities of the people by increasing production and reducing inequalities. Indeed, development is basically enlarging the choices of the people. And the choices of the people, in turn, depend upon the 'economic development and social justice'.

Principles of Decentralization

The following are important principles, among others, that may govern transfer of power to LSGIs.

(i) Autonomy

Autonomy does not mean sovereignty. Among the LSGIs, autonomy is guaranteed by limiting the supervision of the State Government to the obligatory and regulatory functions. It has got three dimensions: (1) financial autonomy; (2) Functional autonomy; and (3) Administrative autonomy. Autonomy implies that various levels of LSGIs should not be seen as hierarchically organised, with unit one controlling the others below it. However, there exists active 'cooperation, coordination, complementation, and integration'. Nevertheless, the State Government has a very pro-active role in formulating the State priorities within the framework of the national perspective. Thus a multi-level exercise of developmental functions implies, "the existence of a sphere of independent action, at each level, a sphere of cooperative and coordinated action, a sphere of delegated agency function, and a sphere of agency from above, in the descending order of magnitude" (Committee on Decentralization, 1996).

(ii) Subsidiarity

This principle governs the division of functions among different tiers of LSGIs. Subsidiarity implies what can be done best at a particular level shall be done at that level and only residual functions are given to the higher level. The process starts from below, transferring functions and powers from the level of Gram Sabhas/ Ward Committees and go up to the Union Government.

(iii) Complementarity

Integration is perhaps the most important task in decentralized planning. The entire system has to work with unity of vision and diversity of means. While integrating the functions, there must not be any chance for overlapping and repetition. This means that the activities of higher levels should complement those of the lower levels and the programmes implemented by all agencies in a given local body will be consistent with local needs and priorities and will in turn, converge into an integrated local plan.

(iv) Uniformity

The principle of uniformity stipulates that norms and criteria for selection of beneficiaries, identification of sites, prioritization of activities and pattern of assistance within a given local body shall be the same for a particular programme irrespective of the agency sponsoring such programmes. This helps in formulating criteria for decision making, which may be made open to the people so that transparency can easily be ensured.

(v) Participation of People

In decentralized governance, participation of the people is envisaged by empowering them to take their own decisions after they analyse their problems themselves. In fact, the local self government provides an institutional framework for participatory democracy. People's participation is expected in all stages of a development programme including identification of needs, formation of scheme, its implementation, monitoring and evaluation. The reservation of seats for women, Scheduled Castes and for Scheduled Tribes is one of the ways of ensuring participation of the vulnerable sections in the mainstream development activities. The institutions like Gram Sabhas/Ward Committees are meant for facilitating people's participation in terms of mobilization of resources in cash, kind and of decision making. Participation also helps in ensuring transparency by examining the activities at various stages. Furthermore, the citizen's pro-active role is expected in augmenting harmony among various sections of the people, popularization of literacy, improvement of public health, etc.

(vi) Transparency and Accountability

Local Self Government Institutions are primarily accountable to the people and this is guaranteed by making transparency in its function. This calls for a social audit system for examining the performance of the local bodies. The social auditing is performed by the Gram Sabhas and Ward Committees by examining the activities of development programme in the respective area. Every decision taken has to be based on certain predetermined norms and criteria, which are evolved on the basis of social consensus and the rationale behind each decision has to be made public. For this purpose, the procedures and the language of administration have to be made people-friendly by simplifying it. In such a system the people have the right to know details of project documents, procedure of its execution, estimates, its monitoring, financial expenditures and evaluation. The people are also expected to play a facilitative role for smooth functioning of the developmental activities.

IV

DECENTRALIZED PLANNING : THE CONCEPT

The concept of the ongoing experimental participative planning process in Kerala has been emerged, primarily, as a critique of centralised planning process. Development planning in India has, so far, been primarily planning for investments, required for building up essential economic overheads such as irrigation, power, transport, mining and heavy industry and social overheads such as in education, health and scientific research. In this centralised planning process, there has been very limited space for people's participation, despite some deliberate attempts in making the process participative.[6] However, there is no disagreement in defining planning in its broad sense, as an attempt by a society to consciously regulate the economic process through collective decisions so that sustainable and equitable growth is achieved. But the departure from centralised planning began when one consider: (1) ideal unit of planning, and (2) separation of sequential stages of planning. Discussions on local level planning have often been preoccupied with the identification of some unique ideal level of planning. This is really a false notion as rightly pointed out by the Report of the Working Group on Block Level Planning (Government of India, 1978). In fact, such an ideal unit of planning neither exists nor is it necessary. In the case of separation of different stages of planning one has to bear in mind that planning is an interactive process wherein the programme itself may undergo several modifications in setting up of organizational arrangements for the design, selection and implementation of projects.

Predetermined sequencing of stages of planning tend to lose sight of the inter-dependencies among different projects in the programme in terms of both technical relations and resource constraint. That is to say, the total money to be spent on different project during a given period of time is limited. Some have, therefore, to be chosen in preference over others. Furthermore, in formulating projects, the basic technical balance between different projects, belonging to different levels of planning needs to be maintained.

In the light of the two points raised above, the conventional procedure of moving from the formation of overall plans to individual projects needs to be reversed. Instead, one has to start from the end use, and end users, of different projects — which would itself indicate the most convenient level at which the particular projects should be implemented. This will, in turn, indicate the appropriate organizational framework/points at which different sets of projects should be implemented.[7] Therefore, in practice, what is required is a system of multi-level planning, where the lowest unit is allowed to plan and implement everything that may be performed most effectively at that level and only the residual is left to the higher levels.

The Concoct of an Experiment in Decentralized Planning

The thoughts on experimenting a decentralized Planning in Kerala State has been coined quite for a long period of time (CDS, 1980). In 1980s it was evaluated that Kerala has a relatively favourable social and political environment for efforts in this direction.[8]

The 73rd and 74th Constitutional amendments and the ensuing Kerala Panchayat Raj Act, 1994 provided an institutional background for the democratic decentralization and participative decentralized planning in the State. A State Finance Commission was also constituted for making recommendations for sharing the resources of the State Government with Panchayats and for improving financial resources of Panchayats. Both the Finance Commission and the Committee on Decentralization have submitted their reports and in the light of these the Kerala Panchayat Raj (Amendment) Act, 1999 has been enacted.[9]

Complementing these developments the State Planning Board introduced a participative planning process, viz. 'The People's Campaign for the Ninth Plan' on an experimental basis. In fact, it is an attempt in the direction of planning from below. The hallmark of it is the massive involvement of people with a campaign mood (Government of Kerala, 1996).

In this approach all LSGIs are to formulate their schemes on the basis of their priorities. These schemes together with departmental proposals and other related funds will go to the District Planning Committee (DPC) which will prepare the plan for the district within the framework of the guidelines given by the State Planning Board. In addition to creating new assets, maintenance and renewals may be included in the schemes. If a DPC finds that some modifications in schemes of lower tiers are necessary, modifications may be made only after mutual discussions with the concerned LSGIs. Gram Panchayats will prepare their plans on the basis of suggestions of Gram Sabha. A project spreading beyond the limits of a Gram Panchayat area will go to the Block Panchayat and that going beyond the area of block will go to the District Panchayat. As noted earlier, the State Planning Board will take care of inter-district schemes.

Expectation from the New System

From the emerging new decentralized governance, the expectations are threefold. First, it is envisaged that the system would break the rampant cynicism among the people regarding the very low rate of growth of the regional economy. It is also important that whatever momentum has been achieved so far has to be sustained in the future. It is envisaged that the participation of the people in the development process, right from the pre-planning stage to the evaluation, would guarantee a significant improvement in productivity. Ultimately, it will tend to reflect further on the standard of living of the people with greater self-reliance.

Secondly, a considerable amount of resource mobilization would become possible as a result of massive people's participation. The contribution from the people may be in the form of cash, kind, or service. Thirdly, the corruption would be reduced by vigilant supervisions of the works and schemes by Gram Sabhas/Ward Committees, People's groups and socially active individuals and organizations.

V

PANCHAYATI RAJ SYSTEM IN KERALA

Earlier System

Historically there were self-governing units at the village level organised on the basis of castes, in different parts of Kerala. These units were not democratic in modern sense. They did not have any voice in the overall governance of villages. However, it is important to note that despite the changes in kings/rulers, these traditional Panchayats survived as basic units of administration. The 'Gramms' of Brahmins, the 'Tharas' of Nairs, the 'Karas' of Ezhavas were examples of village level self-governing units. These units were further divided into sub-units having the nature of a Gram Sabha and they were known as 'kazhagoms' and 'koottams'. The 'koottam' was the base on which the structure of both civil and judicial administration at the local level was built (Ramachandran, 1995).

In Kerala, formal local bodies were first established during the period of the British under Lord Ripon. They were urban local bodies established in the form of municipal boards and sanitary boards initially, and later Panchayats also were constituted in the similar pattern. By 1920 Panchayats became legal entities in Kerala. When the Kerala State was formed in 1956, there were Panchayats and urban local bodies in the three different regions of the State, viz. Travancore, Cochin and Malabar. In addition to these, there was a District Board in the Malabar region, which was abolished soon after the formation of Kerala State.

The first elected government of Kerala in 1957 gave top priority to democratic decentralization. However, the attempts were not successful with the failure to enact the Kerala Panchayat Bill and the District Council Bill as a result of the dismissal of the Government. The next government passed the Kerala Panchayat Act 1960, the Kerala Municipalities Act, 1960, and the Kerala Municipal Corporations Act, 1961.

The executive and financial powers of the Panchayats were very limited under the Kerala Panchayat Act of 1960 (hereafter KPA) and the local bodies were more nominal than real. For instance, the principal functioning of the Panchayats included only items like maintenance and lighting of local roads; drainage, sanitation, garbage disposal and provision of public latrines; arrangements for petty irrigation, potable water, burial, and registration of births and deaths; and maintenance of village courts. For the major developmental activities like agriculture, animal husbandry etc., or even social services like education and health, the role of the Panchayats were merely that of lending its cooperation to the concerned departments of the State Government.

Panchayat Raj in Kerala since 73rd and 74th Amendments of Constitution in 1992

Despite the historical developments in favour of decentralized governance in Kerala, it was the 73rd and 74th Amendments to the Constitution of India that gave a background for the effective initiatives. Within the framework of the Constitutional Amendments, the Kerala Panchayat Raj Act, 1994 was passed with effect from 23rd April 1994. This KPR Act was, in fact, a turning point in strengthening the Panchayat Raj System in the State. However, as a result of the hectic legislation, the KPR Act contained a number of mistakes and omissions, and to rectify the same, the Kerala Panchayat Raj (Amendment) Act, 1995 and the Kerala Panchayat Raj (Amendment) Act, 1996 were passed with effect from 5th August 1995 and 26th March, 1996 respectively.

To incorporate the recommendations of the Committee on Decentralization and the State Finance Commission, and the suggestions of the State Planning Board in the light of their experience in decentralized planning, a new legislation was necessitated and hence the Kerala Panchayat Raj (Amendment) Act, 1999. This may be considered as one of the best legislations in the State since the methodology adopted for the formulation of it was 'learning by doing'.

Kerala Panchayat Raj (Amendment) Act, 1999 (KPR (A) Act)

The KPR (A) Act has taken care of almost all aspects of the process of decentralization ranging from environmental aspects to judicial matters. Notable features of the KPR (A) Act are : (1) strengthening of Gram Sabha; (2) changes in the structure of Panchayats both in terms of number of constituencies and in terms of committees; (3) emphasis on transparency; (4) new institutions such as Ombudsman and Appellate Tribunals; (5) new system of auditing; (6) more decision making powers to elected functionaries; and (7) provisions for wide people's participation.

Present Panchayat Raj System

We attempt to provide an account of the present system of Panchayat Raj incorporating the recent legislation of KPR (A) Act. Therefore, while going through this section one has to bear in mind that certain provisions in the latest Kerala Panchayat Raj (Amendment) Act,

1999 has to be materialised by means of Rules and its implementation. Also important to note is the fact that many of the provisions in the KPR Act are related to other allied Acts.

Structure of Local Self Government Institutions (LSGIs)

In line with the Constitution (Seventy Third Amendment) Act, 1992, the Kerala Panchayat Raj System has a three-tier structure of Panchayats by constituting Village, Block and District Panchayats. There are 1,214 Local Self Government Institutions in Kerala. The distribution of LSGIs is given in Chart 7.1 and the Table 7.2 gives the district-wise distribution of Gram Panchayats, Block Panchayats and Municipalities with average area and population. The broad structure of Panchayat Raj System in Kerala is given in Chart 7.2.

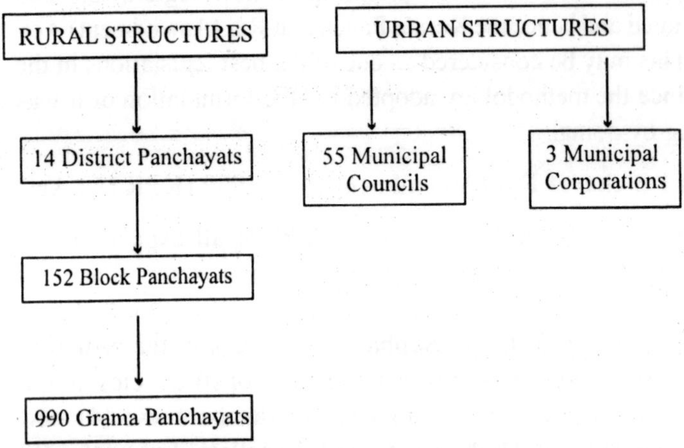

CHART 7.1 : Distribution of Local Self Government Institutions in Kerala

The State Election Commission and the State Finance Commission are the two higher offices set up concerning the implementation of Panchayati Raj system in Kerala. In addition to these, the KPR (A) Act provides for an Ombudsman and an Appellate Tribunal. The Ombudsman is constituted for dealing the cases against the Panchayats or the officials under the Panchayats. The Tribunals, formed by Government for one district or for more than one district, are to make revisions of the appeals against the decisions of the Panchayats.

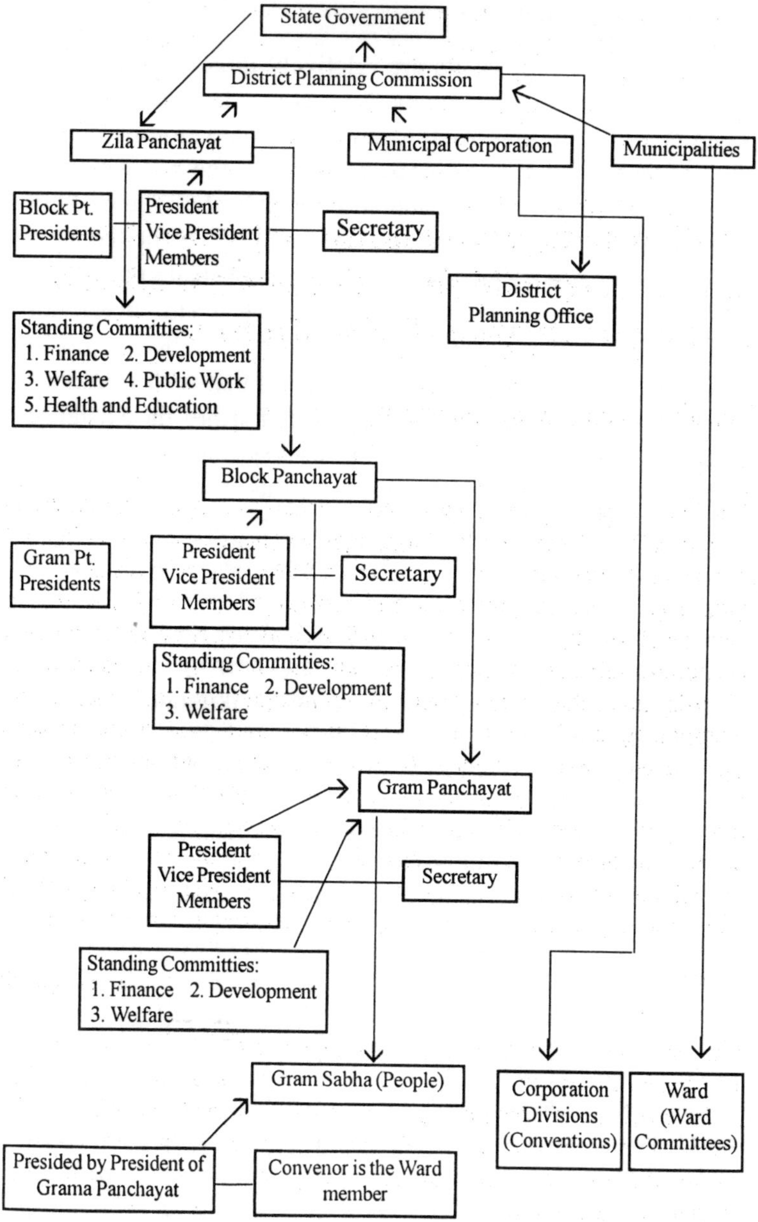

NOTE : For the existing structure of Standing Committee, see Table 7.4

CHART 7.2 : Structure of Panchayat Raj System in Kerala

Gram (Village) Panchayat

In Kerala, Gram Panchayats are relatively larger in size when compared to those in other States. An average Gram Panchayat in Kerala is 37.83 sq. km. in area and has a population of 25,199 (1991 census). There exists wide variation in the population of village Panchayats. The least populous Panchayat of Vattavada in Idukki district had a population of 4,588 in 1991, while the most populous Panchayat of Munnar in the same district had a population of 78343. In terms of area, Valapattanam (2.04 sq. km.) in Kannur district is the smallest Panchayat and Kumily (795.28 sq. kms) in Idukki district is the largest. It is to be noted that such variations seem to be against the spirit of Constitution. Further, the existence of revenue villages not coinciding with the village Panchayats creates difficulties in administration. Gram Panchayats are often larger than the revenue villages. There are 1,384 revenue villages, while there are 990 Gram Panchayats in the State of Kerala.

The number of members of a Gram Panchayat will be decided on the basis of population. The minimum and maximum number of members to the three tiers of Panchayats has been increased by the recent amendment Act. The minimum and maximum number of wards (constituencies) as per the KPR Act and the KPR (A) Act are given in the Table 7.3.

TABLE 7.3 : Minimum and Maximus Number of Wards (Constituencies) according to KPR Act and KPR (A) Act.

Level of Panchayat	Existing As per KPR Act, 1994		Envisaged As per KPR (A) Act, 1999	
	Minimum No. of members	Maximum No. of members	Minimum No. of Members	Maximum No. of Members
Gram Panchayat	8	15	10	20
Block Panchayat	8	15	10	20
District Panchayat	15	25	15	30

TABLE 7.2 : Distribution of Grama Panchayats, Block Panchayats and Municipalities by District

District	No. of GPs	Average Area (Sq.km)	Average Population	No. of of BPs	Average Area (Sq.km)	Average Population	No. of Municipalities	Average Area (Sq.km)	Average Populatiojn
Thiruvananthapuram	84	24.28	27,032	12	169.93	1,89,227	4	1796	37,979
Kollam	71	34.00	30,655	13	186.66	1,68,007	3	24.09	74,439
Panthanamthitta	64	49.36	19,739	09	293.05	1,18,807	3	24.18	40,710
Alappuzha	71	17.62	23,406	12	104.24	1,38,496	5	22.08	67,863
Kottayam	73	29.25	22,863	11	195.73	1,51,727	4	13.43	39,820
Idukki	51	99.38	20,367	08	636.33	1,29,839	1	35.43	40,656
Ernakulam	86	24.76	22,979	15	142.42	1,31,809	8	18.31	34,536
Thrissur	98	30.63	22,479	17	170.68	1,45,943	7	13.81	36582
Palakkad	90	48.02	23,573	13	336.12	1,64,859	4	26.69	59,768
Malappuram	94	36.16	30,181	14	242.80	2,02,647	5	29.40	51,855
Kozhikode	76	29.05	27,235	12	185.77	1,77,306	2	21.33	72,434
Wyanad	24	87.15	27,049	03	697.17	2,16,396	1	34.14	22,949
Kannur	81	35.65	23,866	09	306.96	2,09,380	6	29.34	52,473
Kasaragod	37	51.49	26,060	04	476.27	2,41,054	2	28.11	53,646
Total	990	37.83	25,199	152	296.01	1,70,392	55	24.16	48,784

Note : GP— Grama Panchayat, BP— Block Panchayat

Source : Govt. of Kerala (1999): *Economic Review*, 1998, State Planning Board, Thiruvananthapuram, p.195

The existing Gram Panchayats have been constituted on the basis that Gram Panchayats with population not exceeding 10,000 are entitled to have 8 members and one additional member for every 4500 of the population subject to a maximum of 15 members. All Panchayat members will be elected directly by the people. The President and Vice President of the Gram Panchayat will be elected indirectly from among the elected members of the Panchayat.

The functions and powers regarding the subjects devolved as per the 11th Schedule of the Constitution, is clearly stated in the KPR (A) Act. The latest Amendment Act has revamped the functions of all the tiers of Panchayats. The Third schedule of the Act lists the functions of the Gram Panchayat. There are 27 mandatory functions, 14 general functions, and 29 sector-wise distribution of responsibilities. Every village Panchayat in Kerala has major institutions like Primary Health Centre, Veterinary Hospital, Krishi Bhavan, High Schools, etc. At present the village Panchayats have control over all local level institutions except High Schools.

Presently a Gram Panchayat has only one Standing Committee, which looks into such aspects as taxation, planning, finance, etc. The KPR (A) Act provides for three Standing Committees : (1) Finance, (2) Development and (3) Welfare.

The village Panchayats have their own sources of income and get reasonable amount as grants and shared taxes. Moreover, they have been provided with the major share of plan funds. The following are important taxes assigned to Gram Panchayats:

1. Land tax (tax imposed on land and building in the concerned land)
2. Employment tax
3. Advertisement tax
4. Entertainment tax
5. Service tax
6. Tax on land title transfer (as a surcharge on tax imposed as per the Kerala Stamp Paper Act of 1959)
7. Tax on reclaimed land (or land converted from paddy fields and the like)

The Gram Panchayats have powers to collect fees, and to avail loans for financing development programmes. As per the KPR (A) Act, State Government Grants from basic tax, to Gram Panchayats are of two types - (1) grant, as far as possible, equal to 3/8 portion of the total basic tax collected last year from the area of the Gram Panchayat , and (2) based on population and area of Gram Panchayat, as far as possible equal to 1/8 portion of the total basic tax collected from total Panchayat area of the State shall be given to all Gram Panchayats in the State.

Block Panchayat

An average Block Panchayat in Kerala is 296.01 sq. kms in area and has a population of 1,70,392 (1991 census). There are 152 Block Panchayats in Kerala. The existing Block Panchayats are constituted on the basis that Block Panchayats with a population not exceeding one lakh are entitled to have 8 members and one additional member for every 25,000 population subject to a maximum of 15 members as directly elected members. Each Block Panchayat consist of (a) members who are directly elected by the people, and (b) Presidents of the Gram Panchayats, within Block Panchayat area. The President and Vice-President of Block Panchayat will be elected from among the elected members of the concerned Panchayat. The BDO is the secretary of the Block Panchayat. At present a Block Panchayat is getting assistance from two Standing Committees, one on matters of finance and planning and the other on welfare. The KPR (A) Act provides for three standing committees for Block Panchayats: (1) Finance, (2) Development and (3) Welfare.

The fourth schedule of the KPR (A) Act enlists the functions to be attended to by the Block Panchayats. Apart from the 24 sectoral functions, the Block Panchayats are entrusted to pool technical expertise both Government and Non-Government at the Block level, to provide technical services to village Panchayat to avoid duplication and provide the backward and forward linkages.

Block Panchayats have no powers to tax. However, they have powers to collect fees, and avail loan for financing development programmes. The State Government Grant to Block Panchayat is such that, as far as possible equal to 3/10 portion of the total basic tax collected last year from a district Panchayat area, as grant to all the Block Panchayats in that district. The plan fund is also shared with Block Panchayats.

District Panchayat

There are 14 District Panchayats in Kerala. At present the District Panchayats are constituted on the basis that District Panchayats having a population of 10 lakhs are entitled to have 15 members and one additional member for every one lakh population subject to the maximum of 25 members (directly elected by the people). The District Panchayat consists of (a) members who are directly elected by the people, and (b) the presidents of Block Panchayats, within the territorial limits of the District Panchayat. The President and the Vice-President of the District Panchayat will be elected from among the elected members of the concerned Panchayat. The District Panchayat is at present being assisted by four Standing Committees. The Standing Committees are: (1) finance and planning, (2) welfare, (3) development and (4) public works. The KPR (A) Act provides for five standing committees for a District Panchayat: (1) Finance, (2) Development, (3) Welfare, (4) Public works, and (5) Health and Education.

The fifth schedule of the KPR (A) Act enlists the functions to be attended to by District Panchayat. The District Panchayats are entrusted with plan integration and mobilization of technical expertise in addition to its other sectoral functions.

The District Panchayats have no powers to tax. However, they have powers to collect fees, and avail loan for financing development programmes. The District Panchayats can also issue revenue bonds and raise money for financing developmental works. The State Government Grant to a District Panchayat is, as far as possible equal to 1/5 portion of the total basic tax collected last year from the district Panchayat area. Furthermore, a portion of the State plan fund is distributed among the District Panchayats.

Standing Committees and Steering Committees

The existing structure of Standing Committees for three tiers of

Panchayats as per the KPR Act and the changes provided for in the KPR (A) Act are given in Table 7.4.

TABLE 7.4 : Standing Committees

Levels of Panchayats	*As per Kerala Panchayat Raj Act, 1994*	*As per Kerala Panchayat Raj (Amendment) Act, 1999*
Gram Panchayat	(1) Taxation, Planning, Finance, Welfare, etc.	(1) Finance (2) Development (3) Welfare
Block Panchayat	(1) Finance and Planning (2) Welfare	(1) Finance (2) Development (3) Welfare
District Panchayat	(1) Finance and Planning (2) Welfare (3) Development (4) Public Works	(1) Finance (2) Development (3) Welfare (4) Public Works (5) Health and Education

In order to co-ordinate the functioning of the Standing Committees and to avoid the possibility of conflicting decisions on related issues by different Standing Committees, there is a Steering Committee in each and every Panchayat, headed by the President of the Panchayat.

Full-time Role of Panchayat President

The president is the executive head of a Panchayat. In view of the augmented responsibilities as a result of the transfer of massive resources, the president will be a full-time functionary. He has administrative control over the officials of the Panchayat and of the transferred institutions under the purview of it. Indeed, the president has the power even to suspend an officer, except the secretary and Gazetted officers, in order to take disciplinary actions. On the recommendations of the Panchayat Samiti, the president may request the government for a transfer of the secretary who is the pivotal officer in a Panchayat.

Right of Members

The members have the right to dissent, which is considered to be very essential for the democratic functioning of a Panchayat. Every member who have voted against any resolution has the right to submit a note of dissent giving the reasons for doing so against a resolution. This note of dissent has to be given to the Panchayat secretary within 48 hours of the conclusion of the meeting and the secretary has to forward it to the State government along with the minutes of the meeting.

Panchayat Fund

All the three levels of Panchayats have Panchayat Fund: The Gram Panchayat Fund consists of all receipts of Gram Panchayat except the receipts made for Block Panchayat, District Panchayat or State government; the Block Panchayat Fund consists of all receipts of Block Panchayat except the receipts made for District Panchayat or State government; and the District Panchayat Fund consists of all receipts of District Panchayat except the receipts made for State government.

Plan Grant-in-aid

The Ninth Plan has introduced a basic change in the financial situation of the local bodies of Kerala. About 35 per cent to 40 per cent of the total plan expenditure of the State has been given to the local bodies. The plan fund to Panchayats is in the form of grant-in-aid, which is an untied fund. The total fund included the amount for Sectoral plan for Scheduled Castes and sub plan for Scheduled Tribes. The general category fund has been divided among the Panchayats at a ratio of 70:15:15 for village, Block and District Panchayats respectively. The criteria for intra-tier distribution of plan grant-in-aid are given in Table 7.5.

TABLE 7.5 : The Criteria for Intra-Tier Distribution of Plan Grant-in-Aid

Indicators	*Weightage (percentage)*			
	Gram Panchayat	*Block Panchayat*	*District Panchayat*	*Municipalities/ Corporations*
1. Population (excluding SC/ST)	65	65	55	75
2. Geographical area excluding area under forests	5	10	15	5
3. Area under Paddy	5	—	—	—
4. Own Income of Gram Panchayat	10	—	—	—
5. Composite Index of Agricultural Labourers, Persons Engaged in Live-stock, fisheries, etc. and Marginal Workers	15	25	20	—
6. Composite index of backwardness of houses without latrine and houses without electricity	—	—	10	20
Total	100	100	100	100

Source: Govt. of Kerala (1999): *Economic Review* 1998, State Planning Board, Thiruvananthapuram, P. 211.

Gram Sabha

Gram Sabha is the soul of the Panchayat Raj system in the State and its functions and responsibilities have been strengthened further by the KPR (A) Act. In fact, it has become one of the important institutions involved in decentralized planning in the State.

Gram Sabha consists of all persons included in the electoral roll of a ward (constituency) of a Gram Panchayat. The member of a Gram Panchayat representing the constituency is the Convenor of that Gram Sabha and the meetings of the Gram Sabha has to be presided over by the President of the Gram Panchayat.

It is compulsory to hold general meetings of the Sabha once in three months. The quorum is 10 per cent of the Gram Sabha, but if the Gram Sabha is convened for the second time for lack of quorum at the first convene, the second time needs quorum of only 50 persons. An important development in the recent legislation of KPR (A) Act with an element of direct democracy is the provision for

Special meeting of Gram Sabha when not less than 10 per cent of members demand for such a meeting in writing.

The Village Panchayat shall place before the Gram Sabha reports relating to the developmental programmes of the constituency during the previous year and those that are proposed to be undertaken during the current year and the expenditure therefore, the annual statement of accounts and the administration of the preceding year. Gram Sabha can seek clarifications from the President or Members about the works undertaken by the village Panchayat. The selection of individual beneficiaries of various schemes has to be approved by the Gram Sabha.

The Powers, Functions and Rights of Gram Sabha are given below:

(a) Help collection and compilation of details needed for formulating development plans for the Panchayat.

(b) To generate proposals and indicate priorities for preparation of annual and Five Year Plans.

(c) To prepare the final list of eligible beneficiaries in the case of beneficiary oriented schemes by applying the selection criteria, according to priority, and give to Gram Panchayat.

(d) Rendering assistance in the effective implementation of developmental schemes by providing locally needed facilities.

(e) Mobilization of voluntary labour and contributions in kind and cash needed for developmental schemes.

(f) To suggest the location of streetlights, water taps, public wells, public sanitation units, irrigation facilities, other public utilities, etc.

(g) Establish awareness generating programmes relating to matters of public interest like sanitation, environmental protection, pollution control, etc. and provide protection against social evils like corruption and false and artificial dealings.

(h) To promote harmony and unity among the various groups of people in the area of Gram Sabha and organise arts and sports *melas* to promote good mentality among people.

(i) To monitor and help the beneficiary committees conducting development activities in the area of the Gram Panchayat.

(j) To verify the eligibility of persons getting various kinds of welfare assistance of Government like pensions, subsidies, ration schemes, etc.

(k) To know the detailed estimates of the works proposed to be taken up in the area of the Gram Sabha.

(l) To ascertain from the officials the services they will render and the works they are to do in the succeeding three months.

(m) To know the rationale of every decision of the Panchayat concerning that area.

(n) To know the follow-up action taken on the decision of the Gram Sabha and to know the detailed reasons if some of the decisions cannot be implemented.

(o) To co-operate with staff of Gram Panchayat in cleaning process and provide voluntary service to remove wastes.

(p) To find out the drawbacks in the distribution of pure water and street lighting in the area of Gram Sabha and to suggest remedies.

(q) To help the activities of Parent-Teacher Associations in the schools in the area of Gram Sabha.

(r) To help the public health activities in the area of Gram Sabha, particularly, immunisation and family welfare.

(s) Such other functions as may be prescribed from time to time.

Responsibilities of the Gram Sabha

(i) Dissemination of information on development and welfare programmes.

(ii) Canvassing participation in health, literacy and similar development campaigns.

(iii) Collecting essential socio-economic data.

(iv) Providing feedback on the performance of development programmes.

(v) Resorting to moral suasion to pay taxes, repay loans, promote environmental cleanliness, maintain social harmony, etc.

(vi) Mobilising local resources to augment Panchayat resources.

(vii) Supervising development works and volunteers teams.

(viii) Creating arrangements to report quickly incidence of epidemics, natural calamities, etc.

Role of State Government

The role of State Government has been redefined in such a manner as to ensure the autonomy of LSGIs by limiting its activities to obligatory and regulatory functions. Indeed the Government is attempting to delegate even these functions to such institutions as Ombudsman and Appellate Tribunals. However, the necessary regulatory powers are existing with the Government. For example, if a Panchayat president or secretary fails to discharge any official responsibilities entrusted to them by the government, the government can ask for explanation from them. [section 190 (1) (2)]. The section 191 (1) empowers the government to cancel or withhold a resolution passed by the Panchayat Committee. Government need cancel resolutions only if there is imminent likelihood of breach of law and order, disturbance to communal harmony or danger to life and property. Section 192 States that the annual administration report of Village Panchayat and Block Panchayat should be submitted to the District Panchayat. The District Panchayat should submit their annual report to the State government to be placed before the legislature. Section 193 States that if a Panchayat fails to approve budget for the financial year and experiences financial crisis due to the same, the State Government can dissolve such Panchayat committee through a Gazette notification. The administration of the concerned Panchayat can be put under the control of a Special Officer or an Administrative Committee.

Regarding economic development and social justice, the government has to play a pro-active role. The government has to frame guidelines for technical specifications, planning standards, cost and subsidy norms, environmental safeguards, special measures to protect the interests of Scheduled Castes and Scheduled Tribes, and financial systems and administrative procedures. While forming these norms it has to take care of the national priorities.

Thus government has a guiding, advising and corrective role rather than a punitive or retributory role. That is to say it has a caring and nurturing attitude towards LSGIs.

Functional Autonomy of Panchayats

In order to make the Panchayats 'institutions of local self-government' the powers, functions and responsibilities have been redefined in such a way that the sphere of activity of each local body is fairly clear. Thus, the third, fourth and the fifth schedules— powers, functions and responsibilities of Village, Block and District Panchayats respectively — have been amended accordingly. By doing this, the scope of government interventions has been reduced, on the one hand, and prevent interference of upper tiers of Panchayats in the matters of lower tiers, on the other.

The Panchayats have absolute freedom in deciding their priorities within their functional domains. Generally, the powers of administrative approvals are limited only by their own budget. In the case of technical sanction, the powers have been delegated to the officers available at a particular level for that level of Panchayat.

In Kerala, therefore, there has been a conscious decision to avoid a hierarchy among the three tiers of Panchayat Raj Institutions. Although coordination is envisaged, no formal control over the tiers below is warranted. In sum, the Panchayat Raj System in Kerala has three spheres rather than three tiers.

Accounts and Audits

In the context of massive devolution of funds, audit of local bodies assumes much importance. Audit is not viewed as an instrument of control by the State Government; it is seen as an important professional support system, working as an antenna of the public, keeping track whether the use of public fund is according to accepted laws, procedures and conventions (Committee on Decentralization, 1997).

Under the present system, the elected functionaries have responsibility to keep the accounts of the Panchayats. It is the Panchayat Committee to maintain proper accounts of these institutions. Traditionally, the accounting and auditing system of Panchayats has not been good. The conventional procedures have to be improved and a culture of keeping proper records has to be nurtured. For evolving a proper accounting and book keeping procedure, Audit Manual, Accounts Manual, Budget Manual, etc. are being prepared.

The audit system comprises four types of auditing: (1) Local Fund Audit, (2) Accountant General Audit, (3) Performance Audit and (4) Social Audit.

1. *Local Funds Audit*

It is the conventional system of auditing for Panchayats and this is a statutory audit by the State Government.

2. *Accountant General Audit*

Since the Central Government grants and aids also are given to Panchayats, the accounts are audited by Comptroller and Auditor General (CAG).

3. *Performance Audit*

In view of the more delegation of powers and devolution of funds to LSGIs, a new set of financial procedures have been evolved. The LSGIs requires to be guided properly in maintaining records and following principles of financial procedures and propriety. In this context, a new audit system namely Performance Audit, has been introduced in the KPR (A) Act. It is a running audit system, which is more friendly, helpful and on-line corrective system, which would detect irregularities and deviations, almost simultaneously, allowing for easy rectification.

At the State level the Secretary, Local Administration Department is the Performance Audit Authority. The Authority will be supported by a State Performance Audit Officer, at the State level and by the Performance Audit Officers at the regional level. Under the Performance Audit Officers, Performance Audit Teams will be visiting each Panchayat once in three months for conducting the audit.

4. *Social Audit System*

Another new concept of auditing that has been gaining ground for acceptance is social auditing. Whereas the purpose of Performance Auditing is for concurrent observations and corrections, the social auditing is envisaged for better transparency. Under this system every citizen will have the right to have a look at the estimates, list of beneficiaries, assistance given in each scheme, muster rolls, bills, vouchers, accounts, etc. by providing photocopies of them on payment of actual cost. There may be stipulation that all applications for various licences, certificates, given to a LSGIs are given a queue number and this priority should not be violated. Registers indicating date of application and date of clearance in each case should be available for reference by any applicant. A citizen may examine the tax assessment, granting of exemption, etc. Women's watchdog committees also may be set up at the level of Gram Panchayats and Municipalities.

In addition to these four types of audit, the Panchayats may have Chartered Accountant's Audit for credit rating. The District Panchayats are empowered to raise resources by means of issuing Revenue Bonds.

Transparency and Right to Information

Accountability to the people is best ensured through transparency. Transparent administration enables people to achieve an on-line monitoring of the administrative process. In fact, the citizens' right to information and the level of his access to it would constitute the best indicator of democratisation of a society. When there is democratic decentralization, institutions for people — like Gram Sabha, Parent-Teacher Associations, Watershed Committees, Co-operatives, etc. — would emerge and flourish. In Kerala, these institutions have been gained ground and they have become integral part of the development process.

The public can attend the Panchayat meetings. The public is also allowed to observe all procedures discussions and decision making of the Panchayats, while meetings are convened. In case any member of Gram Sabha is interested in referring the decision of Panchayat, there exists the freedom to do so.

A new chapter for transparency has been introduced in the KPR (A) Act (Chapter XXV A — Right to know). Accordingly, people have right to information that includes the right for taking extracts and obtaining certified copies of documents. It may be any material or information contained in a document relating to the administrative, developmental or regulatory functions of a Panchayat and includes any document or record relating to the affairs of the Panchayat.

Political Panchayats and Anti-defection

Kerala has recognised political Panchayats with elections fought on the basis of political parties. However, Panchayats are expected to be apolitical in their functioning, particularly in decision making on developmental matters. By 'apolitical' we mean narrow divisible functioning on party considerations, but does not exclude larger ideological debates and developmental dialogues. At the same time, party discipline is to be observed in special instances like election of a president or vice president or during no confidence motions. Thus, in Kerala, defection would lead to disqualification of member. Therefore, one cannot wish away the reality of political party identities in the name of freedom of expression of ideas and opinions.

In order to improve the credibility and capability of members new conditions have been introduced for disqualification. These conditions exclude the criminal, corrupt and immoral persons from getting into the Panchayat governance.

Official-Non-official Interface

The traditional division of powers of the political executives and the official executives, with policy making being the function of one and the carrying them out, the function of the other, mingles at all levels of local bodies. For example, there is a policy element in laying down priorities, which requires professional support. Similarly, the elected members have a definite role in implementation. Therefore, a positive official-non-official interface is a pre-requisite for proper functioning of local bodies.

In Kerala, the new system provides an opportunity for professional satisfaction for officials by helping design appropriate projects for local level development and observing the process of implementation. The officials, therefore, would have to enrich their skills.

Compared to the District Panchayats and Block Panchayats, Village Panchayats are functioning effectively from the point of view of friction between officials and non-officials.

Devolution of Functions

In Kerala, all the important subjects listed in the Eleventh Schedule of the Constitution have been transferred to the LSGIs by State legislation. Accordingly the Government has directed the 17 concerned departments to transfer institutions and posts to the respective LSGIs.

For the devolution of functions, the principle of subsidiarity has strictly been followed. Most of the welfare programmes of Central Government have been channelled through Block Panchayats. The functions of the three tiers of Panchayats have been reorganised for the purpose of clarity in functions and responsibilities. Apart from the sectoral distribution of responsibility, the Block Panchayats and District Panchayats are entrusted with pooling of technical expertise and integration of plan from the point of view of backward and forward linkages.

Representation of MPs/MLAs

MPs and MLAs do not have any representation in Panchayats. But they have to be invited for the Gram Sabhas in their respective constituency.

As per the KPR (A) Act, the MPs/MLAs cannot be members of Panchayats simultaneously. In the light of the fact that the work of a Panchayat member is almost fulltime, and that it will not be possible for MPs/MLAs to carry out the duties of a Panchayat member in addition to their parliamentary responsibilities, it has been decided that the MPs/MLAs have to confine their membership either to Parliament/Legislative Assembly or to Panchayat.

New Institutions

For realisation of the ultimate objective of decentralized governance, certain existing institutions, particularly Gram Sabha and State

Election Commission have been strengthened and provisions for establishment of two new institutions have been made in the KPR (A) Act. The two important new institutions are: (1) Appellate Tribunals, and (2) Ombudsman. The Tribunal is meant for dispensing appeals very quickly while the Ombudsman looks into defective administration by the local bodies by employing an investigative approach.

Appellate Tribunals

In the context of the emerging scenario of decentralization in the State, conflicts may arise and dependence on the existing Judiciary for appeals would cause much delay in getting verdict. Justice delayed is justice denied. Therefore, the KPR (A) Act provides for Appellate Tribunals at District level.

An Appellate Tribunal consists of one Judicial Officer, having the rank of District Judge, will be appointed by the Government in consultation with the High Court. The Tribunal will have the same powers as that of a civil court. The Tribunals are expected to be citizen-friendly by means of adopting simple procedures.

Ombudsman

At present there is no institution exclusively to investigate and attend to complaints regarding corruption and defects in the administration of LSGIs and/or the public servants under the LSGIs. Therefore, the KPR (A) Act provides for constituting an Ombudsman which will investigate independently complaints from individuals, groups, and from Government relating to defective administration by local bodies. It is envisaged as a cost-free mechanism for a complaint and is essentially investigative in character. The Ombudsman goes beyond the judicial process, as after redressal of a grievance it can choose to monitor the behaviour of the local authority concerned and it can point out systematically the deficiencies and suggest improvements.

To be more specific, the Ombudsman will conduct investigations and inquiries on any complaint with regard to any action involving corruption, maladministration or irregularities in the administration by the LSGIs and for disposal of such complaints. The following are the members of the Ombudsman for LSGIs.

(1) A High Court Judge, appointed by Government with the approval of the Chief Justice of High Court of Kerala, who shall be its chairman.
(2) Two Judicial Officers of the rank of District Judge appointed by Government with the approval of the Chief Justice of High Court of Kerala.
(3) Two Officers of the Government not below the rank of Secretary to Government, appointed by Government.
(4) Two public men of repute having known integrity, appointed by the Government in consultation with the Leader of Opposition of the Legislative Assembly of the State.

Elections

The State Election Commission is the authority responsible for conducting elections to local bodies. The decisions on the delimitation of constituencies, the reservation of constituencies and chairmanships are of the State Election Commission. The rotation of reserved seats and positions has to be determined by the Commission by means of drawing of lots. The decisions of the State Election Commission in this regard will be final and the decisions cannot be challenged in any court.

The elections to the three-tiers of Panchayats have been conducted on the same date, in the State. The elections to the Nagarapalika institutions also were conducted simultaneously to the elections to PRIs. The elections to local bodies were conducted on two days (23rd and 25th September, 1995) during last election for the convenience of the election machinery.

Simultaneous elections in PRIs and Nagarapalikas will be advantageous because all the people of the State feel they are together in the matters of polity and their constituting the local administrative bodies together will foster such a feeling, and will reduce disparities of being in urban or rural areas at least in the matter of politics. Election procedures also can be made and felt uniform in both Nagarapalika institutions and PRIs. The expenditure on elections also can be reduced considerably as it is conducted simultaneously for all local bodies.

Reservation

In order to achieve the objective of 'social justice', reservation of seats for Scheduled Castes, Scheduled Tribes and women have been ensured in Kerala. The KPR (A) Act has incorporated that the groups of Scheduled Tribe hamlets as Sub-committee of Gram Sabhas enjoying all the powers of Gram Sabha for the purpose of tribal development.

As per the Constitutional provisions, one-third of seats have been reserved for women and proportional representation has been ensured by reserving seats and positions for Scheduled Castes and Scheduled Tribes. But there is no reservation for other backward classes. The same reservation pattern has been followed in all tiers of Panchayats and municipalities.

The Panchayat level development plan projects formulated for the Ninth Five Year Plan have to earmark 10 per cent of the overall grant-in-aid shall be set apart for Women Component Plan. Only those projects, which directly benefit women, and which are organised or managed by women should be included in the Women Component Plan. Furthermore, in the Sub Committees constituted by Gram Sabha, fifty per cent of members shall be women.

The State Women's Commission and Women's Development Corporation are the two important agencies taking cases of gender issues and women's development. The Women's Commission take care of the atrocities against women, while the Women's Development Corporation takes initiative in the development activities for augmenting their economic status, employment, etc.

On an average, the women functionaries are found to have been performed effectively. However, there are exceptions also wherein women elected representatives are controlled from backside by their respective political parties and by other power blocks.

Although all the women contested were not politically enlightened, majority of them found to have a political will and wish. This has led to active participation of a large number of women of the State in election campaigns. The support of men of political parties have inspired and promoted the active participation of women in elections as well as in generating more interest in women in political affairs. Representation of women, Scheduled Castes and Scheduled Tribes in PRIs in 1995 elections is given in Table 7.6.

TABLE 7.6 : Statistical Profile of Women, SCs and STs in Panchayats in Kerala

Local Body	*Total seats (elected)*	*Women*	*% to total*	*SC*	*% to total*	*ST*	*% to total*
Gram Panchayat	10719	3954	36.89	1058	9.87	118	1.10
				153	9.90	17	1.10
Block Panchayat	1546	572	37.19	30	10.00	3	1.00
District Panchayat	300	109	36.33				

Source : Data Bank, Kerala Institute of Local Administration, Thrissur, Kerala.

From Table 7.6, it is evident that around 37 per cent of seats have been won by women in spite of the fact that the reservation of seats for women has been only 33 per cent (one-third of total seats).

The initiative of women headed villages in development planning has been admirable. While scrutinising the developmental projects submitted for the action plan for the Ninth Five Year Plan for the State the State Planning Board has observed that the village Panchayats, which have been headed by women, have submitted largest number of projects, which were relatively realistic as well as technically feasible and economically viable. Women in local administration are mainly new comers to the field. Therefore, they are able to work for the development of the Panchayats without any prejudice. Their civic consciousness and responsibility have increased due to the reservation of seats in local bodies and they have taken it as an opportunity to do more efforts in attaining development of the Panchayats. The informal discussions with the women representatives who have attended training at KILA also corroborate this view.

Political Economy of Official-Non-official Interface

In the recent amendments to the KPR Act, both the official and the elected functionaries have been given balancing powers and responsibilities. To be more specific, a Panchayat president has the power to suspend an official (except the Panchayat secretary and Gazetted officers) when there is a case for a disciplinary action. The president has to ratify the decision in the next Panchayat meeting. In the case of a secretary the president may request the Government to transfer him on the basis of a resolution for such effect by the Panchayat Samiti.

At the same time the secretary has the right to record his opinion, in writing, on all agenda of a Panchayat meeting. If the secretary is not convinced (from the point of view of Acts, Rules, Government Orders and other financial proprieties) regarding the decision of the Panchayat Samiti, he has the right to recommend for reconsideration by the Panchayat Samiti. Even after the reconsideration, if the samithi again passes the same decision, the secretary may refer the matter to the Government. But the decisions have to be implemented when there is no reply from the Government within 15 days. In such a case, both official and the elected representatives are given sufficient opportunities for raising issues relating to malfunctioning.

It is worth noting that the political parties have not, so far, been realised the importance of each tier of Panchayats and the extent of responsibilities entrusted with it. In the emerging scenario, for example, a District Panchayat President may be having a status very near to that of a State Minister; but if we look into the status of candidates, in their respective political parties, the picture is not desirable. As a result of it, it is easy for the higher level political leaders and bureaucrats to influence the decisions of the Panchayat functionaries. The indirect influence of the higher level politicians may come out in the form of a pressure for a change in the leadership in Panchayats through the party politics or in the form of influencing a transfer of an administrator through the State Government. These type of frictions may be avoided if political parties understand and consider the level of operation of respective Panchayats and provide candidature accordingly. In such a situation, an MLA or an MP may not be having any difficulty with Panchayati Raj institutions since they will be working/interacting with leaders who are similar in positions with them. In such an augmented status of Panchayat functionaries, some of the problems of bureaucrats will be solved just as they are comfortable to work with Ministers. In fact, the service and advice of senior level politicians are required for Panchayats particularly in the case of integrated planning for sustainable development of Panchayats.

Kerala has made an attempt in making the District Collector the Secretary and Chief Executive Officer of the District Panchayat. The much acclaimed Committee on Decentralization has recommended that "the District Collector should be made the Secretary and Chief Executive Officer of the District Panchayat" (Committee on Decentralization, 1996, p. 21.). But the recommendation has not been accepted. Surprisingly enough, the Government has decided to appoint another bureaucrat as Secretary of the District Panchayat. In effect, the attempt in curtailing the burden of one bureaucrat has boomeranged and landed the District Panchayats in Kerala with that of two! The District Collector is the Chairman of the District Level Expert Committee (DLEC). The Collector will nominate the Chairman of the Block Level Expert Committee (BLEC) and the Chairman and Convenor of the Subject Committee, the Convenor of the Municipal Level Expert Committee (MLEC) and the Chairperson of the Corporation Level Expert Committee (CLEC). Through these expert committees, the District Collector is able to make his influence.

VI

PEOPLE'S CAMPAIGN FOR THE NINTH PLAN

People's Campaign for the Ninth Plan', the first attempt in the world in decentralized planning with people's participation, was formally inaugurated on 17 August, 1996. Decentralization and people's participation are the hallmarks of this novel approach. In fact, it has inaugurated an era of planning from below. The background of

The primary objective of the Campaign is to ensure that the local bodies prepare and prioritise a shelf of integrated projects in a scientific manner. Besides the schemes that are implemented by the line departments, due care has to be taken to incorporate suggestions made from below. It is envisaged that at least 35-40 per cent of the plan should consist of schemes formulated and implemented by the local bodies within their respective areas of responsibilities. Accordingly, out of the total plan outlay of Rs.16,100 crores for the Ninth Five Year Plan for the State, Rs. 6,000 crores are earmarked for LSGIs. The total plan devolution to local bodies in 1997-98 was Rs.1,025 Crores (36 per cent of the annual plan for 1997-98), and in 1998-99 it was raised to Rs.1,178 crores (around 39 per cent of the annual plan for 1998-99). The amount allotted for LSGIs comprised of Rs. 276 crores for State sponsored schemes and the remaining Rs. 749 crores as plan grant-in-aid for the Annual Plan for 1997-98 and in 1998-99, the plan grant-in-aid component was enhanced to Rs. 950 crores.

In view of the expected massive people's participation, preparation of such a background was found to have been a prerequisite. For this purpose, the planning process has been moulded in a Campaign mode. An idiosyncratic feature of this Campaign is the political consensus by all political parties in the State. The Campaign has been guided by a High Level Council of Guidance and a host of institutions are involved in the process. The organizational framework and institutions involved in the Campaign are given in Chart 7.3. The People's Campaign is markedly distinct from other experiments in decentralized planning attempts elsewhere in the world on the following five counts.

(i) Mass Conscientization

The planning process itself is perceived as an instrument of mass conscientisation. That is to say, the methodology of creating the shelf of projects/schemes itself is as important as the proposals themselves from the point of view of participation of the people. By doing this, it is expected to break the atmosphere of cynicism that exists among the people regarding the economic development of the State.

(ii) Subsidiarity

Under Plan Campaign what is suggested is a system of multi-level planning, where the lowest unit is allowed to plan and implement everything that can be performed most effectively at that level and only the residual is left to the higher levels. Many advantages are claimed for such planning process from below: the plan programme thus would become more responsive to local needs and conditions, it would permit a more integrated development process as distinct from the present watertight departmental development interventions, mobilization of local resources would become feasible, more importantly, by virtue of greater participation of the people it would make planning more transparent and implementation more efficient (Isaac and Harilal, 1997, p.53.).

(iii) Empowering Local Bodies

The campaign is also an attempt to empower the Panchayat bodies. There exists even today a large number of impediments in the way of the efficient functioning of the Panchayats: lack of finance, bureaucratic hurdles, absence of clear rules, out dated related Acts and so on. The Campaign smoothed the process of empowering local bodies. In fact, in Kerala, it is the experience/lessons that formed the planning process which helped in a greater extent in framing the Panchayat Raj (Amendment) Act 1999. Thus, it has facilitated a 'learning by doing' approach in democratic decentralization in the State.

(iv) Institutionalization of the Process

The campaign is an attempt to conceptualise, operationalise and institutionalise a system of multi-level, people centred planning process suitable to the regional specificities of Kerala.

(v) Integrated Approach

While optimum solutions for many problems are to be found at the local level, there are also issues which require to be addressed at higher levels. It is also important that development interventions are integrated both horizontally and vertically among various tiers of decision making so the complementaries are maximised and

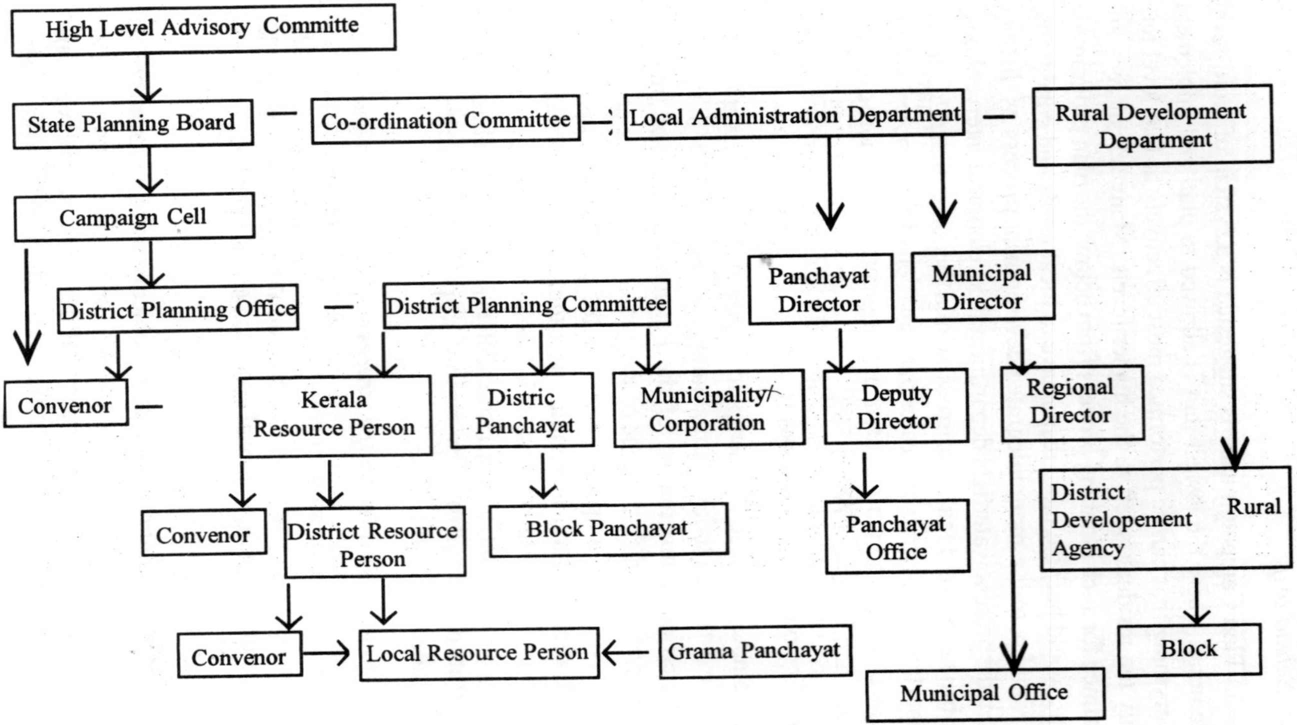

CHART 7.3 : Hierarchy of Offices and Institutions involved in People's Plan

Source : Issac (1997) *Janakeeyasoothranam Sidhanthavum progogavams* Kerala Stte Planning Board, Thiruvananthapuram.

of decision making so the complementaries are maximised and conflicts reduced to the minimum. What is being advocated in the context of the People's Campaign, therefore, is a system of multi-level planning, where the lowest unit is allowed to plan and implement everything that can be performed most effectively at that level and all the rest is left to the higher levels (Government of Kerala, State Planning Board, n.d.).

The People's Campaign is also an effort to consolidate and articulate public opinion in favour of decentralized planning and thereby help the government to translate its commitment to concrete actions. The process of planning from below would not have been possible without the series of measures taken by the State Government to facilitate the same. It should, however, be noted that these measures were not ready in place at the beginning, but have evolved in response to the popular demand from below and requirements of the Campaign as it progressed from one State to other (Government of Kerala, State Planning Board, n.d.) .

Training for the Plan Campaign

An important component of the Campaign has been the extensive training and orientation programme for a large number of resource persons, various functionaries and volunteers. In fact, each phase of the Campaign has been preceded by a training programme. In the first phase a three tier programme of State, district/block /local training, covering more than one lakh resource persons, was undertaken. For conducting the training programmes effectively and time-bound manner a cascade model strategy was adopted. It was difficult to train all the resource persons at one centralised place due to time constrains. Therefore, a three tier training programme had been envisaged: (1) a State level training programme for Key Resource Persons, (2) a district level training programme for District Resource persons, and (3) a Panchayat/Municipal level training for Local Resource persons. The State Level Key Resource Persons (KRP) trained District Level Resource Person (DRP), who in turn trained Local Level Resource Persons (LRP). The course content of each phase of training is given in Table 7.7.

TABLE 7.7 : Course Content of Different Rounds of Training

MODULES	*I*	*II*	*III*	*IV*	*V*	*VI*	*VII*
Challenges of Development	-	+	+	*	*	+	*
Decentralization Philosophy	-	+	+	*	*	+	*
Rules and statutes	-	+		*	-	*	-
Gram Sabhas	-						
PRA Techniques	*	-					
Secondary data	+	-					
Development Report	+	-					
Projects		*	-	-	*	*	+
Plan Documents				-	-	*	+
Appraisal				*		+	-
Sectoral Development Perspectives	+	-	-	+			
Implementation						+	-
Micro Development Models				-			
Integration	*	*	*		-		
SC/ST, Gender	+	+	+	*	*	+	+

+ Main Theme, - Sub Theme, * Minor Theme

Source: Govt. of Kerala (1999): *Economic Review*, 1998, State Planning Board, Thiruvananthapuram , p. 203.

The second phase of training was to impart knowledge regarding the preparation of development reports at the village Panchayat level. In the second phase, more persons were trained and the newly selected persons were selected by the respective District Planning Committees. Training was given on how to prepare development reports and to give importance to various sectors, classes were concentrated on primary sector, secondary sector, etc. Monitoring procedures of the existing programmes, role of financial institutions in local level development, etc. also have been dealt with in the training period. These State level resource persons trained at the second phase took classes for the district level training programme at the second phase. The training to the village Panchayat level resource persons has then been followed.

The third phase of training concentrated on formulation of projects, programmes, etc. Project is the micro operational unit of development action. Combining similar project a programme is formulated. Schemes are formulated at State level as integrated development activities. About one lakh projects have been formulated in the State under various Panchayat Raj institutions. According to the priority at local level and availability of fund, these projects will be implemented at various levels.

The fourth and fifth phases of training concentrated on the preparation and the content of Plan Document. Following this the village Panchayat level and Block level Plan documents were prepared. The participants in the training at the fifth phase were the Block Panchayat Presidents and Vice Presidents, Block Development Officers (Secretaries of Block Panchayats) and the State level Resource persons. In continuation to the training for Block level resource persons, training was also given to the persons involved in the formulation of the District Panchayat development plan. In the sixth and seventh round of the training programmes, issues relating to plan implementation were taken up. Table 7.8 gives the distribution of participants.

The process of decentralized planning may be divided into six distinct phases as follows.

Phase I Gram Sabha/Ward Committees

In decentralized planning the first stage is the elaborate discussion on problems of development and identification of opportunities in the form of local level needs. In Kerala this has been achieved through Gram Sabhas (for Municipalities by ward conventions). As part of the Ninth Plan, Special Gram Sabhas were convened. Special effort was made for ensuring participation of the people on a wider scale. Special emphasis has been given for mobilising women. For popularising the activities, such propaganda measures as quiz, festival of development lamps, *Vilambara jathas*, etc. have been conducted by the Panchayats and colourful posters, advertisements involving all branches of media were resorted to. In order to ensure maximum participation, the Gram Sabhas were convened on holidays.

TABLE 7.8 : Participation in Training/Empowerment Programme

Phase	*State*	*District*	*Block*	*Panchayat/ Municipality*
I	375(5)	11716(3)		100000(1)
II	660(3)	11808(2)		100000(1)
III	300(4)	1146(3)	1500000(2)	
IV	3014(3)		10000(2)	
V	1186(3)			
	304(2)			
VI	150(2)	6000(2)	6000(1)	
	300(3)		6000(1)	
VII	2890(2)		25000(2)	
	3360(2)			

Note: (1) Number in parentheses represents number of days
(2) Do not include one day conferences like 3 State level conferences of presidents and chairpersons, numerous regional conferences of KRPs, VTCs, DLEC members, Block Panchayat Secretaries and District Conferences of DRPs, etc.

Source: Government of Kerala (1999): *Economic Review*, 1998, State Planning Board, Thiruvananthapuram

In order to facilitate proper guidance for the Gram Sabhas adequate preparations were taken in the form of training the Resource Persons. Around 650 Key Resource Persons (KRPs) at the State level, 12000 Resource Persons at the district level and more than one lakh persons at the local level were given training to take active part in the conduct of Gram Sabhas and group discussions on development sector, and to facilitate structured discussions.

After a brief inaugural function, people were encouraged to air their development problems in their ward. Then the participants split theniselves into various subject groups for discussions. In general, there were 12 subject groups, assigned to 12 areas of local development, as suggested by the State Organisers. The groups are: (1) agriculture and irrigation, (2) fisheries and animal husbandry, (3) education, (4) transport, energy and markets, (5) industry, (6) housing and social welfare, (7) public health and drinking water, (8) culture, (9) women's welfare, (10) co-operatives, (11) welfare of scheduled castes and scheduled tribes, and (12) resource mobilization.

The trained resource persons facilitated the semi-structured discussions. A model questionnaire for structuring the discussions, which was to be adopted by the resource persons to suit the local conditions, was also circulated. The aims of the group discussions were three-fold: first, certain qualitative, and to a very limited extent, quantitative information with respect to that particular development sector of the ward is elicited; secondly, development problems of the ward with reference to the sector are listed and the group may prioritise the needs; and thirdly, the people were also guided to analyse the problems on the basis of their experience and, to the extent possible make suggestions of solutions. From each group one or two representatives were selected for participating in the development seminar that was to follow at the Panchayat/Municipal level. The deliberations of each of the group were summed up at the plenary session of the Gram Sabha.

Phase II : Development Seminars

During the second phase, a development seminar was conducted in all local bodies. The seminar was conducted to arrive at broad statement of solutions to various development problems. Apart from representatives selected by Gram Sabhas, the seminars were also attended by all the key officials of the area and invited experts from the locality and outside.

The discussion in the development seminars were based on a printed 'Panchayat Development Report', which provided necessary background information for sector-wise discussions based on socio-economic status of the Panchayat/Municipality. The reports were prepared on the basis of: (1) Consolidation of Gram Sabha reports, (2) Review of ongoing schemes, (3) Collection of secondary data, (4) Geographical study of the area, and (5) a brief survey of local history. These development reports may be considered as bench mark study on development of their respective regions. The preparation of the Panchayat Development Reports was to go on concurrently with the Gram Sabha meetings. All Panchayats (990) and Municipalities (55) produced their development reports. The reports run from 50 to 200 pages. Each has a chapter on each of the 12 task force topics mentioned earlier.

Panchayat Development Report (PDR)

Preparation of the Panchayat Development Report (PDR) is an important focal point of the People's Planning. Felt needs of the people and local problems identified at the Gram Sabhas would be dominated by the subjective aspirations of the local people. To formulate a plan that meets such subjective aspirations, an objective assessment of the problems identified in the Gram Sabhas is essential. Both material and human resources available also has to be made subject to objective assessment so as to understand the resource potential and constraints and to make rational choices. The traditional wisdom of the people together with the theory and practice of modern science help the formulation of development activities. The PDR is envisaged to integrate and incorporate such information as noted above and to lay down a perspective for the comprehensive development of the Panchayat.

The ultimate aim of the development reports was to initiate discussions to prepare the economic development projects. Therefore, each development sector has been analysed and the potential for development identified. Cultural, gender and organizational aspects of development have been incorporated in the analysis. The development report is to have two parts as follows:

Part I (with three chapters)

1. Introduction to the Panchayat and People's Planning
2. Economic and Social History
3. Geo-Physical Conditions and Resources

Part II (with 15 chapters giving the present status, problems and development prospects of each sector).

1. Agriculture and irrigation
2. Animal husbandry
3. Fisheries
4. Forestry

5. Industry
6. Energy
7. Housing
8. Transport
9. Education
10. Health
11. Drinking water and sanitation
12. Women and Development
13. Welfare of SC/ST
14. Resource mobilization
15. Culture.

Before writing the development report, the task force constituted by the Panchayat has ensured that the Gram Sabha reports have been consolidated, ongoing schemes are reviewed, necessary secondary data have been collected, geographical study of the area has been conducted and local history has been documented.

Development Seminars took place in movie theatres, schools, co-operative society halls, Hindu marriage halls, private or public, devoted or rented.

In the seminar integrated solution for various problems, identified at Gram Sabhas/Ward conventions, were arrived at through discussions among people's representatives, officials and experts. The outcome of the second phase may be identified as: (1) Generation of an extensive local data base, (2) a comprehensive survey of all development sectors for all Panchayats and municipalities, (3) a list of possible solutions to the development problems, and (4) formation of task forces to prepare development projects for each development sector. It has been estimated that around 3 lakh people, consisting of representatives from Gram Sabhas, elected representatives, local leaders of political parties, line department officials, local experts, etc. participated in the Development Seminars.

Phase III : Task Forces

In the third phase, the task forces constituted for all sectors expected to convert the solutions suggested in the Development Seminars into projects /schemes proposals in a format that would be included in the plan. The task of project preparation demanded participation of more officials and technically qualified people than the earlier phases. Accordingly, special efforts were made to ensure participation of officials and local level experts. While chairperson of the task force was an elected representative, an officer from the concerned department was supposed to be its convenor.

The task forces were to undertake detailed review of the suggestions made at the seminar and draw up the project/scheme proposals based upon them giving the necessary technical, cost, benefit, time frame and other details mandated by the State Planning Board. The handbook prepared for the purpose suggested a simple format for the projects to be prepared by the task force. It was suggested, to ensure uniformity, that the project reports should generally have the following components:

1. Introduction; explaining necessity and relevance of the project.
2. Objective; in well defined (as far as possible in quantitative/ measurable) terms.
3. Beneficiaries; criteria proposed to be followed in selecting beneficiaries or benefiting areas.
4. Activities; technical analysis and time-frame of all project activities.
5. Organization; agencies and their role in implementing the project activities.
6. Financial analysis; investment needed for each activity and identification of source of funds.
7. Cost-benefit Analysis; preliminary analysis of all direct and indirect benefits and costs including a gender and environment impact assessment.
8. Monitoring; details of the proposed monitoring mechanism.

The State Planning Board had issued a set of guidelines for the preparation of SCP and TSP projects. Further, it was recommended to earmark 10 per cent of the plan assistance for projects meant for development of women.

The task forces prepared around one lakh projects for the consideration of Panchayats. Around 12,000 task forces functioned at the village level alone with a total participation of 1.2 lakh persons for the preparation of these projects.

Phase IV: Panchayat Plan

The fourth phase of the Campaign was to formulate the annual plan of local bodies. For finalising the plan, the Panchayats were expected to: (1) Make a clear assessment of their capacity to mobilise resource from various sources to finance the plan; (2) Evolve a development strategy on the basis of problems identified and resource potential of the locality, prioritise and select projects to be implemented; and (3) Decide a monitoring mechanism for successful implementation of each project selected. An expert group constituted by the Gram Panchayat drew up a Panchayat development plan for every Village Panchayats, on the basis of the reports of the task forces.

Broad guidelines were given to local bodies regarding the sectoral allocation of plan funds provided in the State budget, by the local bodies. While the guidelines for allocation for rural local bodies emphasised productive sector, the urban local bodies have been guided to give emphasis on social service sector. The details are given in Table 7.9.

TABLE 7.9 : Guidelines on Sectoral Allocation indicated to the Local Bodies

Sector	*Rural Local Bodies*	*Urban Local Bodies*
Productive	40-50	20-30
Service	30-40	40-50
Infrastructure	10-30	10-35

Source: State Budget Papers, Appendix IV, 1997-98, quoted from, Isaac, (1999): *People's Planning Towards a Handbook*, Kerala State Planning Board, Thiruvananthapuram

The plan document comprises eight chapters and four appendices. The chapters are on:

1. Preface
2. Development Strategy
3. Resource mobilization
4. Projects, Sector-wise
5. Integrated Development Programmes
6. Scheduled Caste-Scheduled Tribe Development Programme
7. Women's Development Programme
8. Monitoring system

Appendices

1. Various Fora regarding the Plan
2. Project Documents
3. People's Plan Documents
4. Suggestions to higher levels.

Special Component Plan (SCP) and Tribal Sub Plan (TSP)

About 67 per cent of the Special Component Plan and Tribal Sub Plan have been devolved to the local bodies in 1997-98. A large number of schemes for the development of the Scheduled Castes and Scheduled Tribes also have been devolved to the local bodies. The local bodies provided about Rs. 8 crores for the SCP and TSP from their own revenue and this has extended the source of fund for development programmes of the vulnerable sections of the society. The democratic decentralization of SCP/TSP creates opportunity for the weaker sections to directly participate in planning for their own welfare.

Women Component Plan

The campaign gave due importance to gender issues also. Participation of women in the campaign was given emphasis. The training programmes for the campaign incorporated the theme of 'gender and development'. Most important is the incorporation of a mandatory section of 'Gender impact statement' in the assessment of the development projects. And the local bodies were given the guideline to set apart 10 per cent of the plan funds be allotted to the projects directly benefiting women. Although almost all the local bodies prepared special projects for women, in no district the target of 10 per cent was met in 1997-98.

Phase V: Annual Plan of Higher Tiers

The fifth phase of the Campaign was the integration of the local plans and formulation of Block and district plans. The Block and District Panchayats also have their own separate plan schemes. The sequential ordering of the process was made in order to ensure that the plans of the various tiers are integrated and the plans of the higher tiers were complementary to those of the lower tiers. Special emphasis has been given for ensuring backward and forward linkages in projects. The Block and District Panchayats also organised seminars to discuss their draft plans. They have to undertake a detailed analysis of local Development Reports, local Plan Documents and to give attention to the recommendations from below.

District Panchayat Development Plan

The plan proposals of Block Panchayats and municipalities have been integrated at the District level. Broad strategy for district level development has been evolved by the task forces constituted by the District Planning Committee for the purpose. However, at present the laws and rules favours the implementation of planned activities by District Panchayats such that the development plan projects are formulated and implemented only for the Panchayat areas of the district concerned. The Urban areas of the district shall have to be excluded for the purpose of formulating and implementing District Panchayat development plan.

The District Planning Committee forwards the integrated development plan for urban and rural areas of the district to the State. The State Planning Board is the State level co-ordinating agency and the framework for planning also has been set by the same State level agency.

As noted earlier, Kerala has a 'rurban' settlement pattern. The Constitutional stipulation of rural-urban distinction in the Panchayati

Raj system creates the problem of integration at the district level. The District Panchayat's activities are limited to the rural areas. It is the District Planning Committee, the agency which integrates the plans of District Panchayat and Municipalities in a district. At the implementation stage also there are problems in assigning district level officers to District Panchayats. Thus the rural urban linkage found to have been blurred under the present system. Of course, the rectification of this requires an amendment to the Constitution.

State Plan

The State plan has been formulated by the State Level Task Forces constituted by the State Planning Board. The line departments have been directly represented in the Task Forces. The Board ensured that the proposals made by the Panchayat Raj-Nagarapalika institutions through their District Planning Committee are duly incorporated in the State Plan.

Phase VI: Plan Appraisal

The sixth phase of the Plan Campaign was for the appraisal of technical feasibility and financial viability of the projects and plans. Since DPCs did not have sufficient technical expertise, Voluntary Technical Corps (VTCs) were formed requesting retired technical experts and professionals to enrol themselves as volunteer to appraise the projects and plans of local bodies in order to rectify the weaknesses in technical aspects and financial analysis.

Expert Committees

The projects and plan documents prepared by local bodies, and appraised by the local bodies and the District Planning Committees, has to be appraised for technical feasibility, financial viability and procedural acceptability. For this purpose Voluntary Technical Corps (VTC) were constituted at Block Panchayat , Municipality and Corporation level. District Level Expert Committees (DLEC) were also constituted in all the districts for issuing technical sanctions to the projects. However, due to delay in issuing technical sanction to all project by VTCs and DLECs, more Expert committees with official and non-official members have been constituted at Block, Municipality and Corporation levels, namely Block Level Expert Committees (BLEC), Municipal Level Expert Committees (MLEC) and Corporation Level Expert Committees (CLEC). The composition of the DLEC has been revised. The officials in the Expert Committees have been made mandatory members. The DLEC consist of 64 mandatory members, including the District Collector and District Planning Officer.

BLEC, MLEC and CLEC have 15 subject committees each, while DLEC has 24 subject committees. The existing Voluntary Technical Corps/Plan Appraisal Teams at Block Panchayat, Municipality and Corporation levels have been deemed as Expert Committees in Block Panchayats, Municipalities and Corporations. The District Collectors have a prominent role in constituting the Expert Committees, as they have powers to nominate members to the Expert Committees. The non-official members of the DLEC are nominated by the State Planning Board. The District Collector is the Chairman of the DLEC. The District Planning officer is the convenor and the District Planning Office is the secretariat of DLEC.

The District Planning Committees (DPCs) approved the plan of local bodies on the recommendations of these expert committees. It is important to note that the expert committees have no right whatsoever to change the priorities set by the local bodies. Their tasks were clearly confined to technical and financial appraisal of the projects and to suggest such modifications as would make the proposed projects viable and feasible.

Implementation of Development Plan

The basis for the financial backing of the plan projects of the local bodies is the share (35-40% of total plan allotment) of State Plan expenditure for the Ninth plan. However, the local bodies can also implement projects from funds raised on its own and from contributions, voluntary work and such other raised resources. The centrally sponsored welfare programmes are usually implemented through the Block Panchayat.

The actual implementation of the projects may be done in four ways depending upon the nature of the work. First, the beneficiaries may constitute a committee, viz. Beneficiary Committee, and the Committee may undertake the project. In these cases the projects will be benefiting a number of individual beneficiaries. When a particular project is meant for a specific area also, beneficiary committee may be constituted. Secondly, the Panchayat Samithi may execute the works directly. The third preference is given to certain authorised NGOs like CSTFORD and Nirmithi Kendra, which are accredited by the Government of Kerala for carrying out such works. Finally, there is the option for open tender. In all the cases, utmost care has been taken to avoid benami works so that maximum benefit is ensured with minimum cost.

VII

ON EVALUATING THE PROGRESS

Although it is premature to evaluate the experimental decentralized planning, which is considered to be a pioneering attempt in the world, certain impressions may be gathered from the experience of last two-and-a-half years. The achievements made so far has been legendary in the sense that it has attracted worldwide attention and acceptance as a new methodology in decentralized planning. According to World Bank, "The decentralized planning process is largest of its kind in the world".

Our attempts in the direction of evaluating the performance of the process, by means of a rapid appraisal, identifies elements of success on the following nine counts.

1. Qualitative change
2. Speed of the Programme
3. Nature of the schemes
4. Attitudinal change of the staff
5. Level of participation
6. Equitable prioritisation
7. Participation of women in development
8. General response of the people
9. Technical advice and its acceptability.

Justice Krishna Iyer, renowned social activist and thinker, observes the Campaign as follows:

> "The people's campaign marks the beginning of a social revolution in Kerala. The failure of democracy in India consists in the failure to share power with the people. In Kerala today political power is in the hands of the people."
>
> (Iyer, 1998)

NOTES

1. Popularly known as Sen Committee since the Chairman of the Committee was Shri. S.B. Sen.
2. There is disagreement among scholars regarding calling 'Kerala Model', because a model is meant to have possibility of replication/ adoption. Some are of the opinion that the Kerala experience may not be replicable because of its unique features. Therefore, according to them, it is not appropriate to call the experience as a model.
3. For basic data on Kerala, see *Gazetteer of India* (1986, 1989), and for socio-economic details see Government of Kerala (1999).
4. A detailed account of trends in urbanization is available in Sreekumar (1990).
5. On details of public action and development in Kerala, see Ramachandran (1996).
6. The Community Development approach during the fifties had been envisaged to ensure people's participation. However, the attempts have not been successful. It may also be noted that information theorists and specialists in organizational design have demonstrated that the delays in implementation as well as costs in terms of information handling, human and material resources are minimised when the organizational distance between the point of decision and the point of implementation is minimum.
7. The legislation for setting up of District Administration Councils stands to this reason.
8. We will discuss the salient features of this Amendment later in section V.
9. Apart from the historical background other forces that resulted in the introduction of the Campaign are:
   (1) the prevailing critique of centralised planning and administration in the country; (2) failure of hitherto efforts at decentralization and the intimidating long list of obstacles that new attempts at genuine decentralization face; and (3)The contemporary development

challenges of the State of Kerala which by consensus demand a decentralized approach to planning as also a revival of the participatory spirit to project the widely acclaimed gains of the past.

REFERENCES

Amin, Samir (1991): "Four Comments on Kerala", *Monthly Review*, New York, January 1991.

Centre for Development Studies (CDS) (1980): Some Notes on Possibilities of Decentralized Development in Kerala, Working Paper No. 106, Thiruvananthapram.

Committee on Decentralization (1996): Interim Report, Government of Kerala, Thiruvanathapuram.

Committee on Decentralization (1997): Final Report, Volume 1, Part A and B, Government of Kerala, Thiruvananthapuram.

Gazetteer of India (1986): Kerala State Gazetteer, Volume I (by Adoor K.K. Ramachandran Nair), published by the State Editor, Kerala Gazetteers, Thiruvananthapuram.

Gazetteer of India (1989): Kerala State Gazetteer, Volume III Economic Affairs, published by the State Editor, Kerala Gazetteers, Thiruvananthapuram.

Government of India (1978): Report of the Working Group on Block Level Planning, Planning Commission, New Delhi.

Government of Kerala (nd.): *The People's Campaign for Ninth Plan in Kerala: An Introduction*, Kerala State Planning Board, Thiruvananthapuram.

Government of Kerala (nd.): *Power to the People's Plan - Ninth Plan*, State Planning Board, Thiruvananthapuram.

Government of Kerala (1996): *People's Campaign for Ninth Plan in Kerala: An Approach Paper*, Kerala State Planning Board, Thiruvananthapuram.

Government of Kerala (1999): *Economic Review 1998*, State Planning Board, Thiruvananthapuram.

Isaac and Harilal (1997): "Planning for Empowerment: People's Campaign for Decentralized Planning in Kerala", *Economic and Political Weekly*, Jan. 4-11, p. 53

Isaac, Thomas T.M. (1996): *People's Campaign for Ninth Plan: An Approach Paper*, Kerala State Planning Board, Thiruvananthapuram.

Isaac, Thomas T.M. (1997): *Janakiyasoothranam: Sidhanthavum Prayogavum* (in Malayalam), Kerala State Planning Board, Thiruvananthapuram.

Isaac, Thomas T.M. (1999): *People's Planning: Towards a Handbook*, Kerala State Planning Board, Thiruvananthapuram.

Iyer, Krishna (1998): 'Beginning of Revolution', *Mathrubhumi*, 17 August 1998.

Oommen, M.A. (n.d.): 'Development Experience, Development Priorities and Fiscal Resources of Kerala', in *People and Development*, Centre of Science and Technology for Rural Development, Thrissur.

Ramachandran, V. (1995) : "Kerala", *Status of Panchayats in the State of India, Institute of Social Sciences*, Concept, New Delhi.

Ramachandran, V.K. (1996): *On Kerala's Development Achievements*, in Dreze, Jene and Amartya Sen, (1996) Indian Development: Selected Regional Perspectives, Oxford University Press, Delhi.

Sreekumar, T.T. (1990): 'Neither Rural Nor Urban: Spatial Formation and the Development Process', *Economic and Political Weekly*, 1-8 September.

Woodcock, George (1967): *Kerala - A Portrait of the Malabar Coast*, Faber and Faber, London.

8

NEW PANCHAYATI RAJ SYSTEM AT WORK: KARNATAKA

N. SIVANNA

INTRODUCTION

With the passing of the 73rd Constitutional Amendment, the Panchayati Raj Institutions (PRIs) have acquired a statutory status, become an integral part of our polity and, more importantly, they have been recognized as 'institutions of self-government' (Article 243 G, 73rd Amendment). Consequently, this has given an impetus to decentralised governance and planning as strategies for initiating socio-economic transformation in rural areas with a prime objective for developing rural infrastructure and improving the living conditions of the rural people, especially the weaker sections.

Set in the above framework, this chapter analyses Karnataka's experience in the area of decentralised governance and planning, particularly under the new Panchayati Raj Act of 1993. The data[1] for this chapter were collected from the Chitradurga Zilla Panchayat, one of the twenty-seven Zilla Panchayats in Karnataka, three Taluk Panchayats and six Gram Panchayats. Of the three Taluk Panchayats one (Hiriyur) was developed, second (Hosadurga) developing and the third (Challakere) underdeveloped. Out of the six Gram Panchayats — Iknur, Babur in Hiriyur, Bokikere, Lakkihally in Hosadurga and Nannivala, Obalapura in Challakere — two each from a Taluk Panchayat, one was near to the Taluk headquarters and the other away from the headquarters. The analysis has been carried out keeping in view the parameters and some of the issues that arise from the theory of decentralization (Russell Nicholson 1981 Rondinelli 1989, Maddick 1963). The parameters and issues are: there should be access to decision-making to all of those sections which are likely to be affected by such decisions; decentralised institutions should enjoy both political and financial autonomy; both officials and non-officials should be accountable to people; the planning process should be carried out in an integrated area development framework; implementation should be cost effective to promote sustainability; and planning process should be integrated into the State system of planning and development administration. The related relevant issues are what subjects (powers) and resources be devolved from the centralised to decentralised decision-making level?, how should these powers and resources be used to plan and implement projects? and what sort of relationships emerge among the various actors involved in decentralised governance? (Abdul Aziz 1993, Abdul Aziz *et al.* 1998). This chapter is divided into four sections: Section I narrates, in brief, the evolution of Panchayats in Karnataka; Section II examines the salient features of the 1993 Act and about the recent amendments. Section III analyses working of Panchayats under 1993 Act; and Section IV makes an overview.

I

The genesis of PRIs in Karnataka dates back to 1862 when a 'Local fund' was established for constructing roads and other subsidiary works. However, in the history of Panchayati Raj of Karnataka, the period between 1950 and 1954 was seen as a period of great significance (Sivanna 1998). During this period, the Government had appointed two review committees to strengthen the working of the then existing district boards and Village Panchayats. The 'Integration and Co-ordination Committee', under the Chairmanship of Venkatappa, which submitted its report in 1950, recommended a 'two-tier' system with Group Panchayats and District Boards. The District Boards were composed of members elected indirectly by the directly elected members of the Panchayats. The major thrust of its suggestions was with regard to co-ordination and integration. Based on these suggestions, the then Government passed the Mysore Village Panchayat and District Boards Act of 1952. Meanwhile, the Government had appointed one more committee, the Local Boards Enquiry Committee, under the Chairmanship of D. Chandrashekaraiah, to examine the working of local bodies which submitted its report in August 1954. The Committee recommended a 'three-tier' structure of local self-government with District Boards at the apex, Taluk Boards at the middle and village Panchayats at the base. One of the significant recommendations of this committee was that both District Boards and Taluk Boards should function as 'executive bodies' and these bodies should be assisted by a 'special agency' to implement public works. However, there was no positive response from the Government and it could not implement the recommendations of the above committees owing mainly to impending reorganization of the State.

Karnataka had inherited varying patterns of local-self government and experiences when it was to constitute Panchayats under the new Act, the Mysore Village Panchayats and Local Boards Act, 1959, although it was very much a by-product of the 'blue-print' provided by Balwantrai Mehta Committee report, which provided a new impetus and a new rationale for Panchayati Raj. Following the recommendations, the Government had constituted a directly elected village Panchayat for every village or a group of villages, with a population ranging from 1,500 to 10,000. The membership of the Panchayats was between 11 and 19. Seats were reserved for Scheduled Castes and Scheduled Tribes in proportion to their population and for women, whose membership in no case should be less than two. Chairman and Vice-chairman were elected from amongst the members. There was a Secretary to look after the administrative matters.

The Taluk Development Board (TDB), which was an executive body, was constituted as an intermediary tier for each Taluk. The membership of the TDB varied depending on the population; Taluks, with a population of less than one lakh, could elect 19 members. Like Panchayats, even in TDB, seats were reserved for Scheduled Castes, Scheduled Tribes in proportion to their population and for women, the number being not more than two. The office bearers were elected from amongst the elected members. Members of the State Legislature were members of the TDB with a right to vote, but not to hold office. The BDO (Block Development Officer) was the Chief Executive Officer of the TDB.

The apex institution created under 1959 Act was the District Development Council (DDC), constituted for each district. The institution was visualised purely as an advisory and co-ordinating body. All the presidents of the TDBs together with MPs, MLAs and MLCs and some official members constituted this body. The Deputy Commissioner (head of the district administration) was the ex-officio President of the Council. Its main functions were to give approval to the budgets passed by TDBs, to review the work of TDBs and to provide guidance and assistance to, and co-ordinate the works of the TDBs. The DDC was not assigned with any independent sources of revenue.

As regards working of Panchayats, the TDBs were involved in the formulation and implementation of rural development programmes. The involvement was seen in two ways: first as a feedback providing and implementing agency, and, secondly, as an independent institution involved in the planning of the developmental works of their own. Even the village Panchayats were involved in the planning process, particularly in identifying the local needs and resources and prioritising the needs and schemes (Sivanna 1990).

In Karnataka, when the Janata Party came to power in 1983, there was a revival of interest for strengthening Panchayati Raj system with genuine transfer of powers and functions. The Asok Mehta Committee Report came in as handy for the Government to introduce reform measures. The Government was successful in its maiden attempt at giving powers to people. By enacting Karnataka Zilla Parishads, Taluk Panchayat Samitis, Mandal Panchayats and Nyaya Panchayats Act 1983, a new era of Panchayati Raj began in the history of local government in India, as it demonstrated for the first time willingness of a State Government to divest itself of substantial powers and functions in favour of sub-State institutions (Chandran 1994, Meenakshisundaram 1994).

The 1983 Act provided for a directly elected 'body corporate' both at the district and the mandal levels, apparently greatly influenced by the strong role such institutions had in Maharashtra and Gujarat and the model suggested by Asok Mehta Committee report. The Zilla Parishad members were directly elected with 25 per cent of the seats reserved for women, and reservation of seats for the Scheduled Castes and Scheduled Tribes was in proportion to their population (minimum 18 per cent); incidentally, the proportion of seats reserved for women was one of the highest in the PRIs in India. Apart from this, reducing the voting age to 18 years was another radical measure introduced by the Government, which enabled the rural youth to actively participate in the political process at the grassroots. The members of Parliament and State Legislature were entitled to take part in the proceedings and had voting rights, but could not hold office. The Adhyaksha and the Upadhyaksha, elected from amongst the members of the Zilla Parishad, were given the status and salary of minister of State and deputy minister of the State government respectively.

The administrative wing of the Zilla Parishad was headed by the Chief Secretary, a person senior in service to the deputy commissioner of the district. The Chief Secretary had the operational responsibility for all development programmes/ schemes, works and staff. However, he had to work under the supervision of Adhyaksha, who was incidentally the 'executive head' of the Zilla Parishad. There were subject specialists in the fields of planning, statistics, accounts and so on. All the district level officers and the staff of development departments functioned under the Zilla Parishad, which was like an 'umbrella'. The two important merits of this arrangement were that (a) it ensured an effective mechanism for identifying and articulating people's needs and aspirations and (b) it helped to co-ordinate the efforts and resources of the various district development departments (Abdul Aziz, 1994).

Karnataka was the first State to legislate for constituting Mandal Panchayats, as recommended by the Asok Mehta Committee. The Mandal Panchayat was comprised of a cluster of villages with a population of 8,000 to 12,000. Seats were reserved for women and for Scheduled Castes and Scheduled Tribes to the extent of 25 per cent and 18 per cent, respectively. Wherever members of the backward communities were not elected to the Mandal Panchayats, the Zilla Parishad could nominate two persons representing these groups. The Pradhan and Upapradhan who were indirectly elected were empowered to convene meetings and supervise officers and employees. Each Mandal had a Secretary and it is significant to note that the Mandal Panchayat had powers to appoint its own employees.

The 1983 Act had provided for the intermediary tier, i.e., Taluk Panchayat Samiti between Zilla Parishad and Mandal Panchayats. It was essentially an advisory body and designed to assist the Mandal Panchayat in the effective implementation of programmes and schemes. The Samiti had powers of supervision, review and co-ordination. The Block Development Officer was the Secretary of the Samiti devoid of any executive powers as this officer had in erstwhile TDBs. The MLA representing the Taluk was the President of the Samiti.

The 'Gram Sabha' was regarded as the 'soul' of the Panchayati Raj System. It was a council of all those on the electoral roll of a revenue village (around 27,024 in the entire State). The main functions of the Gram Sabha, which should meet at least twice a year, were to discuss, consider and review the work of Mandal Panchayats, to select beneficiaries for the beneficiary oriented programmes and to prepare specific village development plans. In addition, the Gram Sabha had the responsibility of mobilizing voluntary labour and contribution (cash) and assisting Mandals in the implementation of village development schemes. The meetings were attended by voters of the village, people's representatives and officials, thereby facilitating an interface between Government officials and elected members and providing an opportunity for the people to put forth their needs, aspirations and day-to-day problems.

Compared to the 1959 Act, as far as local governance and planning is concerned, the 1983 Act provided genuine centres of decentralised units. The then Government made a revolution in the art of local governance and planning; it was indeed a radical measure. The merits of decentralization could well be seen in the structure and functioning of Zilla Parishads and Mandal Panchayats. The Act had given enough powers and resources to undertake rural development activities. The local polity was almost parallel to State level polity as far as the nature and style of functioning was concerned. Seen in terms of representation, the Zilla Parishads and Mandal Panchayats were almost representing the rural society with members drawn from scheduled castes and scheduled tribes, backward classes, women and other sections. More strikingly, through Gram Sabha meetings, the accountability of elected members and officials to general public was ensured to a great extent.

II

The process of real decentralization that began under 1983 Act, started diminishing with the change of Government at the State level. This clearly indicated that the PRIs lacked political stability and their legitimacy was always in question and depended very much on the empathy shown by the State and Central leadership. Seen in this background, the Constitution Seventy-third Amendment provided a much awaited statutory status to PRIs making these institutions integral part of our polity. This Amendment had facilitated for the establishment of a uniform three-tier structure of Panchayati Raj, with exception given to North-East States, for conducting elections regularly, once in five years, reservation of seats and authority positions for scheduled castes and scheduled tribes in proportion to their population, women and for backward classes if the concerned States wished to do so, for constituting State Finance Commission and Election Commission. Thus, the Amendment provided a firm base for the PRIs to grow as centres of local self-government institutions.

In Karnataka there were efforts to redesign PRIs, by the new government, and this was done keeping in view the broad framework of the 73rd Amendment. It is significant to note that Karnataka was the first State to pass a new legislation in 1993, namely, The Karnataka Panchayat Raj Act, 1993. The new Act provides for a three-tier structure of Panchayati Raj with Zilla Panchayats (at the district level) Taluk Panchayats (at the Taluk level) and Gram Panchayats (at the village level). The Bill for constituting

Panchayats, which was introduced on 1st April 1993, came into force from May 18, 1993.

Elections were held first to Gram Panchayats (December 1993) and elections to Taluk and Zilla Panchayats in January 1995. Elections to Gram Panchayats were held on non-party basis whereas to Taluk and Zilla Panchayats on party basis. As reported in press and based on field experiences the elections were to a greater extent free and fair. Instances like booth capturing, dummy voting, clashes etc., were hardly cited in the press and the media. The entire process was democratic and voters-friendly (Subha 1995). All the three Panchayats are directly elected bodies. To facilitate people's participation in the governance and planning, the Act provides for the Gram Sabha, convened twice in a year, with the functions of mobilizing voluntary labour and contributions, identifying beneficiaries for the development schemes and rendering assistance in the implementation of programmes/schemes pertaining to the village. In its preamble the 1993 Act resolves for promoting greater participation of the people and ensuring more effective implementation of rural development programmes. It also recognises Panchayats as 'Units of Local Self Government'.

One of the salient features of 1993 Act, compared to previous Acts, is that it has provided reservation not only to membership seats but also to executive positions — Adhyaksha and Upadhyakshas. It has provided reservation to women (one-third in each category of seats), backward classes (one-third) and to Scheduled Castes and Scheduled Tribes (with a minimum of 18 per cent) in proportion to their population. One fifth of the Gram Panchayat's Adhyakshas are represented in the Taluk Panchayats by annual rotation and the adhyakshas of the Taluk Panchayats in the Zilla Panchayats. Members of Parliament and State Legislature are members of both the Zilla Panchayat and the Taluk Panchayat with right to vote (except in the election of the Presidents of Zilla Panchayats and the Taluk Panchayats) but not to hold office. The Adhyakshas and the Upadhyakshas are elected by the elected members only. The Adhyaksha of the Zilla Panchayat and the Taluk Panchayat can be removed by a simple majority whereas the Adhyaksha of the Gram Panchayat by a two-thirds majority.

In conformity with the Eleventh schedule of the Constitution, the 1993 Act has entrusted a wide range of functions (Schedule I, II and III) to Panchayats. To carry out these functions, the Gram Panchayat receives Rs. one lakh annual grant and has powers to levy tax on buildings and lands, levy water rate, tax on entertainment, vehicles, advertisement and hoarding, market fee, fee on bus stands and on grazing cattle. Both the Taluk Panchayat and the Zilla Panchayat are allowed to charge fee on their property used by others and they do not have powers to levy taxes. In addition, both the Gram Panchayats and the Taluk Panchayats get proceeds from cess on land revenue, surcharge on stamp duty levied by the State Government. Except for these, the Panchayats have to depend solely on the resources transferred from the Government.

A close look at the various sections of the 1993 Act, enacted by the Congress-I Government revealed that unlike the 1983 Act, it had certain disturbing aspects which went against the idea of giving 'power to the people'. The State Government had vested considerable powers of supervision, control, even suspension of resolutions, issue of directives and supersession with higher level bureaucracy. As a consequence, the bureaucracy could intervene at the critical levels of Panchayats' functioning. Chapters XVI and XVIII, dealing with Inspection, Supervision and Miscellaneous, had given discretionary powers to individual officers of the State to intervene. For instance, the Divisional Commissioner had the powers to dissolve Gram Panchayats, Chief Executive Officer of Zilla Panchayat to annual the resolutions passed by the Zilla Panchayat and Assistant Commissioner of Sub-division appealing powers. The new Government, the Janata Dal, committing itself for enriching the status and functioning of the Panchayats, initiated necessary reform measures to rejuvenate and reinvigorate Panchayats.

In order to strengthen Panchayats both organizationally and functionally, the Government had appointed an 'Expert Committee' under the Chairmanship of P.R. Nayak. The Expert Committee had made very useful and meaningful recommendations to make Panchayats more viable both politically and administratively. The recommendations of the Expert Committee were: making the elected body superior to bureaucracy; 'executive head' status to presidents of Zilla Panchayat and Taluk Panchayat; vesting dissolution and annulling powers with the next higher level institution; checks and balances to ensure accountability; enthusing Panchayats to prepare perspective plans of 15 years duration; constituting high power committee to make a classification of schemes under appropriate levels; excluding MPs, MLAs, MLCs from the membership of Panchayati Raj; Constitution of State Panchayat Council; giving compulsory representation to women members in all Standing Committees; empowering Zilla Panchayats to transfer Group C and D personnel, making Adhyakshas of Zilla Panchayat and Mayor of the Principal City Corporation as the Chairman and Vice-Chairman of the District Planning Committee respectively, constituting Nyaya Panchayats and a host of other recommendations which have definite bearing on the functioning of Panchayats (Sivanna 1996).

Taking note of these recommendations, the Government have, so far, passed three amendments to the Act. The first phase of amendments included the bifurcation of backward classes into two categories — Category 'A' and Category 'B' and reserving seats in Panchayats accordingly. For category 'A' 80 per cent and category 'B' 20 per cent seats were reserved from among the total 1/3rd of seats allotted to Backward Classes. Secondly, amendments were also made to sections 152 and 193 of the Act to recognise Adhyakshas of Zilla Panchayat and Taluk Panchayat as 'Executive Heads' of respective Panchayats. The Second phase of the Amendment directed towards reducing the term of Adhyaksha and Upadhyaksha of both Zilla and Taluk Panchayat from five years to twenty months. The Third phase of the Amendment aimed at promoting capabilities and capacity building among Panchayats. The important amendments are: strengthening the hands of the elected body by giving powers of dissolution, appealing, supervising and monitoring; retrenching many powers given to the officials under Chapters XVI and XVIII of the Act; making officials to come under the supervision and control of the President; entrusting obligatory functions on the Panchayats; providing provision for constituting additional standing committees and joint committees between two or three Panchayats for promoting functional linkages; Constitution of State Panchayat Parishad; making the President of the Zilla

Panchayat as the Chairman of the District Planning Committee and the Mayor of the City municipality as the Vice-Chairman; statutorily sanctioned Chief Planning Officer; authorising Chief Executive Officer of Zilla Panchayat to report to the Government about the irregularities and; disqualifying membership if any member fails to have a lavatory facility within the gap of six months from the date of his or her becoming a member (Sivanna 1997).

III

About the District

Chitradurga district, which was the northernmost district in the old Mysore State, now occupies a central place in the geographical map of Karnataka. It is one of the six districts falling within the Bangalore division. In the overall State development index (1985-86) the district takes the seventh position, almost close to the State average. With 10,852 square kilometers in area, the district has a population of 21,80,443 (1991 census), of which 73 per cent of the persons are in the rural area and 27 per cent in the urban area. Out of the total population, 51.44 per cent constitutes males population and 48.56 per cent are females. The scheduled caste population is 19.84 per cent and the scheduled tribe population is 14.60 per cent of the total. The growth rate of the population between 1981 — 1991 is 23.25 per cent which is above the State average of 21 per cent. As for literacy rate, of the total population, 66.11 per cent of males and 37.89 per cent females are literate whereas in the State 67.26 per cent males and 44.34 per cent females are literate. Compared to the State level literacy rate of 56.05 per cent the district's literacy rate is 46.25 per cent.

As for land utilization pattern (1994-95), 8.94 per cent of the land is under forest, which is below the State average of 16.14 per cent. However, more than 68.34 per cent of the land has been put to productive use. With regard to agricultural land holding pattern, it is quite revealing to note that large farmers (10 hectares and above), who constitute 3.07 per cent of the total, exercise the ownership to the extent of 18.62 per cent whereas 27.85 per cent of marginal farmers (less than 1 hectare) control only 6.18 per cent of the total holdings. Small farmers (between 1 and 2 hectares) and semi-medium farmers (between 2 and 4 hectares) constitute 30.49 per cent and 27.73 per cent together control over 43.39 per cent of the total land holdings. There are around 13.84 per cent of medium farmers (between 4 and 10 hectares) controlling 31.81 per cent of the land holding. Put together both medium farmers and large farmers exercise control over 50.43 per cent of the total holdings. This is indicative of the skewed distribution pattern of land holding in the district. And, more so, bulk of the land is concentrated in the hands of the relatively small number of farmers. This is true of the State also because 13.24 per cent of both medium farmers (11.01 per cent) and large farmers (2.23 per cent) own 46.58 per cent of the land holdings.

The picture that emerges from the above account is that the Chitradurga district is on the average path of development. It is regarded neither as fully developed nor underdeveloped. In this path of development process the Panchayats have a significant role to play.

In Karnataka, there are 5640 Gram Panchayats, 175 Taluk Panchayats and 27 Zilla Panchayats. There are around 80,160 members in Gram Panchayats, 3340 in Taluk Panchayats and 919 in Zilla Panchayats. One of the salient features of the 1993 Act, compared to previous Acts, is that it has provided reservation not only to membership seats but also to executive positions — Adhyakshas and Upadhyakshas. In compliance with the provision of the 73rd Amendment, the Act has provided one-third reservation to women, one-third to Backward Classes and to Scheduled Castes and Scheduled Tribes in proportion to their population. Through an amendment, the Backward Classes have been grouped under 'A' and 'B' categories. Category 'A' was considered most backward and category 'B' more backward. The former was given reservation to the extent of 26.6 per cent (almost 80 per cent) and the latter 6.4 per cent (almost 20 per cent). Under Category 'A' 190 castes were listed and nine castes under Category 'B'.

Tables 8.1, 8.2 and 8.3 present the percentage distribution of seats in the Panchayats for the State as a whole and for the district understudy, it is significant to note from the Tables about the representation of weaker sections in local governance which is a suggestive of the growing political socialization and political mobilization among the vulnerable sections of the society. With regard to party-wise distribution of seats (Tables 8.4 and 8.5) in the Panchayats both at the State level and at the district under study, the Janata Dal, the ruling party in the State, had bagged more seats compared to other political parties.

The above information testifies to the fact that the reservation policy has, in a way, brought in the hitherto neglected and disadvantaged communities of the society into the system of governance. With the reservation accorded to both membership seats and authority positions — Adhyaksha and upadhyksha — the vulnerable groups have taken the reigns of local democracy. This, in fact, has widened the social base of the Panchayat system and thereby paved the way for promoting social interaction between the citizens and the Panchayats. With regard to participation of these new groups in the functioning of Panchayats the collected field information from the district has both positive and negative aspects, and more importantly it varies between the lower level Panchayats and the higher level Panchayats. For instance, the participation of women members in Zilla Panchayat found to be very encouraging since they were found attentive, vocal in putting across their views, opinions and arguments. Whereas in Gram Panchayats, their participation was not so encouraging. They feel shy and reluctant for getting themselves involved in the discussions. Field experiences are an indicative of the fact that in higher level Panchayats we have women members drawn from different socio-economic and political backgrounds. Particularly in terms of better educational background, good family support, family members political experience and their better economic status acting as strong motivating factors on their effective performance.

TABLE 8.1 : Reservation of Seats in Village Panchayats [Category-wise, District-wise (in %)]

District	*SC*	*ST*	*BC*	*OTHERS*	*WOMEN*
Bangalore (U)	26.68	7.06	33.27	32.99	44.77
Bangalore (R)	21.71	7.05	33.48	37.76	43.22
Chitradurga	23.42	17.65	32.72	26.21	41.62
Kolar	26.79	10.40	33.00	29.81	44.49
Shimoga	26.37	11.48	33.29	28.86	48.77
Tumkur	21.82	9.77	33.31	35.10	42.44
Chikamagalur	24.87	10.62	33.09	31.41	49.34
D Kannada	18.34	8.22	33.17	40.27	43.80
Hassan	22.94	7.60	33.43	36.03	44.88
Kodagu	19.80	12.56	33.73	33.91	46.65
Mandya	19.23	6.41	33.41	40.95	42.09
Mysore	23.96	7.80	33.37	34.87	42.21
Belgaum	17.75	7.60	32.21	41.44	43.81
Bijapur	21.86	6.70	33.34	38.10	43.26
Dharwar	20.16	8.44	33.38	38.02	43.93
U Kannada	19.99	9.07	33.39	37.55	47.25
Bellary	23.53	12.90	32.93	30.64	42.53
Bidar	24.08	12.28	33.55	30.09	42.75
Gulbarga	26.36	8.67	33.48	31.49	44.27
Raichur	20.66	11.34	33.26	34.74	41.87
Average	*22.22*	*9.40*	*33.27*	*35.11*	*43.79*

Source : Computed from the information provided by the Department of RD & PR, Government of Karnataka.

Legend : S C-Scheduled Caste, S T-Scheduled Tribe, B C-Backward Caste

As for participation of members belonging to SC/ ST groups, the available information indicates that wherever educated and experienced members were in the control of the Panchayats, their participation was quite effective and they were able to assert their position and powers. Whereas, wherever the membership was weak, in terms of illiteracy, poor economic status and lack of political experience, its participation was not to the desired level. In such cases one could see the active role of other members belonging to locally dominant communities and groups. And, more so, one could

TABLE 8.2 : Reservation of Seats in Taluk Panchayats [Category-wise, District-wise (in %)]

District	*S C*	*S T*	*B C - A*	*BC - B*	*OTHERS*	*WOMEN*
Bangalore (U)	26.09	1.45	27.54	5.80	39.13	39.13
Bangalore (R)	20.98	3.50	26.57	6.29	42.66	39.86
Chitradurga	22.09	17.44	26.74	6.98	26.74	40.70
Kolar	26.34	9.14	27.42	5.91	31.18	43.01
Shimoga	18.92	4.05	27.03	6.76	43.24	41.89
Tumkur	18.72	8.37	26.60	6.90	39.41	39.41
Chikamagalur	20.00	1.90	27.62	6.67	43.81	43.81
D. Kannada	7.28	4.37	26.21	6.80	55.34	39.81
Hassan	18.18	0.00	25.87	7.69	48.25	39.16
Kodagu	14.58	10.42	27.08	6.25	41.67	39.58
Mandya	14.97	0.00	25.85	7.48	51.70	38.10
Mysore	21.40	3.29	26.75	6.58	41.98	38.68
Belgaum	11.15	2.09	26.13	6.62	54.01	37.28
Bijapur	18.58	0.88	26.99	6.64	46.90	37.17
Dharwar	12.50	2.82	27.02	6.85	50.81	42.74
U. Kannada	8.94	0.81	26.83	8.94	54.47	46.34
Bellary	21.90	10.95	27.01	6.57	33.58	40.15
Bidar	22.43	9.35	28.04	5.61	34.58	40.19
Gulbarga	25.49	4.90	26.96	5.88	36.76	39.71
Raichur	17.95	9.23	26.67	6.15	40.00	41.54
Average	*17.99*	*5.06*	*26.77*	*6.68*	*43.50*	*40.21*

Source : Computed from the information provided by the Department of RD & PR, Government of Karnataka.

Legend : S C-Scheduled Caste, S T-Scheduled Tribe, BC-A - Backward Caste Group A and BC-B - Backward Caste Group B.

TABLE 8.3 : Reservation of Seats in Zilla Panchayats Category-wise, District-wise (in %)

District	*SC*	*ST*	*BC-A*	*BC-B*	*OTHERS*	*WOMEN*
Bangalore (U)	5.00	0.00	27.78	5.56	38.89	38.89
Bangalore (R)	8.00	2.63	26.32	7.89	42.11	39.47
Chitradurga	21.33	17.39	26.09	6.52	28.26	36.96
Kolar	13.00	8.00	28.00	6.00	32.00	38.00
Shimoga	8.00	4.88	26.83	7.32	41.46	36.59
Tumkur	10.00	7.41	25.93	7.41	40.74	37.04
Chikamagalur	7.00	3.03	27.27	6.06	42.42	39.39
D. Kannada	4.00	5.45	25.45	7.27	54.55	34.55
Hassan	7.00	0.00	27.03	5.41	48.65	35.14
Kodagu	3.00	7.41	25.93	7.41	48.15	37.04
Mandya	5.00	0.00	25.64	7.69	53.85	35.90
Mysore	14.00	3.13	26.56	6.25	42.19	34.38
Belgaum	9.00	2.63	26.32	6.58	52.63	35.53
Bijapur	11.00	1.67	26.67	6.67	46.67	36.67
Dharwar	9.00	2.99	26.87	5.97	50.75	35.82
U. Kannada	3.00	0.00	26.32	7.89	57.89	36.84
Bellary	8.00	10.53	26.32	7.89	34.21	39.47
Bidar	7.00	10.34	27.59	6.90	31.03	37.93
Gulbarga	14.00	5.45	25.45	7.27	36.36	34.55
Raichur	10.00	9.26	25.93	7.41	38.89	35.19
Average	*17.95*	*5.11*	*26.44*	*6.86*	*43.63*	*36.45*

Source : Computed from the information provided by the Department of RD & PR, Government of Karnataka.

Legend : S C-Scheduled Caste, S T-Scheduled Tribe, BC-A - Backward Caste Group A & BC-B - Backward Caste Group B.

also see the intervention of locally dominant leaders (local elite) influencing the minds of the SC/ST and women members. As regards participation of members belonging to backward classes, particularly members belonging to Group B, the field level data indicate that

TABLE 8.4 : Party-wise Distribution of Seats in Zilla Panchayats in the State

District	*No. of ZP seats*	*BJP*	*Cong (I)*	*CPI*	*CPI (M)*	*IND*	*J.D.*	*KRRS*	*KCP*
1. Bangalore (U)	18 (7)	2	4	0	0	0	11	0	0
2. Bangalore (R)	38 (15)	4	1	0	0	0	33	0	0
3. Chitradurga	46 (17)	6	14	0	0	2	24	0	0
4. Kolar	50 (19)	0	15	0	1	0	34	1	5
5. Shimoga	41 (15)	7	10	0	0	0	18	0	0
6. Tumkur	54 (20)	4	16	0	0	5	29	0	0
7. Chikmagalur	33 (13)	0	3	0	0	2	28	0	0
8. D. Kannada	55 (19)	25	14	0	1	0	15	0	0
9. Hassan	37 (13)	0	3	0	0	1	33	0	0
10. Kodagu	27 (10)	7	5	0	0	0	15	0	0
11. Mandya	39 (14)	0	7	0	0	0	30	2	0
12. Mysore	64 (22)	2	19	0	0	3	40	0	0
13. Belgaum	76 (27)	0	10	0	0	12	54	0	0
14. Bijapur	60 (22)	0	9	0	0	0	51	0	0
15. Dharwad	67 (24)	0	15	0	0	0	52	0	0
16. U. Kannada	38 (14)	2	0	0	0	0	36	0	0
17. Bellary	38 (15)	0	10	0	0	1	27	0	0
18. Bidar	29 (11)	2	5	0	0	0	22	0	0
19. Gulbarga	55 (19)	2	16	0	1	0	27	0	9
20. Raichur	54 (19)	0	17	0	0	2	34	1	0
Total	*919 (335)**	*63*	*193*	*0*	*3*	*28*	*613*	*4*	*14*

Note: * Figures in parentheses indicate number of women members.

BJP = Bharatiya Janata Party
Cong (I) = Congress (I)
CPI = Communist Party of India IND = Independent
CPI (M) = Communist Party of India (Marxist)

JD = Janata Dal
KCP = Karnataka Congress Party
KRRS = Karnataka Rajya Raitha Sangha

TABLE 8.5 : Party-wise Distribution of Seats in Taluk Panchayats in the State

District	*No. of TP Seats*	*BJP*	*Cong (I)*	*CPI*	*CPI (M)*	*IND*	*J.D.*
1. Bangalore (U)	69 (27)	12	19	0	0	1	37
2. Bangalore (R)	143 (57)	11	15	0	0	2	115
3. Chitradurga	172 (70)	18	56	0	0	11	81
4. Kolar	186 (80)	0	69	0	3	2	112
5. Shimoga	148 (62)	26	38	0	0	11	59
6. Tumkur	203 (80)	15	66	0	0	15	102
7. Chikmagalur	105 (46)	2	17	2	0	7	77
8. D. Kannada	206 (82)	79	60	0	1	2	61
9. Hassan	143 (56)	2	15	0	0	4	122
10. Kodagu	48 (19)	18	4	0	1	0	25
11. Mandya	147 (56)	3	40	0	0	19	85
12. Mysore	243 (94)	7	77	0	0	27	129
13. Belgaum	287 (107)	0	68	0	0	46	172
14. Bijapur	226 (84)	10	57	0	0	5	154
15. Dharwad	248 (106)	9	63	0	0	10	166
16. U. Kannada	123 (57)	10	9	0	0	0	104
17. Bellary	137 (55)	1	48	0	0	4	82
18. Bidar	107 (43)	12	32	0	0	6	57
19. Gulbarga	204 (81)	4	59	0	4	6	101
20. Raichur	195 (81)	1	75	0	1	9	109
Total	*3340 (1343)**	*240*	*887*	*2*	*10*	*187*	*1950*

Note: * Figures in parentheses indicate number of women members.
BJP = Bharatiya Janata Party
Cong (I) = Congress (I)
CPI = Communist Party of India
CPI (M) = Communist Party of India (Marxist)

IND = Independent
JD = Janata Dal
KRRS = Karnataka Rajya Raitha Sangha
KCP = Karnataka Congress Party

their participation in the functioning of Panchayats, at all the three levels, was quite an imposing one. In fact, members belonging to locally dominant communities like Lingayats were found to be dominant and interfering in the discussing and meetings of the Panchayats. This is particularly so wherever Panchayats headed by members belonging to SC/ST, Group A and women categories.

Powers and Functions

It is clear from the above that Karnataka has provided a Panchayat system which promotes closer social interaction between the governing and the governed. In order to make this more substantial and meaningful the recent Third Amendment to the 1993 Act recognizes the Panchayats as 'units of self-government'. For this purpose, necessary powers and functions have been devolved to all the three Panchayats keeping in view the spirit of the eleventh schedule of the 73rd Constitution Amendment. These powers and functions of the Gram Panchayats, Taluk Panchayats and Zilla Panchayats have been listed in Sections 58, 145 and 184 and in the Schedules I, II and III respectively. An underlying principle of Karnataka Panchayat system is that the Panchayats have to function in accordance with the 'cardinal' principle that what is appropriate at a given level of the three-tier system should be done at that level and not necessarily at the higher level. The three schedules authorise the Panchayats to carry out functions such as preparation of annual plans; annual budgets and sectoral schemes for promotion of agriculture, animal husbandry, rural housing, drinking water, roads and bridges, rural electrification, education, rural sanitation, public health, women and child development, social welfare, public distribution system, maintenance of community assets, cooperative activities and promotion of libraries.

In an effort to demarcate functions between the Panchayats, the Government of Karnataka have, taking note of the recommendations made by P.R. Nayak Committee, so far, passed two orders — No. RDP 472 ZPS 93 (1) dated 16.7.1994 and No. RDP 121 ZPS 98, dated July 16, 1998 — to reallocate certain functions and to add certain activities, schemes and programmes to Schedules I, II and III.

Under the 1994 order, the Government had transferred some of the Zilla Panchayat schemes to Taluk Panchayats and added some more activities, programmes and schemes such as sports and youth services and sericulture relating activities to Schedule II and III. A point to be noted in this context is that no such exercise was done to Gram Panchayats. Under the 1998 order the Government had transferred some of the schemes, programmes of Taluk Panchayats, particularly under information, tourism and youth services, fisheries, animal husbandry and veterinary, forest, sericulture, education, health, rural water supply, rural communication and monitoring and co-ordinating of programmes like IRDP, TRYSEM to Zilla Panchayats. Likewise some of the Zilla Panchayat schemes and programmes coming under animal husbandry, education, rural water supply, public works, giving IRDP subsidy, toolkits, TRYSEM have been transferred to Taluk Panchayats. They are, for instance, integrated cereals development programme, minor forest produce, AIDS Control Programme, desert development programme, Ashraya scheme — all to Zilla Panchayats; rural group life insurance scheme, 15 per cent JRY, Indira Awas Yojana, Planning unit to Taluk Panchayats and 70 per cent JRY to Gram Panchayats. All these come under the district sector schemes and programmes. As for State sector schemes and programmes concerned, the Government has transferred sports promotion in rural areas, providing facilities for teaching Sanskrit in secondary schools, supply of power operated plant protection equipment on subsidy to Zilla Panchayats; national project on improved *chullas* to Taluk Panchayat and; construction and maintenance of community sanitation latrines, assistance to households for constructing sanitary latrines to Gram Panchayats.

The role of Zilla Panchayat, in the entire framework of decentralised governance and planning, was one of a facilitator and co-ordinator. It has the responsibility of integrating plans submitted by the Taluk Panchayats, giving approval to JRY action plans, allocation of finances to Development Departments and more importantly to keep an eye over the functioning of the Taluk Panchayats and the Gram Panchayats. Both the Executive Head and Chief Executive Officer have the general powers of supervision and inspection. However, the Chief Executive Officer has more executive and controlling powers compared to the President of the Zilla Panchayat. For example, he has every right (Section 198) to requisition, from Taluk and Gram Panchayats, records pertaining to property, recovering arrears of land revenue, seeking information pertaining to concealed property or amount, and to supervise and control the execution of the Zilla Panchayat works.

As regards Taluk Panchayats, the prime responsibilities of these Panchayats were (a) giving approval to JRY action plans submitted by the Gram Panchayats; (b) giving concurrence to 'action plans' prepared by development departments such as education, social welfare, health and family welfare; (c) maintenance of hostels, (d) distribution of house sites and houses under various housing schemes; (e) discussing and ratifying works suggested by the Standing Committees, and (f) to make contracts or agreements.

In regard to exercising powers, the Zilla Panchayat was found to be in the driver's seat. In respect of all the development programmes, which are to be implemented by the eighteen development departments, Taluk/ Gram Panchayats, all the money that comes to Taluk Panchayat (EAS grants, housing schemes, money under drinking water supply) and to Gram Panchayat (JRY grant, annual grant of 1.00 lakh) the Zilla Panchayat takes a final look; and all the correspondence between the State Government and the Panchayats has been routed through the Zilla Panchayat. In this process, clear cases of discrimination by the Zilla Panchayat while allotting benefits coming under Ashraya, Ambedkar Housing Schemes and EAS works were reported during our field work. The members of the Zilla Panchayat, including the President and the Vice-President and the Adhyakshas of the Taluk Panchayats, were able to corner a lion's share compared to other members. For instance, the Zilla Panchayat had allotted 900 houses to Challakere Taluk, from where the President of the Zilla Panchayat hails, and just 400 houses to Hiriyur Taluk. Under EAS works Challakere was allocated Rs. 97 lakhs whereas Hiriyur got Rs. 67 lakhs. When questioned by the Hiriyur Taluk Panchayat President, the ZP President replied that Challakere Taluk has larger size population (2,41,018 persons) and more number of villages (190 villages) compared to Hiriyur which has a population of 1,91,194 and 157 villages. However, the former fought back and got an additional amount of Rs. 20 lakhs under EAS and 50 to 60 more houses (Aziz *et al.* 1998).

Furthermore, there were hurdles coming in the way of functioning of the Panchayats. For instance, although Gram Panchayats have powers of giving licenses, no objection certificates, laying of roads and construction of building, there are always hurdles particularly the interference of higher leadership, both of political and administrative, in their day to day activities. A related issue in the above context is that there have been apparent mismatch between what has been specified in the Schedules and what has been going on in practice. For instance, according to Schedule I of the Act the Gram Panchayat is expected to carry out 31 activities but in practice it is found to be executing only 30 to 40 per cent of these activities.

With regard to Constitution and functioning of the Standing Committees at the Gram, Taluk and Zilla Panchayat levels, there were divergent views pointing towards the low-working profile of these committees. Except for their reasonably functioning well at the Zilla Panchayat level the working of these committees at the Gram and Taluk Panchayat levels was below the desired level. There appeared to be a lukewarm attitude towards these committees from all sides. Although, all the six Gram Panchayats had constituted these committees, no Panchayat was serious enough to call meetings at regular intervals. Similarly, even the Taluk Panchayats had not made any efforts to call the meetings, except for one Taluk Panchayat. Half of the Gram and Taluk Panchayat members were not even aware of such committees and their responsibilities. However, at the Zilla Panchayat level, the meetings of all the five Standing Committees were called regularly. One of the reasons given by the Taluk Panchayat executive functionaries and members, at the time of the field work, is that when there are no specified planning and financial powers. The Government now, has sanctioned for separate planning unit and accounts wing for Taluk Panchayats. The committees such as Finance, Audit and Planning have no role to play in the promotion of Panchayat's working.

The Third Amendment to the Act has introduced certain changes at Zilla, Taluk and Gram Panchayat levels. At Gram Panchayat level, the Amendment has inserted new Section 61A which authorises Gram Panchayat to appoint one or more committees in addition to the existing three Standing Committees for any specific purpose and it may devolve necessary powers and functions to such committees for fulfilling the purpose for which they are appointed. Further, Amendments to Section 148 and Section 186 enjoin Taluk Panchayats and Zilla Panchayats respectively to constitute Standing Committees with each committee consisting of six members at the Taluk Panchayat level and seven members at the Zilla Panchayat level including the Chairman. Prior to the amendment these committees had five members each.

A close look at the devolution of powers and functions reveals that the State Government has been making efforts through amendments either to delete certain provisions which go against the democratic functioning of Panchayats or to add new sections to strengthen the process of local governance. This is not to State that the State Government has been able to devolve a greater amount of powers and functions to Panchayats. In fact, the Government has retained many regulatory, controlling, supervising powers and some important functions like public distribution system (PDS)[2]. More importantly, the personnel of the Panchayats is very much controlled by the State Government, both in terms of recruitment and transfers. In fact, P. R. Nayak committee had strongly recommended that Zilla Panchayats should be given the powers of transferring Group C and D staff of the Panchayats. But the Government is yet to give its green signal.

Devolution of Financial Resources

Sections from 199 to 208 of the 1993 Act deal with taxes, fees, levy of cess and grants relating to financial assistance given to Panchayats. Of the three levels of Panchayats, the Gram Panchayat enjoys taxation powers and it has powers to levy taxes and fees. But the Taluk Panchayats and the Zilla Panchayats do not have taxation powers; instead they receive grants from the State Government, can raise loans and earn income from assets, if any owned.

Income and Expenditure Pattern of Gram Panchayats

The Gram Panchayat can levy (rates as specified in Schedule-IV in the Act) tax on buildings and lands, water rate, tax on entertainment, non-motor vehicles, advertisement, pilgrim fee, market fee, fee on the registration of cattle, on buses, taxies and auto stands and on grazing cattle in the grazing lands. In addition, the Gram Panchayat gets an annual grant of Rupees one lakh to be utilised for meeting the electricity charges, maintenance of water supply, sanitation and other welfare activities. Furthermore, these Panchayats also get annually JRY grants to the tune of Rupees two to three lakh.

The income pattern of Gram Panchayats (Table 8.6) reveals that the Gram Panchayats depend more on grants — per capita grants — provided by the State Government. Almost 46 per cent of their financial resources come from such grants and the remaining from their own tax and non-tax revenues (39 per cent), a source on which the Gram Panchayats have some financial autonomy to spend as they prefer. Considering the fact that the Gram Panchayats have a poor resource base, the revenue from tax and non-tax revenues is quite encouraging. However, Gram Panchayats have to take necessary steps, rather harder ones, to collect taxes from the people and augment locally available resources. Some of the Panchayats have gone in for auction of 'fish tanks', construction of shopping complexes to earn additional revenue.

As for expenditure pattern (Table 8.7) is concerned, the major share of expenditure has been on public development works (21.54 per cent), public security works (24.45 per cent) like purchase of street lights, civic amenities which include drinking water maintenance, maintenance of library, cow-shed, construction and maintenance of roads, drainage, buildings, water works etc. However, much of the expenditure has gone towards salaries to staff, so much so, on an average 17.21 per cent of Panchayats expenditure is being spent on general administration. In addition to this, on an average, 12.06 per cent of the expenditure is incurred for promoting the welfare of Scheduled Castes and Scheduled Tribes.

TABLE- 8.6 : Income Pattern of Six Selected Gram Panchayats of the Study Region 1994-95 to 1996-97

*Category of Income**	*1994-95***	*1995-96*	*1996-97****	*Average of Three Years*
Tax Revenue	494,568.00	529,283.00	452,979.00	492,276.67
	(34.05)	(33.44)	(33.83)	(33.77)
Non-Tax Revenue	66,900.00	57,300.00	106,100.00	76,766.67
	(4.61)	(3.62)	(7.92)	(5.38)
Grants-in-aid	621,100.00	472,100.00	630,000.00	664,400.00
	(42.76)	(46.89)	(47.05)	(45.56)
Other receipts	54,700.00	45,650.00	14,000.00	38,116.67
	(3.77)	(2.88)	(1.05)	(2.57)
Dept. Heads	104,759.00	114,157.00	42,450.00	87,122.00
	(7.21)	(7.21)	(3.17)	(5.86)
Opening Balance	110,561.00	94,295.00	93,517.00	99,457.00
	(7.61)	(5.96)	(6.98)	(6.85)
TOTAL	*1,452,589.00*	*1,582,785.00*	*1,339,046.00*	*1,458,140.00*
	(100.00)	*(100.00)*	*(100.00)*	*(100.00)*

SOURCE: Computed from information provided by the Gram Panchayats under study.

NOTE: Figures in parentheses denote percentage to the total
*: This does not include JRY Grants.
,*: Details pertaining to income Statement for the years 1994-95 and 1996-97 of the two selected Gram Panchayats viz., Nannivala and Babbur are not computed due to non-availability of relevant records.

An important aspect of income and expenditure of Gram Panchayats is their extent of dependency on the external financial assistance provided by the State and Central Governments mainly in the form of grants and funds to implement various poverty alleviation programmes like JRY. Taken together these grants and funds, the Panchayats own financial position is quite low; Table 8.8 reveals this. As seen from the Table 8.8, 57.77 per cent of

Gram Panchayats income and expenditure is covered by the JRY funds, whereas the remaining (42.33 per cent) income and expenditure is from both tax and non-tax resources. Put together, both grants and JRY funds take the major share (almost 80 per cent) of Panchayats income and expenditure. This clearly points out the extent of tied and untied finances which the Gram Panchayats have at their command.

Income and Expenditure Pattern of Taluk Panchayats

As for the finances of the Taluk Panchayats, they hardly have any regular source of income except the income derived from stamp duty. According to Section 205 of the Act, the Government may levy a surcharge on duties imposed by the Karnataka Stamp Act 1957 on instruments of sale, gift, mortgage, exchange and lease in perpetuity of immovable properties situated within the area of a Taluk Panchayat at a rate not exceeding three per cent. The amount so collected will be passed on to Taluk Panchayats in proportion to latter's population.

The Taluk Panchayats under study, on an average, were getting receipts from sur-charge made on stamp duty and deposits to the tune of Rupees ten to fifteen lakh per year. This amount is being released by the Zilla Panchayat in 2 to 3 instalments. However, this practice was questioned by the Taluk Panchayats on the ground that the Zilla Panchayat has no powers to deposit the amount collected in the form of stamp duty in to its fund. In one of its meetings (2/11/95), Hiriyur Taluk Panchayat had passed a resolution by quoting Section 205 of the Act that the amount should be credited in the name of the Taluk Panchayat fund and that the Zilla Panchayat should refrain from crediting the amount in to its own fund. Also the Panchayat was against the practice of releasing money in instalments; instead it wanted the amount to be released in one instalment and on time.

Discussion with the Taluk Panchayat officials and non-officials, and inspection of records of the proceedings of the Finance, Audit and Planning Committee indicated that, by and large, the amount collected under the stamp duty was spent for constructing office buildings for Taluk Panchayats, staff quarters, shopping centres,

TABLE 8.7 : Expenditure Pattern of Six Selected Gram Panchayats of the Study Region in 1994-95 to 1996-97

*Category of Expenditure**	*1994-95***	*1995-96*	*1996-97****	*Average of Three Years*
General Administration	270,750.00	264,510.00	218,060.00	251,106.67
	(18.64)	(16.71)	(16.28)	(17.21)
Public Security	258,600.00	349,800.00	355,500.00	354,633.33
	(24.69)	(22.10)	(26.55)	(24.45)
Public Development Works	301,000.00	339,807.00	300,500.00	313,769.00
	(20.72)	(21.47)	(22.44)	(21.54)
Civic Amenities	161,700.00	217,550.00	165,000.00	181,416.67
	(11.13)	(13.74)	(12.32)	(12.40)
Development Works under SC/STs 20%	147,670.00	200,455.00	178,903.00	175,676.00
	(10.17)	(12.66)	(13.36)	(12.06)
Donations and Assistance	5,687.00	9,645.00	5,263.00	6,865.00
	(0.39)	(0.61)	(0.39)	(0.46)
Debt Heads	71,760.00	100,357.00	75,317.00	82,478.00
	(4.94)	(6.34)	(5.62)	(5.64)
Closing Balance	136,412.00	100,661.00	40,503.00	92,525.33
	(9.39)	(6.36)	(3.02)	(6.26)
TOTAL	*1,452,589.00*	*1,582,785.00*	*1,339,046.00*	*1,458,140.00*
	(100.00)	*(100.00)*	*(100.00)*	*(100.00)*

Source : Computed from information provided by the Gram Panchayats under study.

Note : Figures in parentheses denote percentage to the total expenditure.
*: This does not include JRY Expenditure.
, * Details pertaining to Expenditure Statement for the years 1994-95 and 1996-97 of the two selected Gram Panchayats viz., Nannivala and Babbur are not computed due to non-availability of relevant records.

TABLE - 8.8 : Actual Income and Expenditure including JRY of five Selected GPs for the years 1994-95 and 1995-96

	1994-95	*1995-96*	*Total of two years*	*Average per year/ GP.*	*Percentage to the grand total*
I. Category of Income					
Tax Revenue	124,384.95	238,639.85	363,024.80	36,302.48	9.72
Non-Tax Revenue	12,350.00	9,065.00	21,415.00	2,141.50	0.57
Grants-in-aid	413,717.50	406,250.00	819,967.50	81,996.75	21.96
Other Receipts	18,250.00	3,543.00	121,793.00	12,179.30	3.26
Debt. Heads	33,413.10	12,403.15	45,816.25	4,581.63	1.23
Opening Balance	88,822.93	116,203.94	205,026.87	20,502.69	5.49
Total	*790,938.48*	*786,104.94*	*1,577,043.42*	*157,704.34*	*42.23*
JRY Income	1,034,773.68	1,122,247.10	2,157,020.78	215,702.08	57.77
Grand Total	*1,825,712.16*	*1,908,352.04*	*3,734,064.20*	*373,406.42*	*100.00*
II. Category of Expenditure					
General Administration	234,086.00	195,238.00	429,324.00	42,932.40	11.50
Public Security	101,649.00	42,973.00	144,622.00	14,462.20	3.87
Public Development Works	55,115.00	90,712.00	145,827.00	14,582.00	3.91
Civic Amenities	173,104.00	240,719.00	413,823.00	41,382.30	11.08
Development Works Under SC/ST 20%	34,383.00	65,548.00	99,931.00	9,993.10	2.68
Donations and Assistance	38,771.30	2,330.00	41,101.30	4,110.13	1.10
Debt Heads	37,626.25	–	37,626.25	3.762.63	1.01

Contd......

	1994-95	*1995-96*	*Total of two years*	*Average per year/ GP*	*Percentage to the grand total*
Closing Balance	116,204.08	148,584.94	264,789.02	26,478.90	7.09
Total	*790,938.63*	*786,104.94*	*1,577,043.57*	*157,704.36*	*42.23*
JRY Expenditure	1,034,773.53	1,122,247.10	2,157,020.63	215,702.06	57.77
Grand Total	*1,825,712.16*	*1,908,352.04*	*3,734,064.20*	*373,406.42*	*100.00*

Source : Computed from Audit Reports provided by the Local Audit Circle, Chitradurga

Note : Since the details of the audit reports for the years 1994-95 and 1995-96 of the remaining one Grama Panchayat was not available at the time of field work, we computed the data of five Gram Panchayats only.

purchasing and repairing of typewriter machines, fans and for giving contribution to festivals and sports events etc. Taluk Panchayats also had proposed 20 per cent of their finances towards ameliorating the living conditions of the SC/ST. However, hardly in any case, the above amount was spent for the same purpose.

Income and Expenditure Pattern of Zilla Panchayats

The Zilla Panchayats, unlike the Gram Panchayats, have no financial resources to levy and collect taxes or duties. Hence they depend heavily on the transfer of funds from the State Government; Chitradurga Zilla Panchayat was no exception to this. Sector-wise allocation of resources was followed while devolving both plan and non-plan grants to Zilla Panchayat and there were 45 major heads of account. The sectors were education, medical and public health, water supply and sanitation, welfare of scheduled castes and tribes and other backward classes, social security, agriculture, animal husbandry, rural employment, rural development programs, village and small scale industries, fisheries, forestry, roads and bridges and minor irrigation.

As for allocation of plan and non-plan grants, the Zilla Panchayats have been allocated with more of non-plan grant than plan grant. The State level picture indicates that on an average 56 per cent of non plan grant is allocated to Zilla Panchayats against the plan grant of 42.20 per cent. The non-plan grant is provided mainly for meeting the establishment charges, salaries, maintenance and repair charges, grants-in-aid to schools, construction of schools and health centres. In the study area on an average (computed for five years i.e., from 1994-95 to 1998-99), Chitradurga Zilla Panchayat annually had received 43.12 per cent of plan grant and 56.88 per cent of non-plan grant. In absolute figures it had received between Rs. 59 crores and Rs. 80 crores of plan grant and between Rs. 71 crores and Rs. 103 crores of non-plan grant.

A close look at the sectorwise expenditure pattern (Table 8.9) of Chitradurga Zilla Panchayat reveals that out of the total expenditure incurred on different sectors, expenditure on social infrastructure takes the major share. On an average, 45.64 per cent of the expenditure was incurred for promoting social sectors like education (most expenditure was on salary), nutrition, water supply and sanitation etc. This is true even at the State level. On an average, across various Zilla Panchayat sectors, 26.90 per cent and 25.34 per cent of the amount was spent on the promotion of education and water supply and sanitation respectively. This was followed by rural development sector which includes expenditure on rural employment (JRY grant) and other special rural development programmes. On an average 21.24 per cent of the total expenditure was incurred on this sector. The third in the priority of Zilla Panchayats expenditure was on agriculture and allied activities. Of the total, the expenditure on this sector accounted only for 17.90 per cent. The last in the priority of expenditure was the expenditure incurred on the welfare of Scheduled Castes and Scheduled Tribes. During the years 1993-94, 1994-95, 1995-96 Chitradurga Zilla Panchayat had spent only 5.94 per cent, 7.96 per cent and 8.02 per cent respectively towards ameliorating the living conditions of these groups. It is significant to note in this context that even at the State level expenditure incurred on the development of Scheduled Castes and Scheduled Tribes is nowhere near the desired expenditure of 20 per cent. Between the years i.e., 1994-95 to 1996-97, across the Zilla Panchayats, on an average only 13.75 per cent was spent on the welfare of the Scheduled Castes and Scheduled Tribes. However, this proportion of expenditure falls short of the Section 227 (1) of the Act which States that not less than 20 per cent of the funds meant for welfare activities should be utilised for the welfare of the Scheduled Castes and the Scheduled Tribes.

With regard to the criteria followed for the devolution of financial resources, the executive functionaries informed us that generally the criteria followed were total population of the district/ Taluk/ village and the percentage of Scheduled Caste and Scheduled Tribe population. Further, they told that although they were aware of Gadgil's formula of five criteria, it was hardly given any importance. In fact, there were instances wherein the factors like sense of belonging to a region, party affiliation were given due consideration while allocating sites, identifying beneficiaries under IRDP, housing schemes and EAS schemes. As reported by some of the opposition members, the Presidents of the Panchayats had a final say in the allocation of such resources and benefits. However, State level authorities have confirmed that the Gadgil's formula is being followed for allocating grants to Zilla Panchayats.

TABLE 8.9 : *Sectorwise Expenditure Pattern of Chitradurga Zilla Panchayat*

Sector	*1993-94*	*1994-95*	*1995-96*	*Average of Three Years*
1. Agriculture and Allied Activities	37.95	8.01	7.74	17.90
2. Village and Small Industries	0.20	0.46	0.30	0.32
3. Rural Development	15.74	24.24	23.72	21.24
4. Social Infrastructure	34.35	50.26	52.30	45.64
5. Economic Infrastructure	2.75	4.76	3.84	3.78
6. Social Security and Social Welfare	3.01	4.23	4.05	3.76
7. Welfare of SCs and STs	5.94	7.96	8.02	7.31
8. Administrative Expenses	0.06	0.08	0.03	7.31
Total	*100.00*	*100.00*	*100.00*	*100.00*

Source : Computed from information provided by the Chitradurga Zilla Panchayat under study.

In order to streamline the process of devolution of financial resources between the State Government and the Panchayats, the Government had appointed State Finance Commission under the chairmanship of Prof. G. Thimmaiah. The Commission, keeping in view the prevailing drawbacks, had recommended for devolving finances to Panchayats in percentage terms and not in absolute amounts. Accordingly, it had recommended for transferring 36 per cent of Government's 'non-loan gross own revenue receipts' every year to Panchayats and urban institutions. However, this amounted to a marginal rise of 1.73 per cent from the existing 34.27 per cent. Further the commission had specified five indicators for devolving finances. They are: population (33.33 per cent), area (33.33 per cent), illiteracy rate (11.11 per cent), number of persons per hospital bed (11.12 per cent), and road length per square kilometer (11.12 per cent). Out of the total 36 per cent, the relative share of Panchayats is 30.60 per cent and the remaining is for the urban bodies. On the whole, the Panchayats would get 85 per cent and the urban bodies 15 per cent. In terms of share of each tier, the Gram Panchayat would get 25 per cent, Taluk Panchayat 35 per cent and Zilla Panchayat 40 per cent. Notwithstanding this the commission did not make any recommendation regarding giving taxation powers to both Taluk Panchayats and Zilla Panchayats. There is a great demand from these Panchayats to have some taxation powers.

The State Finance Commission had made in total thirty four important recommendations in its report. Out of these thirty four, seven have been accepted, only one is not accepted and remaining twenty-six are under the consideration of government. The accepted recommendations are : to take into account both plan and non-plan expenditure requirements of Panchayats, 36 per cent devolution of funds to local bodies, devolution to be based on percentage terms and releasing funds to Gram Panchayats and Taluk Panchayats directly from the Zilla Panchayats. The one which is not accepted is regarding treating one lakh grant, which is given at present to Gram Panchayat, as additional financial assistance and should not be adjusted from the funds recommended under devolution scheme. While not accepting this, the government has Stated that the amount (one lakh grant) should form a part of overall devolution. Recommendations like giving weightages to the criteria, respective shares of Panchayats, and many other recommendation are under the consideration of the government.

Planning and Decision-Making

The analysis of the process of identification of people's needs and aspirations, decision-making, prioritization and implementation of the programmes reveals both positive and negative points. During the initial stages, attempts were made by the Gram Panchayats to identify the felt needs and aspirations of the people by holding Gram Sabha meetings. All the six selected Gram Panchayats had convened the Gram Sabha meetings. These meetings were called by giving enough publicity by distributing pamphlets, and by beating the drum (tom-tom). Two types of meetings were held by these Panchayats. The first type were called mainly to identify the felt needs and demands not only of the people but also of the villages. These meetings were called mostly in the initial phase of the Panchayat's working. The second type of meetings were called at the behest of the Executive Officer, Taluk Panchayat mainly to identify the beneficiaries of IRDP, Indira Awas Yojana, Ashraya and Dr. Ambedkar Housing Schemes.

The meetings held in the initial phase were mainly for listing the felt needs of the people and the villages. The proceedings of the meetings and interviews with the people reveal that works like providing drinking water and drainage facilities, putting street lights, constructing culverts, laying link roads and repairs to school buildings were discussed and proposed. However, the feelings of the citizens were that such initial type of meetings are hardly called now. Instead, a good number of meetings were called mainly to identify beneficiaries and to discuss JRY Action Plan. Under JRY Action Plan, the meetings were called to identify the works under different categories such as social forestry, drainage, fencing around school and anganawadi buildings, roads and bridges and works for improving the welfare of the Scheduled Castes and Scheduled Tribes. However, we were told by the citizens that, by and large, the number and place of works were decided earlier in the Panchayat meeting and the same were placed before the Gram Sabha meetings for its ratification!

In regard to participation of people in the Gram Sabha meetings, on an average 25 to 30 per cent of the electorates had participated in the meetings. There was a strong feeling among the electorate that President, Vice-President, senior members, influential leaders and officials like Secretaries of the Panchayats, Panchayat Extension Officers were found to be in the forefront as far as initiating the projects and taking final decisions which smacks of the requirement of people's participation in decision-making process.

The integration process of planning was seen in the context of annual plans and JRY plans. Gram Panchayats are expected to prepare annual plans, budget proposals and JRY action plans. For illustration, under 80 per cent JRY, the Gram Panchayat prepares an action plan under various heads. The money that is allocated and spent is as follows. Of the total sanctioned amount, 5 per cent is kept for administrative expenditure, 10 per cent as maintenance expenditure, 25 per cent amount is incurred towards the development of social forestry, 17.5 per cent for road construction and buildings, 22.5 per cent for improving the living conditions of SC/ST and 35 per cent of the expenditure for the promotion of development works which would fetch returns to Panchayats. Under this programme works related to infrastructure and the list of individual beneficiaries were chosen and finalised in the Gram Sabha meetings. The President of the Gram Panchayat called for such meetings in the respective villages to identify the works. For instance, Nannivala Gram had called for three Gram Sabha meetings in the three main villages wherein the villagers had opted for laying of roads, anganwadi buildings, community hall, houses for SC/STs, repairs to school buildings, drainage, maintenance of nursery under social forestry programme and so on.

Planning at the Taluk Panchayat and Zilla Panchayat levels is still a by-product of sectoral planning. Thus, generally speaking, the Zilla Panchayat informs and allocates finances to all the sectoral departments located at district and Taluk levels. Being aware of the financial limits, each department prepares a list of activities to be carried out and the same is submitted to the Panchayats. A point to be noted here that the members of the Panchayats bring to the notice of the concerned development departments the works to be taken up in their respective constituencies. Generally members provide this requirement by submitting memorandum to the concerned officers of the departments. Majority of members use their letter-head pads for giving such memorandums. Some of the officials expressed the view that while preparing action plans for their departments they did take note of the memorandum submitted to them. After preparing draft action plans the same will be submitted by the departments to the Taluk Panchayat for its consideration and approval. Similar exercise is done at the district level also. An important aspect of the above process is that the proposals submitted by the departments are being scrutinised at the various Standing Committee meetings before such proposals are sent to General Body meetings for the final assent. Since the Taluk Panchayat and the Zilla Panchayat have approving powers some changes could be incorporated into the prepared plans. The Zilla Panchayat will ultimately send the plan details to State Planning Department for the latter's final integration and approval.

It is significant to note in the above context that with the Constitution of District Planning Committee (Section 310 of the Act) under the chairmanship of Zilla Panchayat President and Mayor of the municipal corporation, as vice-president, the preparation and integration of district draft development plan for rural and urban areas will be now with this committee. This committee, comprising of MPs, MLAs, MLCs and elected members of the Zilla Panchayat and the City Municipal Corporation, has the responsibility of forwarding, particularly by the chairperson, the district development plan for integrating the same into the State Plan. The Chief Executive Officer (CEO) will be the Secretary of the Committee. As far as functioning is concerned, although majority of Zilla Panchayats have constituted their district planning committees, still necessary modalities have to be finalised for their effective functioning. Some Panchayats have begun their efforts in this direction.

Seen in the integrated planning framework, the Government of Karnataka, as an innovative step, has constituted a 'State Panchayat Parishad' (Section 310A of the Act) with Chief Minister in the Chair, Minister for Rural Development and Panchayati Raj as Vice-chairman, five ministers nominated by the Government, Presidents of all 27 Zilla Panchayats, and Secretary, Rural Development and Panchayati Raj, as the member-secretary. This 'nodal institution', created particularly for promoting integration between Panchayats, is assigned with the task of initiating amendments to schedules dealing with functions, and more importantly, to internalise the externalities and for motivating Panchayats to adopt a 'self-regulatory mechanism'. This institutional arrangement is expected to facilitate sustainability and viability to the system and its process.

As for the process of prioritisation of the works, the available information suggests that this process takes place specially during the Gram Sabha and the Panchayat meetings. The Gram Panchayat functionaries informed us that in the first-two Gram Sabha meetings people preferred drinking water supply and street lighting as their priority works and gave second preference to works like drainage, laying of roads and repair works. Accordingly, the Panchayats had initiated the works in that order of priority.

In the Panchayat meetings, prioritization process was subjected to available funds and other financial resources. In majority of the meetings, much of the discussion centered around identification of works and allocation of money under JRY programme. Under JRY, preference, priority wise, was given to laying of roads, construction of buildings, drainage, distribution of benefits to Scheduled Castes and Scheduled Tribes. There were instances of diverting funds meant for social forestry to laying roads, building samudaya bhavans. However, prior permission was sought by the Gram Panchayats from the Taluk Panchayat to do so.

There were mixed reactions with regard to whether the planning process resulted in improving the choices of the people in terms of employment, income generation and meeting the basic needs of the people. Discussions with the members, officials and the general public brought out different results. The implementation of the programmes like JRY and EAS had provided employment opportunities to rural poor, IRDP programmes and housing schemes enabled quite a few beneficiaries to improve their living standards. People were happy that their basic needs such as water, housing, street lighting were provided.

Relationship between Non-officials and Officials

For the effective functioning of decentralised institutions, co-ordination between the institutions and inter-personal relationship between the functionaries are necessary prerequisites. The status on this issue is presented in the following paragraphs.

The system provides for strong institutional linkages between the Panchayats. Section 120 of the Act States that one-fifth of the Adhyakshas of the Gram Panchayats, on a rotation basis for a period of one year, are represented on the Taluk Panchayat and all the Adhyakshas of the Taluk Panchayats on the Zilla Panchayat (Section 159 of the Act). It is significant to note that the recent Third Amendment effected to the State Panchayat Act with a view to ensure effective and meaningful functional linkages between the lower Panchayats and the higher Panchayats has made a provision for constituting additional 'joint committees' between two or three Gram Panchayats (Section 61 B). Through such integrated approach Panchayats would be able to formulate and implement programs and assist each other in the development of the villages and welfare of people.

Although Panchayats have vertical linkages (organizational) between them, that is members of lower Panchayats participating in the proceedings of the higher Panchayats, there appears to be gaps as far as 'role perception' and 'role performance' of the different Panchayats and among the functionaries. Seen in terms of priorities, the Gram Panchayats had their own priorities, and so do the Taluk Panchayats and the Zilla Panchayats. It was observed that hardly there prevailed a cordial relationship between the members of the lower level and those of the higher level Panchayats. Their relationship appeared to be a 'love-hate' relationship with one always being suspicious of the other. For instance, the Constitution of coordinating committees like EAS (Employment Assurance Committee) Committee under the Chairmanship of the President, Taluk Panchayat, along with the MLA and Zilla Panchayat members, had created considerable animosities among the Taluk Panchayat members. This was mainly because of the fear that the Zilla Panchayat members would corner the benefits and take credit for executing the EAS works. Both the Gram Panchayat and the Taluk Panchayat members, at present, look upon the Zilla Panchayat members as their main opponents in the development process. In fact, the Zilla Panchayat, which is in driver's seat for all operational purposes, is seen as the 'Big Brother'. Such a misunderstanding, coupled with personal egos, is contributing to the development of unhealthy inter-personal relationship in the system.

Commenting on the question of accountability, the non-official members were of the view that the officials should be accountable to the respective Panchayat heads and that the elective body should always have an edge over the official body. Sections giving powers to Divisional Commissioner to dissolve Gram Panchayats and Chief Executive Officer to annul the resolutions passed by the Zilla Panchayat, in the opinion of these members, should be deleted from the Act. However, the recent Amendments have withdrawn such powers given to officials under Chapters XVI, XVIII of the Act and strengthened the hands of the elected body by giving powers of dissolution, appealing, supervising and monitoring. As a result of this, the officials now come under the supervision and control of Executive Heads. Further, the Amendment specifies that wherever individual officers had the final say, they will now be placed in the custody of higher level Panchayats, State Election Commission and the State. The Amendment reposes its faith in the supremacy of the elected non-officials over the officials.

While upholding the supremacy of the elected body over the bureaucracy, the P.R. Nayak Committee had observed that 'the role of government officials within the Panchayati Raj Institutions should thus be facilitative and executive rather than authoritative'. As for organizational linkages between higher level bodies and lower level bodies, the Committee had recommended for vesting dissolution and annulling powers with the next higher level institution. An underlying principle of this is that Panchayats should be able to adapt 'self-regulatory mechanism'. In carrying out all these important tasks the committee had opined that 'the authority should go well with accountability'. With a view to ensuring both authority and accountability, the committee, keeping in view of this 'cardinal principle' recommended for constituting a high power committee consisting of Secretaries and Heads of various Departments to make a classification of schemes under appropriate Panchayat levels.

Relationship between the officials and the non-officials centered around their performance. For instance, non-official members always complain about misappropriation of funds by the officials while making purchases, showing tardiness in implementing the programmes, non co-operation especially from the engineering staff.

On the other hand, officials complain against the non-official members about their non co-operation, taking unilateral decisions, interference and putting pressures in day-to-day administration. These allegations, in fact, have created a considerable amount of confusion in regard to inter-personal relationships. Even news papers have reported matters like irregularities in the departments especially in the areas of transfer and recruitment of teachers, purchase of food items, purchase of low quality materials by the Zilla Panchayat Engineering Division, giving contracts and calling tenders without the consent of the Panchayats.

IV

The foregoing analysis of the process of decentralised governance and planning presents both positive and negative points. They are as follows: The State Government, by initiating necessary amendments, has made some positive efforts to strengthen Panchayats and their governance. With regard to devolution of powers and functions, the Government, by constituting a High Power Committee, and passing two necessary orders, has been able to sort out the confusions prevailed in the allocation of functions between the three-tier Panchayats. However, as for devolution of financial resources, the Panchayats, by and large, depend on the grants released by the Government and funds devolved through various rural development programmes. In order to ensure financial autonomy and to streamline the financial transfers and exchanges, the Government should consider and implement some of the other recommendations made by the State Finance Commission.

As for planning process, there were many operational constraints which came in the way of meaningful planning process, although serious efforts were made by the Panchayats to plan for their Panchayat region. Both inter-institutional and inter-personal relationship, between the Panchayats, and between the officials and the non-officials, appears to be superficial and marked by 'red-tapism' and 'formalism'.

Notwithstanding the above, the Panchayats were able to observe some norms and procedures laid down by the Act. One of the important revelations of the study is that the reservation policy has provided ample opportunities to the hitherto neglected sections of the society to come closer to the 'power center'. An urge for learning was very much in the minds of the members, especially among women, which incidentally may be seen as a welcome step towards 'capacity building'.

NOTES

1. The data for writing this paper are drawn heavily from the Ford-Foundation Project on Decentralised Governance and Planning in Three Southern States conducted at the Institute for Social and Economic Change, Bangalore with the prior permission from the Project Director, Prof. Abdul Aziz. The present author, in the capacity as the Joint Project Director in the project, was involved in studying Karnataka chapter (See for details Abdul Aziz *et al.*, 1998).
2. Recently, the Union Food Ministry has issued guidelines to all State Governments to include PDS as one of the core functions of the Panchayats.

REFERENCES

Aziz, Abdul, 1993. *Decentralised Planning : The Karnataka Experiment.* New Delhi: Sage Publications.

Aziz, Abdul, 1994. *Decentralised Governance in Karnataka: The Mandal Panchayat System.* Hyderabad: National Institute of Rural Development.

Abdul Aziz, Sivanna N., Babu Devendra, Sekher Madhushree, Nelson C Charles, 1998. *Decentralised Governance and Planning : A Comparative Study in Three South Indian States* (Ford Foundation Project), Institute for Social and Economic Change, Bangalore (mimeo).

Bhargava, B.S., Bada, C.R., and Vijay, N Torgal, 1982. *Panchayati Raj System in Karnataka*, New Delhi: Jackson Publications.

Cheema, G.S., and D.A. Rondinelli (eds.), 1983. *Decentralization and Development: Policy Implementation in Developing Countries.* Beverly Hills, Sage Publications, London.

Conyers, D., 1993. "Decentralization: The Latest Fashion in Development Administration", *Public Administration and Development*, Vol.3.

Government of India, 1957. *Report of the Team for the Study of Community Development Projects and National Extension Service* Vol.1., New Delhi.

Government of Karnataka, 1959. *The Karnataka Village Panchayats and Local Boards Act.* Bangalore: Department of Law and Parliamentary Affairs.

Government of Karnataka, 1985. *The Karnataka Zilla Parishads, Taluk Panchayat Samitis, Mandal Panchayats Act.* Bangalore.

Government of Karnataka, 1993. *The Karnataka Zilla Panchayats, Taluk Panchayats and Village Panchayats Act*. Bangalore.

Government of Karnataka, 1996. *Report of the Expert Committee on Karnataka Panchayat Raj Act 1993*, Bangalore.

Government of Mysore, 1949. *Report on the Integration and Coordination Committee for Local Bodies*. Bangalore.

Government of Mysore, 1953. *Report of the Local Boards Enquiry Committee*. Bangalore.

Government of Mysore, 1963. *Report of the Committee on Panchayati Raj* (Chairman: Kondajji Basappa). Bangalore.

Harris, R., 1983. "Centralisation and Decentralization in Latin America", G.S. Cheema and D.A. Rondinelli (eds.), 1993. *Decentralization and Development: Policy Implementation in Developing Countries*, Beverly Hills, Sage Publications, London.

Klibanoff, P., and J. Morduch, 1995. "Decentralization, Externalities and Efficiency", *Review of Economic Studies*, Vol.62.

Maddick, H., 1963. *Democracy, Decentralization and Development*, Asia Publishing House, Bombay.

Mathew, George, *1986. Panchayati Raj in Karnataka Today*. New Delhi: Concept Publishing Company.

Meenakshisundaram, S.S. 1994. *Decentralization in Developing Countries*. New Delhi: Concept.

Satish Chandran, T.R., 1994. *'Karnataka' in Status of Panchayati Raj in the States of India*. New Delhi: Concept.

Sivanna, N., 1990. *Panchayati Raj Reforms and Rural Development*. Allahabad: Chugh Publications.

Sivanna, N., 1996. A Fillip to 'Power to the People', *Deccan Herald*, Bangalore, April 27.

Sivanna, N., 1997. Amendments to the Panchayati Raj Act, *Deccan Herald*, Bangalore, September 28.

Sivanna N., 1998. Decentralised Governance and Planning in Karnataka, *Social Change*, Vol. 28, No. 1, pp. 28-53.

Slater, Richard and Watson, John, 1989. 'Democratic Decentralization or Political Consolidation: The Case of Local Government Reform in Karnataka'. *Public Administration and Development*, 9(1): 147-157.

Subha K, 1995. *Karnataka Panchayat Elections 1995, Process, Issues and Membership Profile*, New Delhi: Concept.

The Karnataka State Finance Commission, 1995. *Report of the Karnataka State Finance Commission*, Government of Karnataka, Bangalore.

9

RURAL LOCAL GOVERNMENT IN ANDHRA PRADESH

M. SARUMATHY

Introduction

Andhra Pradesh is one of the pioneering States in the country in the implementation of rural local government. The performance in this field had its own ups and downs since 1952 when the Panchayati Raj Institutions were established in the State. But very recently they have been constituted under the policy of democratic decentralization. The Andhra Pradesh Panchayati Raj Act, 1994 was enacted on 25.4.1994 as a comprehensive single act in accordance with the principles of the 73rd Constitutional Amendment. A three tier system of Panchayati Raj constituting Zilla Parishads (ZPs) at the district level, Mandal Parishads (MPs) at the intermediary level and Gram Panchayats (GPs) at the village level, was thus reintroduced by merging the Andhra Pradesh Gram Panchayats Act, 1964 and the Andhra Pradesh Mandal PRaja Parishads, Zilla PRaja Parishads, Zilla Pranalika Abivrudhi and Samseeksha Mandals Act, 1986. There are 22 Zilla Parishads 1,093 Mandals and 2,194 Gram Panchayats in the State.

The elections to these newly constituted Panchayati Raj bodies were held by the State Election Commission for the first time, which has been appointed on 12.9.94 for a fixed tenure of five years. The elections to Mandal Parishads and Zilla Parishads were held on 6.3.1995 and 10.3.1995 respectively. The elections to GPs took place on 24.6.95, 27.6.95, 30.6.95 and 3.7.95. Reservation to Scheduled Castes, Scheduled Tribes, has been given according to the size of their population. As many as 34 per cent of the seats have been reserved for the backward classes and one-third of the seats for women at all the levels in all position. The ward constituencies have been divided as follows.

Sl. No.	*Ward Constituency*	*Size of Population*
1.	Gram Panchayat Territorial Constituency (GPTC)	350
2.	Mandal Parishad Territorial Constituency (MPTC)	3,500
3.	Zilla Parishad Territorial Constituency (ZPTC)	1 Mandal

There are 2,08,586 GPTCs out of which 1,87,620 ward members were elected leaving the GPTCs in the Scheduled Areas (20,966) located in nine districts in the State. Besides, 14,644 MPTC members and 1,093 ZPTC members were also elected from their respective constituencies. At present there are 20,142 Sarpanches of GPs, 1035 Presidents of MPs and 20 Chairperson of ZPs in the offices. Annexure Table 9.1 provides the details of number of seats reserved for different categories of people. The seats for women under different category are provided in Annexure Table 9.2. The election details of different category of posts of PRIs can be seen from Annexure Table 9.3.

Structure of the Panchayati Raj System

Gram Sabha (GS)

A Gram Sabha is constituted for every village and consists of all electorate of the Gram Panchayat as its members. The Gram Sabha meets at least twice in a year for considering the following matters.

(a) Annual Statement of accounts and audit reports,
(b) Report on the administration of the proceeding year,
(c) Programme of works for the year or any new programmes not covered by the budget as the annual programme,

(d) Proposals for fresh taxation as for enhancement of existing tax,
(e) Selection of schemes, beneficiaries and location, and
(f) Such other matters as may be prescribed.

All the meetings of the Gram Sabha are convened by the Executive Officer and will be presided over by the Sarpanch. The quorum for convening the meeting of the Gram Sabha has not been mentioned in the Act.

Gram Panchayat (GP)

The Gram Panchayat is the body constituted for the village administration for revenue village or hamlet. A Gram Panchayat consists of members elected from the Gram Panchayat territorial constituency (GPTC) constituted for 350 population each. The Sarpanch of the Gram Panchayat is directly elected by the method of secret ballot on non-party basis. Out of the total strength of the elected members, seats are reserved for the members of Scheduled Castes and Scheduled Tribes on the basis of their population. Besides, one-third of the seats are reserved for women, which includes those belonging to Scheduled Castes and Scheduled Tribes based on their population ratio. The Amendment No. 5, dated February 3rd 1995 to the Act, stipulated reservation of not less than thirty-four per cent of the seats for the Backward Classes. The term of office of the Gram Panchayat is five years. The office of the Sarpanch is again reserved for different categories of people like Scheduled Castes, Scheduled Tribes, women and Backward Classes on the scale of reservation adopted for electing the members. One of the persons is elected as the Up-Sarpanch from amongst the members. The Act has adopted two children norm as a qualification for the members of the Panchayat. In addition, all other members except women who are absent for a period of ninety days from the date of the commencement of the term of office or absent for three ordinary meetings countineously are disqualified. In the case of women a period of not less than four months at a time is excluded if the lady is physically disabled or due to advanced stage of pregnancy and delivery.

Mandal Parishads (MP)

The Mandal Parishad (MP) is constituted for a Revenue Mandal. Each Mandal Parishad consists of persons mentioned below:

1. Persons elected from wards (MPTC),
2. Members of Legislative Assembly as co-opted members,
3. Members of Parliament,
4. A Member co-opted by the Government from Minorities,
5. Chairman of Agricultural Co-operatives,
6. All Divisional Level Officers,
7. Sub-Collector,
8. Executive Engineer,
9. Divisional Executive Engineer for Panchayati Raj,
10. Divisional Executive Engineer for Road and Water Supply (RWS),
11. Divisional Executive Engineer for Irrigation,
12. Divisional Executive Engineer for Road and Building (R&B),
13. Industry,
14. Mandal Revenue Officer (MRO),
15. Veterinary Doctors,
16. PHC, Doctor,
17. Extension Officer for Panchayats, and
18. All Sarpanchs in the Mandal.

Zilla Parishads (ZP)

The Zilla Parishad has been constituted for a district which consists of the following members.

1. Persons elected from the ZPTC,
2. The President of Agricultural Marketing,
3. The Members of Legislative Assembly,
4. The Members of Parliament,
5. Two persons co-opted from minorities,

Functions of the Panchayati Raj Bodies

Gram Panchayat

The functions of the Gram Panchayat include mandatory functions and obligatory functions. The mandatory functions are maintenance of buildings , roads, bridges, culverts etc., Lighting of road and public places, construction of drains, disposal of drainage, cleaning of streets, removal of rubbish etc., and improvement of sanitary conditions, providing public lavatories, maintain cremation and burial grounds, prevention and remedy of epidemics, sinking and repairing of wells, preparation of compost, registration of births and deaths, maintenance of cattle pounds etc., The laws also specifies a list of 26 functions, which the Gram Panchayats may undertake depending on their convenience, and availability of funds. The list includes welfare as well as development functions, such as construction of rest houses, planting of trees, promotion of elementary education, maintenance of dispensaries, libraries, promotion of improved methods of cultivation, organization of voluntary labour for community development, maintenance of maternity and child welfare centres, famine relief, maintenance of public markets, slaughter houses, implementation of land reforms etc. In practice, Gram Panchayats with their meagre funds available are not in a position to execute a number of obligatory functions. The 29 items listed in the Eleventh schedule are being reproduced in the Schedule-I of the Andhra Pradesh Panchayati Raj Act.

Mandal Parishad

The functions of the Mandal Parishad includes the functions listed in Schedule-11 of the Act, 1994. This list includes community development, agriculture, animal husbandry and fisheries, health and rural sanitation, education , social education, Co-operation, cottage industries, women welfare, social welfare, emergency relief, collection of statistics, self-help programme and trusts. The other functions of the Mandal Parishads include the items listed in the Schedule-I which specifies the functions mentioned in X Schedule of the Central Act, 1993. Further, the Mandals are also to complete local statistics. Besides, the Government has power to entrust any functions at its direction. Although there are 29 functions specified in the Amendment, State Act lists out of about 50 functions. This shows that the Mandal Parishads have been entrusted all other functions except Judiciary and Police.

The Mandal Parishads, if need, with prior approval of the Zilla Parishad can levy contributions from funds of the Gram Panchayats in the Mandal.

Broadly speaking the functions of the Mandal Parishad consists of functions related to development, social welfare and social security.

Zilla Parishad

The Zilla Parishad performs its functions entrusted under Schedule-I of the Act, which includes the twenty nine functions listed in the Eleventh Schedule of the Constitution. In addition, Zilla Parishad also has power to:

1. Examine and approve the budget of Mandal Parishads.
2. Distribute the funds allotted to the district by the Central and the State to the mandals.
3. Prepare district plan by consolidating the plans prepared by the mandals.
4. Execute the plans, projects, schemes and other works in the mandals.
5. Exercise powers to levy taxes.
6. Advise Government on all matters relating to development activities.
7. Advise and coordinate works between the government and the other two bodies at the lower level.
8. Collect data and publish statistics relating to local activities.
9. Accept trusts for any purpose for which its funds may be applied.
10. Establish, maintain or expand secondary, vocational and industrial.

Broadly speaking, the functions of Zilla Parishad can be classified as executive, supervisory, advisory and co-ordinate.

Committee System

Generally the Panchayats at any level functions through the committee system. Accordingly Andhra Pradesh has provided for a Committee System at all three levels of the Panchayats.

Zilla Parishad Level

There are seven Standing Committees in which the members of Zilla Parishad are distributed. The functions of the standing Committees mentioned are as follows:

1. *Planning and Finance* : District plan, budget taxation, finance and co-ordination of work.
2. *Rural Development* : Poverty Alleviation Programme, Area Development Programme, employment, housing, cooperation, thrift and small savings, industries including cottage, village and small scale industries, trusts and statistics.
3. *Agriculture* : Agriculture, animal husbandry, soil reclamation including social forestry, fisheries and sericulture.
4. *Medical and Education* : Education including social education, medical services, public health and sanitation including drainage, relief and distress in grave enterprises.
5. *Women welfare* : Development of women and welfare of children.
6. *Social welfare* : Social welfare of Scheduled Castes, Scheduled Tribes and backward classes and cultural affairs.
7. *Works Committee* : Communication, rural water supply, power and irrigation.

The total number of members of each Standing Committee includes the Chairman also. The Chairman of Zilla Parishad is the ex-officio member of the committees except Standing Committee on agriculture. The vice-chairman, Zilla Parishad is the ex-officio member of the Standing Committee on agriculture. The Chairman, Zilla Parishad can be the chairman of any four Standing Committees and for two standing committees, the chairman's post can be filled by nomination by the chairman, Zilla Parishad. A women member of the Zilla Parishad is nominated as chairman for standing committee on women's welfare.

The District Collector has the right to participate in standing committees without voting right.

The decisions of the standing committee are subject to ratification by the general body of the Zilla Parishad that has power to approve, modify and reverse them.

The following officials are the permanent invitees to the meetings of the Zilla Parishad.

(a) The Chairman, District Co-operative Marketing Society.
(b) The Chairman, Zilla Granthalaya Samiti.
(c) The Chairman, District Co-operative Central Bank.
(d) The District Collector.
(e) All the presidents of the Mandal Parishads in the District.

The chairman of the standing committees have power to invite any office bearers other than any political party having experience and specialisation, knowledge in the subject to attend the meetings.

Mandal Parishad Level

The Standing Committees are formed at the Mandal Parishad also. As per section 175 of the Act, each Mandal Parishad can appoint one or more Joint Committees for any activity. However, no such Committee has been constituted both at Pochampally Mandal Parishad and at Chotuppal Mandal Parishad.

Gram Panchayat Level

Even at the Gram Panchayat Level, Beneficiary Committee and functional committees on agriculture, public health,water supply, sanitation, family welfare, education and communication can be formed. But Gram Panchayats are not able to constitute these committees since the Government has not issued appropriate orders as mentioned in section 49 of the Act.

Planning Process

The Planning process as expected by the Constitution under the new democratic decentralization has not undergone any change in the State. Although, Gram Sabha is called on twice in a year, Gram Panachayat and Mandal Parishads are set up at the respective levels, planning is done only at the district level. It is understood that even at the district level planning has been done only by DRDA. The budget has been given to Zilla Parishad for distribution of funds to the Mandal Parishads and Gram Panchayats. Neither the electorate nor the elected representatives are involved in the preparation of the district plan.

District Planning Committee (DPC)

The DPC has not yet been constituted. A separate Act, for bringing the constitution of DPC is being prepared and is to be placed before the House of Legislature.

Organizational Structure of Panchayati Raj

The organizational structure of Panchayati Raj and Rural Development Department in the State comprises of three wings such as:

1. Panchayati Raj Wing
2. Rural Development Wing
3. Panchayati Raj Engineering Wing

Chart 9.1 shows the organizational structure of Panchayati Raj in the State.

Minister for PR & R.D.
Principal Secretary (Panchayati Raj & RD)

Secretary (PR) Deputy Secretary (3) Assistant Secretary (4)	Commissioner (PR)	Commissioner (PR)

Additional Commissioner (PR)

Administration	Accounts	Elections JRY Legal
Chief Executive Officer	Chairman	Zilla Parishad
District Panchayat Officer	President	Mandal Parishad
Divisional Development Officer		Sarpanch
		Gram Panchayat
		Executive Officer

CHART 9.1 : Organizational Structure of Panchayati Raj in the State

The department of Panchayati Raj is responsible for planning and execution of the rural development programmes.

District Level

At the district level the Chief Executive Officer (CEO) is the head of the administration for Zilla Parishads and Mandal Parishads. Chart 9.2 provides the hierarchy of the Nalgonda Zilla Parishad's administration.

Chairman - Zilla Parishad | Chief Executive Officer

Deputy CEO	Accounts Officer	Parishad Education Officer	Executive Engineer Panchayats	Executive Officer RWS

1. Superintendent Planning Wing - Establishment
2. Superintendent Works Wing - JRY and other works
3. Meeting Wing - General body and standing committees of ZP and elections
4. Accounts Wing - All accounts pattern related to Zilla Parishad
5. Education and Accounts - Establishment pattern and Accounts relating to Teaching staff
6. GPF and Pension - GPF and pension of teachers and institutional staff

CHART 9.2 : Nalgonda Zilla Parishad Administration

As far as the administration of the Gram Panchayats is concerned, the District Panchayat Officer (DPO) is the authority for monitoring and supervising at the district level. For instance, the Nalgonda district Panchayat administration has been divided into three divisions where Divisional Panchayat Officers are appointed. Five Extension officers are also working under the control of the Divisional Panchayat Officers for day to day administrations. Chart 9.3 shows the line of control of the office of the DPO at Nalgonda district.

District Panchayat Office
(DPO)
Divisional Panchayat Officer

Nalgonda	Mirralguda	Bhongir

Extension Officers (15) each 5
Superintendentant
Senior Assistant (1)
Junior Assistant (3)
Typist (1)
Ministerial Staff

CHART 9.3 : Administration of Nalgonda District Panchayat Office

Mandal Level

The Mandal Parishad's Development Officer (MPDO) is the Chief Executive Officer of the Mandal Parishad. The MPDO is responsible for implementing the resolutions of the Mandal Parishads. The MPDO is also responsible for convening the meetings of the Mandal Parishads with the approval of the President within 90 days from the last meeting. The establishment of the Mandal Parishad and the staff working in the Mandal Office and the schemes transferred by the Government are under the administrative control and supervision of the MPDO. For a better clarity, the line of control of Pochampally Mandal Parishad administration is given in Chart 9.4.

Mandal Parishads Administration
Mandal Parishad Development Officer

Asst. Executive Eng. (PR)	Extension Officer (RD)	Senior Asst.	Mandal Education Officer (MEO)
Pump Mechanic	VDO Grade I & Grade II (Men & women)	Junior Asst(2)	Mandal Key Resource Persons
		Typist	Mandal Resource Persons

Ministerial Staff

CHART 9.4 : Organizational Set-up of Mandal Parishad

Gram Panchayat Level

The administration of the Gram Panchayat consists of the executive officer, bill collector, sweepers and cleaners. The executive officer is either full time or on part time worker for a Gram Panchayat or for a group of Gram Panchayats. Except the Executive Officer all other staff members are temporary and the pay and other service conditions rest with the Gram Panchayat. The executive officer is the executive authority for the Gram Panchayat.

Staffing Pattern

The staffing pattern of the Panchayat administration at each level has been discussed in detail under the organizational structure of the Panchayati Raj System of this report. Different charts are drawn to indicate the staffing pattern at each level.

The transfer of personnel to Zilla Parishad from each of the department is indicated below :

1.	Panchayat DPO	Extension Officer Panchayat for notified area
2.	Co-operative department	Co-operative
3.	Education department	Panchayat Education department
4.	Agriculture department	Asst. Agricultural Officer
5.	Animal Husbandry dept.	Veterinary Assistant
6.	Medical dept.	PHC Doctor ANMS
7.	Engineering	Executive Engineer AEO, JEO
8.	Women Welfare dept.	EO Women Welfare

The CEO (ZP) writes the annual confidential report of all staff of ZP including the staff from other line departments.

There is no Panchayat cadre separately in the State. Although the heads of the departments [Commissioner RD & Commissioner (PR)] are different, below the State level again RD & PR are put in two in one — DRDA is separate from ZP administration. The Chief Planning Officer is again a separate officer maintaining only the district level statistics. The district collector is the overall administrator of all these organizations in the district.

The cadre strength of Panchayat was fixed two decades ago as per G.O. No. 850 P.R. (Est.viii) department dated 30th August 1977. These divisions of Panchayats as notified and non-notified Panchayats are based on the normal income of the Panchayats as Rs. 40,000 and more respectively. At present there are many Panchayats with an income of Rs. 20 lakhs and this criterion needs to be revised. The staffing pattern of these two Panchayats category are different. The notified Gram Panchayats get full time Village Development Officer and for the non-notified Gram Panchayat part time VDO is appointed. The VDO is the Chief Executive Officer of the Gram Panchayat.

For example Nalgonda district has 52 Gram Panchayats in the district out of 1178 GPs in 3 divisions.

Panchayats in the Scheduled Areas

The elections to the Panchayats in the Scheduled Areas in the State were also held along with the elections to other Panchayats. But the election results are not yet announced due to high court order. There are nine districts in the State, which contain tribal population of about 42 lakhs accounting to 6.3 per cent of the total population of the State. Annexure Table 9.4 shows the data pertaining to the status of Panchayats in the Scheduled Areas in the State.

As far as the seats reserved for the STs are concerned the State was in trouble in the allocation of seats. When the State prepared to conduct election in 1995, 33 seats were reserved in favour of STs, out of 46 Mandal Parishads and districts in the State. As a result, the Vice-President and the Godwana Sangharsh Samiti and the other tribals filed writ petitions. The petition was to plea that after the enactment of 73rd Constitutional Amendment Act, 1992, the State Legislature has no power to make any law with respect to Panchayats extending its operation to Scheduled Areas in view of the specific mention incorporated in Article 243-M. The Petitioners also pleaded saying that due to large influx of non-tribals here it has decreased to a considerable position resulting in the demographic composition of the Scheduled Areas. More than 48 per cent of the agriculture land in the Scheduled Areas went into the hands of non-tribals in spite of the protected legislation forbidding non-tribals from owning lands in the tribal areas. This resulted in losing of 13 Mandal Parishads in the Scheduled Areas which were brought into the open pool as the percentage of the tribal population is less than 50%. The High Court passed interlocutory order to the State Government to complete the elections and instructed to publish the results of the 46 Mandal Parishads.

After the enactment of the Extension of Panchayats to Scheduled Areas Act, 1996, the State appointed a Cabinet sub-committee to examine the various aspects of the Central Act. The convener of the cabinet sub-committee was the Minister for P.R. & R.D. Based on the recommendations made by the committee the State Legislature passed amendment to the Act, 1994 as Act No. 7 of 1998 on January 16, 1998. Thus the Panchayats in the Scheduled Areas are brought in conformity with the Central Act, 1996. But the election results are not announced due to court order. As on today there is no Panchayati Raj set-up in the Scheduled Areas.

Performance Analysis

The Act empowers the Gram Panchayats alone to levy taxes while the other two tiers are permitted to impose surcharge on the taxes levied by the Panchayats, which is not being exercised by the Mandals and Zilla Parishads.

Revenue of the Gram Panchayat

The revenue of the Gram Panchayat includes tax-revenue, non-tax revenue assignments and grants in aid. The tax revenue has been collected by two method of taxes called compulsory and obligatory. The non-tax revenue includes Vehicle tax (other than Motor Vehicles), tax on agricultural land for a specific purpose and land cess at the rate of two paise in a rupee on the annual rental value of occupied land. Among the non-tax revenues, mention may be made of the income from the remunerative sources such as rents, income from fruit bearing trees on Panchayat lands etc. The Gram Panchayats are not levying the taxes and cesses referred to. Under the assigned revenue and collected revenue in respect of certain items and there are specific provisions under which revenues levied and collected by the State government in respect of certain items may be assigned to the local bodies. The revenue collected by way of Land Cess/Local Cess, surcharge on Stamp Duty Tax on Minor Minerals and the Government assigns Entertainment Tax to the rural local bodies. Panchayati Raj bodies also receive a variety of Grants-in-aid which are not specific purposes, while others are tied up funds. The per capita grant of Re.1 per head population and salary grant accounts to 10 per cent.

Further, house tax continued to be the main source of income of the Gram Panchayat accounting for 10 per cent including Jawahar Rojgar Yojana funds. Gram Panchayats are allowed to levy the tax either on the capital value or the annual value of the property. But in practice the Gram Panchayats are reluctant to levy this tax for fear of antagonizing the electorate. The Gram Panchayat is not levying kologaram tax as a compulsory tax. This could have been another source of income if properly managed. Vehicle tax is an another option of income on bicycle to the Gram Panchayats, which amounts to 1.5 per cent. The Panchayats do not find this item as an income yielding area. There are also remunerative enterprises and special taxes which give about 5.4 per cent and 3.9 per cent of revenue respectively. In total the own sources of income of the Gram Panchayats come around 20.57 per cent. The Assigned revenue, which consists of Entertainment tax, Profession tax, land cess, local cess, and surcharge on stamp duty work out to be 6.15 per cent.

The own sources of income of the Mandals and the Zilla Parishads amount to 5 per cent. Such income are drawn from rent on buildings and commercial complexes, fee from markets, ferries and other miscellaneous items. Grant-in-aid is also given to Mandals and Zilla Parishads at the rate of Rs. 5 to Mandals and Rs.2 to Zillas. Grants are released to Mandals and ZPs for different developmental works.

State Finance Commission

The distribution of financial resource in Andhra Pradesh has been carried out as per the State Finance Commission's recommendations, which was constituted in 1994. The Commission consists of a Chairman and four other members including the Member-Secretary. The Commission submitted its report entitled "Report of the First

State Finance Commission 1997-2000". It recommended 39.24 per cent of State revenue both taxes and non-taxes be entitled to the local bodies. An additional devolution of 10.93 per cent has been given to the rural and urban bodies which amounts to be Rs. 979.10 crores. The Commission also categorised the Panchayats into the following four categories for the purpose of distribution of funds:

1. Ordinary - X (16.67%)
2. Advanced - 2/3X (11.11%)
3. Backward - 1-2/3X (27.77%)
4. Tribal - 2-2/3X (44.44%)

The Government accepted the recommendations and granted Rs. 364 crores per annum to Panchayati Raj bodies. This amounts to be 12 per cent of the State revenue, in addition an amount of Rs. 150 crores was added as assigned revenue to strengthen the Panchayati Raj bodies. Annexure Table 9.5 gives details of financial allocation to the PRIs and DRDAs during the last four years.

In addition, the Tenth Finance Commission has made an *ad hoc* allocation of Rs. 351.00 crores for a period of 4 years from 1996-97 to 1999-2000 accounting to Rs. 85.75 crores per year. From the year 1997-98 it is proposed to distribute this Tenth Finance Commission Grant as Rs. 4, Rs. 6, and Rs.6 among Zilla Parishad, MP and GP respectively. All PRIs are expected to utilise these funds for taking up permanent works.

The Chairmen of the ZPs get Rs. 2500 per month towards honorarium and are eligible to use 250 liters of fuel (petrol) per month. The Vice-chairmen and others of ZPs get Rs. 1500 per month. An amount of Rs. 700 is being paid towards TA per month to the Chairmen of ZPs. If any other vehicle than Government vehicle is used for official purpose, charges can be claimed at the rate of Rs. 2. At present after frequent representation made to the Government the Sarpanchs and other members of the Panchayats would be getting monthly salary, which is yet to be finalised.

Devolution of Powers and Functions

The State has not attempted so far to devolve the powers and functions with regard to the 29 items listed in the XI Schedule of the Constitution. To add the ingredients of the Constitutional Amendment, the State has initiated steps towards proper devolution of powers to the PRIs. A committee of Secretariats was constituted with the Principal Secretary as the Chairman. The Principal Secretary, Panchayati Raj and Rural Development, MLAs and Heads of the departments are the members of the Committee to study the pattern of devolution of powers and functions. This attempt is to take steps cautiously after a thorough examination of the issues involved and an in-depth study of existing field conditions so that the ultimate arrangement could be made to achieve durable results.

In Andhra Pradesh, agencies like DRDA, SC & ST Welfare corporations, District Industries Centre, BC Welfare Corporations are involved in the implementation of poverty alleviation programme. Therefore, the transition of devolution of powers and functions should go in with regard to the empowerment of PRIs, deployment of field level functionaries, of the activities of various agencies presently involved in the areas of rural development so that there is no let-up or slowing down of the process of rural development. And therefore to say to the transfer of programmes and schemes to PRIs is yet to take place. The first meeting of the committee was held on 14th July 1998. The action taken with regard to the suggestions made in the meeting is yet to be initiated.

Performance of Women/Scheduled Caste Members

The performance of the women and the scheduled caste members in the functioning of the Panchayats is not uniform. In the study area majority of the members are having poor educational background and their ignorance is bliss for the Sarpanch. Particularly, while operating Joint cheque system of the Gram Panchayat. The law also permits the Gram Panchayats to select any one member amongst the elected representatives. Some of the Sarpanchs found it convenient of having members who are illiterate can put only thumb impression or only signatories. Generally these types of people come from socially and economically backward class.

Issue of Autonomy

PRIs in Andhra Pradesh are not autonomous neither functionally nor financially. Out of three-tier Panchayats only the Panchayats at the district level is stronger and the other two levels of Panchayats i.e., the Mandal Parishad and the Gram Panchayats are treated as the subordinates to ZP. Thus the Panchayats at the Mandal, Gram level are not independent. While analysing the functioning of ZP, it is understood that ZP is autonomous functionally and financially, but not politically. This means that for each district, one Member of State Legislature is appointed as the Minister of the district. For instance, Nalgonda district has got the Home Minister of the State Cabinet as the Minister of the district. By this, the State policy is riding the house of Zilla Parishad. The Chairman of Zilla Parishad is thus brought under the control of the political party in power. The autonomy of the PRIs is limited through the mechanism of Collector and DRDA in the State. PRI has absolutely no role to play either in planning or in preparing budget. The State has provided a capsuler formula in which the funds provided to PRI body could be spent. For instance, the Pochampally Mandal Parishads followed the method given below for spending the fund allotted to them for the year 1998-99.

5% For the Welfare of SC
6% For the Welfare of ST
40% For works regarding Road and Building
5% Women Welfare
10% drainage and water supply
20% Office Management
4% Miscellaneous

By providing such directions as mentioned above, the PR bodies have no chance to accommodate the interest of the problem of people. In case, if any Mandal Parishad needs to utilise the resources more than the allotted money it ought to obtain prior approval of the Government through Zilla Parishad. By involving this process the execution of the Panchayats Work amounts to delay and curtail the freedom of the elected member to the respective constituency. The Sarpanchs of the Gram Panchayats are not psychologically free from the political clout. Although, the elections to the Sarpanchs were held on non-party basis, the politicization has been so strong amongst the members of the Gram Panchayats and there by the Sarpanchs have not tried to make them free from political policy.

Merger of DRDA

There are 22 DRDAs in the State. DRDA has not been merged with Zilla Parishad. The budget of PRI and DRDA is allocated separately and quoted the works of independent agencies at the State level.

Special Features in the Act

* One of the innovative features of PR system in the State is limiting the qualification of members of PRI who has more than 2 children. By this provision in the PR Act, the State has made attempt to implement to bring down the population in the State and also introduced that the members of the Panchayat or the public leader or a politician should be a mode to the society.
* PRI in Andhra Pradesh has provided organic linkage between the three-tiers which means that all Sarpanchs of the Gram Panchayats attend the general body meeting of the Mandal Parishads. Similarly, all the Presidents of the Mandal Parishads attend the general body meetings of the Zilla Parishad. But they have no right to vote.
* A member who is absent for three consecutive meetings becomes disqualified and thereby insisted regularity of the members in attending the meetings to and in effective the functioning of Panchayats.
* Joint cheque power for the operation of Gram Panchayats fund has been provided to the Sarpanch of the Gram Panchayat along with any one member purposively selected by the Gram Panchayat.
* The grant-in-aid of the State Government is being still operated through the Government treasury only.
* The scheme of selection of best Gram Panchayat is an another unique feature in the State. Committees have been at the

State, Zilla and Mandal level for the selection of best Gram Panchayats and incentives are provided to encourage the Panchayats. At the State, district and Mandal level Committees are formed for this purpose. At the State level the Commissioner Panchayati Raj and Rural Development is the Chairman. The Commissioner of Agriculture and Engineer-in chief are the members. The Commissioner, PR is the Member-Secretary. At the district level the Chief Executive Officer, ZP is the Chairman District Panchayat Officer and the Executive Engineer, PR are the members. The Mandal level team includes the Mandal Parishads Development Officer as the Chairman and the Divisional Officer and the Extension Officer, Panchayats are the Members. Statement - I provides the norms fixed for the selection of the best Gram Panchayat.

* The power to call information from Village Development Officer (VDO) has been entrusted upon to the Gram Panchayats (Section 134)
* Co-option to Minorities is given to provide adequate representation to all sections of the community in the village.

Issues related to Performance

A number of issues come up in the functioning of the Panchayats.

1. *The Size of the Gram Panchayat*

The size of the Gram Panchayats varies from 5,000 - 50,000 in the State. This limits to the raising of income of the Panchayats and for a Panchayat with a small size of population it cannot be feasible to hold any developmental activity specifically. It is, therefore, necessary to regroup the Panchayats with the size of population, which the State Government may feel appropriate to make the Panchayat viable.

2. *The Grouping of Panchayats*

All the Gram Panchayats in the State have been classified as notified and non-notified based on the income of the Gram Panchayat that is Rs.40,000 which has been fixed in the year 1972. There are numbers of Panchayats having income of more than Rs. 40,000 which does not fall under notified Panchayats. Moreover, at present an average income of any Gram Panchayat including JRY funds account to be 5-6 lakhs. Therefore, the classification of Panchayats need re-grouping.

3. *Representation of Members in the Higher Level*

The representation provided to the Sarpanches of the Gram Panchayats in the General body meetings of the Mandal Parishad and to the Presidents of the Mandal Parishads in the general body Meetings of the Zilla Parishads seem to be incomprehensible and duplicated. For the constitution of Zilla Parishad one member is being elected from each Mandal which is otherwise known as (ZPTC). thereby representation from each Mandal is being already provided by the Act. This accounts to a huge crowd including the officers. For example, Nalgonda Zilla Parishad has nearly 250 members in its General body. Suitable formula should be worked out to limit the persons to participate in the General body meeting of the Mandal Parishad and Zilla Parishad, so that a better platform could be provided to the members for more meaningful participation.

4. *Appropriate Legislative Measures*

The text of PR act, 1994 includes that necessary orders, guidelines, instructions may be issued by the government for further implementation by many activities. The Gram Panchayats constituted have not any committees for its functioning for the reason that the legislature has not passed any further orders.

5. *Profession Tax*

Profession Tax was compulsory until 1987 and was taken over by the Government. The State collects the tax and distributes to local bodies. After the State taking over the collection of profession tax the collected tax has increased more than two times. Even then, the eligibility of a particular democratically elected body has been seized. Therefore, the Gram Panchayat should be given powers of implementing such taxes so that the procedural delay in transferring money to the local bodies can be avoided.

6. *The Staff of Gram Panchayat*

The staff of Gram Panchayat are still placed under Nominal Muster Roll (NMR) system which was introduced in 1985. Payment to the Panchayat staff has not been regular. The Public Water Supplier (PWS) collects his own payment from the water users which causes inconvenience to the PWS since not all the water users are genuine in paying and regular PWS is placed at the mercy of the water users.

7. *The Village Development Officer*

The VDOs are under the control of the revenue department and should be brought under the control of Gram Panchayats so that issue of caste, income certificates can be made regular.

8. The Problem of Teachers

Since the subject of primary education has been dealt by the Mandal Parishads the transfer and appointment of teachers in the State became a puzzle.

9. *Problem of Group Executive Officer*

There are Executive Officers for more than one Gram Panchayat and called as Group Executive Officers, which is an another hurdle in the functioning of the Panchayats. The Group Executive officers are found nowhere and do not a hold any responsibilities of any Gram Panchayat. Therefore the Sarpanch who have Group Executive officers felt that each Gram Panchayat should be given an Executive Officer.

10. *Overlapping of Functions*

The Andhra Pradesh Panchayati Raj Act did not make any attempt to avoid the overlapping between the obligatory and the discretionary functions.

11. *Role of District Panchayat Officers*

The District Panchayat Officers have been appointed when the Gram Panchayats were considered as the viable unit of development in the sixties. But in the present context of the functioning of the PRIs, where the ZP is made as the unit of implementing all the developmental programmes the role of the District Panchayats Officers have not been defined so far.

12. *Audit Objection*

There are number of audit objections which are pending before many of the Gram Panchayats and are not in a position to reply.

Case Study of Nalagunda Zilla Parishad

Nalagunda district consists of 59 Mandal Parishads and 1178 Gram Panchayats. It has the population of 28.5 lakhs, which includes 5.04 lakhs Scheduled Castes and 2.7 lakhs Scheduled Tribes. The literacy rate of the district is 31.4 per cent, which is about 13 per cent less than the State literacy rate. Out of the total population of 28.5 lakhs, 25.1 lakhs population live in rural areas. At present Nalagunda Zilla Parishad consists of 59 members. Its general body meeting includes the persons listed below.

1.	Members elected from ZPTC	59
2.	Co-opted Member from Minorities	1
3.	Member of Legislative Assembly (Bhongir)	1
4.	Member of Parliament	1
5.	Presidents of Mandal Parishads	59
6.	Line Departments Officers	41

Consequently, Nalagunda ZP also functions vibrantly through Committee system, which are mentioned below

Sl. No.	*Name of the Committee*	*No. of Persons*
1.	Planning and Finance	12
2.	Rural Development	12
3.	Agriculture	12
4.	Medical & Education	11
5.	Women Welfare	9
6.	Social Welfare	10
7.	Works Committees	11

The Chairman of the Standing Committees have power to invite any person who has expertise in the field. The Nalagunda

Zilla Parishad has formed seven Standing Committees and the Chairman, Zilla Parishad is the Chairman of the Standing Committees for 1, 2, 4 and 7. The Vice-Chairman is the Chairman of the Standing Committee on agriculture. For the standing committee on Women Welfare and Social welfare two women of Zilla Parishad have been nominated as the Chairman of the Standing Committee.

Nalagunda ZP has been classified into three divisions such as Bhongir, Mirralguda and Nalagunda for facilitating the administration of Gram Panchayats, where District Panchayats officers are posted. There are 130 Non-notified Gram Panchayats whose income is below 40 thousand. As on June 1998 there were 1,60,450 audit objections in the district involving an amount of Rs. 4,52,26,360 out of which only 871 audit objections were dropped involving an amount of Rs. 52,19,651. All the Executive Officers are not to comply with the problem and give proper reply and many of them are not able to settle the account.

The working system of Nalagunda ZP shows that the Government although made the ZP as the strong functioning unit the ZP is not able to perform satisfactorily due to different reasons. One of the reasons is that there are too many officials involved on the functioning of the Panchayats, whose role is not clear in the Act. The ZP also plays the role of an executing agency. The Planning process that was expected by the Constitution to make these units as truly the agent of democracy is not with the Panchayati Raj bodies.

Case Study of Chotuppal Mandal Parishad

Chotuppal Mandal includes 25 villages having the total population of 52 thousand with 27.8 thousand males and 27.2 thousand females. It spreads over 264 sq.km. area there are 25 Gram Panchayats in the Mandal. The Mandal has the literacy rate of about 47 per cent, which is higher than the State literacy rate. The details of the members of Chotuppal Mandal is given below :

Particulars of the Members of Chottuppal Mandal Parishad

Sl. No.	Age	No.	Party	No	Caste	No.
1.	30-40	9	CPM	7	BC	9
2.	41-50	5	TDP	4	OC	6
3.	51-55	2	CONI	5	SC	1
Total		16		16		16

Similarly, the Chotuppal Mandal's General Body consists of the members listed below :

1.	Elected Ward Members	16
2.	Co-opted Member from minorities	1
3.	Member of Legislative Assembly	1
4.	Member of Parliament	1
5.	Other Department Officers	18
6.	Mandal Revenue Officer	1
7.	Veterinary Doctor	1
8.	PHC doctor	1
9.	Sarpanches	25
10.	Extension Officer Panchayat	1
11.	Mandal Panchayat Development Officer	1
12.	Mandal Revenue Officer	1
13.	Divisional Engineer	1

Although the Act provides for formation of one or more Joint Committees Chotuppal Mandal Parishad has not formed any such Committee so far due to the reason that the State Government has not issued further directions. The own resources of the Mandal are nothing but the grant-in-aid provided by the Government only. The Joint Mandal Credit Plan given to Chotuppal Mandal Parishad by the district for the year 1998-99 is mentioned below

1.	Integrated Rural Development Programme (IRDP)	-	100 units
2.	IRDP loans	-	3 cores
3.	Modified Area Development Agencies (MADA)	-	50 Nos
4.	Scheduled Caste Action Plan (50% subsidy)	-	35 Nos
5.	Minorities Development Action Plan	-	6 Nos
6.	Prime Minister Rozgar Yojana	-	12 Nos

7.	Chief Minister Employment Yojana (50% subsidy) Proposal for a project from 6th class—SSC qualified persons such as weaving,Brass work, etc.	- -	Group
8.	Backward Community Action Plan irrigation work like current motors and submersible motors etc.	-	Individual
9.	Khadi and Village Industries	-	District beneficiaries level
10.	Million Well Scheme (MWS) Corporations sanctions 3HP/5HP motors free supply for the MWS beneficiaries	-	SC
11.	Janmabhoomi Programme Programme for Village Development	-	Community based

Road	50 %	Beneficiary cost
Pipe Line	30 %	Beneficiary cost
Mahila Mandal Activity	5 %	Women Welfare fund
Public Latrine	20 %	Beneficiary cost
School building	30 %	Beneficiary cost

The works mentioned above proves that the Mandal Parishads are the implementing agency of the Zilla Parishads and have no autonomy of functioning. The specific units, which are supposed to be covered under each item, have been mentioned and accordingly it should be implemented.

Case Study of Chotuppal Gram Panchayat

This Gram Panchayat has 2 villages located at one and half km from the Mandal headquarters. The total population is 8,940 with 8,000 voters in it. There are about 2,042 households. It has one ZP residential School and one Balwadi centre. One Government hospital with one doctor, 2 Health workers and 2 ANMS. The sources of drinking water in the Gram Panchayat are from 5 open wells, 18 Borewells, 10 Hand Pumps and 500 Taps. A reasonably good sandies located at the reach of people within the Panchayat. This Panchayat includes 15 elected members including the Sarpanch. The particulars of the members of the GP is given below:

Socio-Economic Particulars of the Members of Chottuppal Gram Panchayat

Sl. No.	Age	No.	Party	No.	Caste	No.
1.	30-40	09	CPM	07	BC	09
1.	30-40	10	TDP	05	BC	11
2.	41-50	05	CON-I	05	OC	03
3.	51-60	Nil	CPM	03	ST	01
4.			INDIP	01		
5.			BJP	01		
Total	15		15		15	

The socio- political scenario in the Chotuppal Gram Panchayat also is similar to that of the Mandal discussed earlier. The General body Meeting takes place once in three months. The issues discussed in this GP for most of time are related to housing facility, income and expenditure and developmental activities. Although the Act provides scope for formation of Beneficiary Committees and Functional Committees, this Gram Panchayat has not constituted any such committees for want of further orders from Government. The staff of the GP consists of the following members:

Executive Officer (1) full time employee Government salary
Junior Assistant (1) full time employee Government salary
Bill Collector (1) full time employee Government salary
Sweepers (9)
Night Watchman (1)
Attender (1)
Water Supply (PWS) (1)

The Mandal is also held up with the problem of Muster role system implemented in the State as there are ministerial staff mostly sweepers working for more than 15 years (. . . . .) still working on the Muster role system. Long Back Court decision was obtained to observe them as regular employees; the State Government has not taken further action. Incidentally these people are also being not paid regularly. Their wage payment is being made once in two or three months. Surprisingly, this Mandal earns nearly two crores rupees by auctioning public market and fish tanks which adds to its own revenue. This is the picture of the major Panchayats. In the case of small Panchayats even the own resources is reduced to a non sizable income without any staff for their own.

Conclusion

The analysis of the working of PRIs in the State is left to a confused State of affairs. The State could not fulfill any of the promises with regard to the functioning of rural local bodies. For instance conducting election to the Scheduled areas is still pending. Another issue is the formula of devolving powers and functions, which is still an on-going process. Majority of the developmental activities has been diverted under the umbrella of Janmabhoomi—the State sponsored programme, which is the most celebrating developmental programme. This involves almost all the developmental departments and phase-wise special activities are taken up. Although Janmabhoomi created a good impact over the society the State Government sidelined the participation of PRIs. It has also been considered to be the programme of development Party Cadres. This is proved to be evident when in one of the district a councillor attempted drastic action against himself for the denial of any developmental activity in his ward under Jhanmabhoomi in spite of his frequent request in the meetings. Jhanmabhoomi has occupied the minds of all officials and the elected representatives in the State and beyond it nothing seems to be successful. The Self-Help Groups and the water User Association have created parallel power structure in the villages to the Gram Panchayats. To conclude it can be said that the rural local government units are neither successful nor can be identified as the institutions, which are completely unsuccessful. These institutions have their own validity in the domain of development and can only prove its image when these bodies are made independent with sufficient financial resources.

REFERENCES

Balaramulu, C.H., and Raghvender., "Political Leadership in Panchayati Raj : A Study of Mandal PRaja Parishad Leadership in Andhra Pradesh" *Administrative Change* 22 : 20, 1995, pp.168-176.

Chaturvedi, Y.S., "Micrology of Mandal Administrative Arrangements in Andhra Pradesh" *Indian Economic Panorama,* 3 : 3 1993, pp.30-41.

Devolution of Powers, Function and Finances to Panchayats in Andhra Pradesh Gramin Vikas, 13:1 1997, pp. 13.

Haragopal,G., and Sudarshanam,G., "Andhra Pradesh" in George Mathew (ed) *Status of Panchayati Raj in the States of India,* New Delhi. Concept Publishing Company, 1995, pp. 15-27.

Ram Reddy, G., Panchayati Raj and Rural Development and Local Organization in Andhra Pradesh in J. Milton and Norman T Uphoff (eds) *Rural Development and Local Organization in Asia,* New Delhi, Mcmillan and Company 1982.

Report of the First State Finance Commission, Government of Andhra Pradesh 1997.

Sarumathy, M., "Panchayati Raj in Andhra Pradesh" in R.C. Choudhry & S.P. Jain (eds) *Patterns of Decentralized Governance in Rural India*, Hyderabad, NIRD, 1999, pp. 25-63.

Sarumathy, M., "Panchayati Raj in Andhra Pradesh : A Democratic Step" *Southern Economist,* 11 : 5 1992, pp. 3-5.

Sastry, K.R., and Vithal, C.P., and Ramachandriah, G., "Panchayati Raj in Andhra Pradesh: An Analytical Study" in NIRD (ed.)., *Panchayati Raj Institutions in Selected States: An analytical Study*, Hyderabad : NIRD, 1995, pp. 1-6.

The Andhra Pradesh Panchayati Raj Act, 1994, Government of Andhra Pradesh 1994.

ANNEXURES

TABLE 9.1

Details showing the Number of Seats Reserved for Different Categories in the State

	Number of Seats reserved (both men and women) for			
	SCs	*STs*	*BCs*	*Women (General)*
1. Gram Panchayat				
(a) Ward member	37,524	10,990	71743	26,196
(b) Sarpanches	3,786	1,075	7615	2,775
2. Block Panchayat Members, Mandal Parishad Territorial Constituencies	2,564	1,111	4,869	2,174
3. District Panchayat				
(a) Members, Zilla Parishad Territorial constituencies	195	99	367	159

TABLE 9.2

Details of Seats for Resereved for Women

	Number of Seats reserved for women			
	SCs	*STs*	*BCs*	*Total*
1. Gram Panchayat				
(a) Ward member	12,882	3,194	2,4771	40,847
(b) Sarpanches	1,247	300	2,537	4,084
2. Block Panchayat				
Members, Mandal Parishad Territorial Constituencies	913	340	1,625	2,878
3. District Panchayat				
(a) Members, Zilla Parishad Territorial constituencies	65	33	122	220

TABLE 9.3

Elections to Panchayat Raj Bodies

upto December, 1997

S. No.	Name of the Office/ Seat	Total No.of Seats/ offices in the State	Whether election is on party/non-party basis	Whether election is direct or indirect	Period within which casual vacancy shall be filled up	No. of offices for which elections were conducted so far.	No. of. Offices covered by agency area	No. of. Casual vacancies reported so far
1.	ZPTC Member	1,093	Party Basis	Direct	120 days	1,093	47	8
2.	Chairman, Zilla Parishad	22	Party Basis	Indirect	6 months	20	2	-
3.	Vice-Chairman, Zilla Parishad	22	Party Basis	Indirect	6 months	20	2	-
4.	Co-opted Member, Zilla Parishad	44	Party Basis	Indirect	8 weeks	40	4	-
5.	MPTC Member	14,644	Party Basis	Direct	120 days	14,600	474	154
6.	President, Mandal Parishad	1,093	Party Basis	Indirect	6 months	1,035	47	5
7.	Vice President Mandal Parishad	1,093	Party Basis	Indirect	6 months	1,035	47	1

TABLE 9.3 — *contd.*

S.No.	Name of the Office/ Seat	Total No.of Seats/ offices in the State	Whether election is on party/non-party basis	Whether election is direct or indirect	Period within which casual vacancy shall be filled up	No. of offices for which elections were conducted so far	No. of. Offices covered by agency area	No. of. Casual vacancies reported so far
8.	Co-opted Member, Mandal Parishad	1,093	Party Basis	Indirect	8 weeks	1,035	47	2
9.	Sarpanch, Gram Panchayat	21,943	Non-Party Basis	Direct	120 days	20,142	1,207	250
10.	Upa-Sarpanch, Gram Panchayat	21,943	Non-Party Basis	Indirect	30 days	20,142	1,207	232
11.	Ward Member, Gram Panchayat	2,08,586	Non-Party Basis	Direct	120 days	1,93,273	12,000	2115

TABLE 9.4

Statement showing the Information on Panchayati Raj Bodies

(Scheduled and Non-Scheduled Areas)

S. No.	Name of the District	No. of Gram Panchayats		No. of MPTCs		
		Scheduled Area	Total	Scheduled Area	Non Scheduled Area	Total
1.	Adilabad	235	866	42	433	475
2.	East-Godavari	121	1,000	57	985	1,042
3.	Khammam	375	774	178	371	549
4.	Mahaboob Nagar	30	1,351	—	815	815
5.	Srikakulam	16	1,112	15	605	620
6.	Visakapatnam	243	974	133	463	596
7.	Vizinagaram	78	930	12	507	519
8.	Warangal	64	1,016	11	658	669
9.	West Godavari	45	887	20	88	808
	Total	1,207	8,920	468	5,625	6,473

TABLE 9.4 (Contd.)

S. No.	Name of the District	No. of ZPTCs			Presidents (Mandal Parishads)			Chairman (Zilla Parishads)		
		Scheduled Area	Non Scheduled Area	Total	Scheduled	Non Scheduled Area	Total	Scheduled	Non Scheduled Area	Total
1.	Adilabad	5	47	52	5	47	52	—	1	1
2.	East-Godavari	7	50	57	7	50	57	—	1	1
3.	Khammam	19	27	46	19	27	46	1	—	1
4.	Mahaboob Nagar	—	64	64	—	64	64	—	1	1
5.	Srikakulam	1	36	37	1	36	37	—	1	1
6.	Visakapatnam	11	28	39	11	28	39	1	—	1
7.	Vizinagaram	1	33	34	1	33	34	—	1	1
8.	Warangal	1	49	50	1	49	50	—	1	1
9.	West Godavari	2	44	46	2	44	46	—	1	1
	Total	47	378	425	47	378	425	2	7	9

TABLE 9.5

Financial Allocations to Panchayati Raj Institutions

(Rs. in Crore)

Year	*Panchayati Raj Institutions*	*RDAs*	*Total*
1993-94	1,447.28	66.87	1,514.15
1994-95	1,373.51	82.25	1,455.76
1995-96	1,545.41	77.75	1,623.16
1996-97	1,712.05	91.53	2,215.18
1997-98	2,788.89	152.19	2,941.08

STATEMENT - I

NORMS FOR JUDGING THE PERFORMANCES OF THE GRAM PANCHAYAT

Name of the Gram Panchayat

(i) Augmenting the Resources

(a) Rate of Tax
(b) Percentage of Taxes
(c) Promptness in collection
(d) Additional resources mobilized

(ii) Remunerative Enterprises

(a) Social Forestry Scheme
(b) Market and Shopping Complexes
(c) Other Enterprises

(iii) Meetings

(a) Whether regularly held
(b) Whether unanimity is there

(iv) Implementation of Schemes

(a) I.R.D.P. Schemes
(b) Housing Schemes
(c) Literacy Achievements
(d) Family Welfare
(e) J.R.Y. Schemes

(v) Amenities Provided

(a) Water Supply
(b) Latrines for Women
(c) Street Lights

BIBLIOGRAPHY

Amin, Samir, "Four Comments on Kerala", *Monthly Review*, New York, January, 1991.

Aziz, Abdul and P.V. Shenoy, "District Planning: Principles and their Operationalisation", *Journal of Rural Development*, Vol. 16, No. 4, 1997.

Aziz, Abdul., Decentralised Planning : *The Karnataka Experiment*, New Delhi, Sage Publications, 1993.

Aziz, Abdul, *Decentralised Governance in Karnataka: The Mandal Panchayat System*, Hyderabad, National Institute of Rural Development, 1994.

Aziz, Abdul, N. Sivanna, Babu Devendra, Sekher Madhushree, Nelson C. Charles, *Decentralised Governance and Planning: A Comparative Study in Three South Indian States*, Bangalore : Institute for Social and Economic Change, 1998.

Balaramulu, C.H. and Raghvender., "Political Leadership in Panchayati Raj : A Study of Mandal Praja Parishad Leadership in Andhra Pradesh" *Administrative Change*, 1995.

Bandyopadhaya, D., Land Reforms in West Bengal Calcutta : Government of West Bengal, 1978.

Beck T., *The Experience of Poverty*, U.K.: International Technology Publication, 1994.

Bhargava, B.S., C.R.Bada, N.Vijay and Torgal, *Panchayati Raj System in Karnataka*, New Delhi : Jackson Publications, 1982.

Centre for Development Studies, "Some Notes on Possibilities of Decentralised Development in Kerala", Working Paper No. 106, Thiruvananthapuram : Centre for Development Studies, 1980.

Chandran, Satish T.R., *'Karnataka' in Status of Panchayati Raj in the States of India*, New Delhi: Concept Publishing Company, 1994.

Chaudhury S., *Study on Food For Work in West Bengal*, Santiniketan: Agro-Economic Research Centre, 1980.

Cheema G.S., and D.A. Rondinelli, (eds.), *Decentralisation and Development: Policy Implementation in Developing Countries*, Beverly Hills : Sage Publications, 1983.

Conveyers D., "Decentralisation: The Latest Fashion in Development Administration", *Public Administration and Development*, Vol.3, 1993.

Chaturvedi Y.S., "Micrology of Mandal Administrative Arrangements in Andhra Pradesh", *Indian Economic Panorama*, 3(3), 1993.

Dahl, Robert A., *Democracy and its Critics*, USA : Yale, 1988.

Dasgupta, P., *Desh Hitaishi* (in Bengali), Calcutta : April 7, 1978.

Dasgupta, B., "Institutional Reforms and Poverty Alleviation in West Bengal" *Economic and Political Weekly*, October, 1995.

Datta, P., *Land Reforms Administration in West Bengal*, New Delhi: Daya Publishing House, 1998.

Datta, P., "The Gram Sabha Experience", *Frontline*, July 30, 1999.

Datta, P., "Political Panchayats in West Bengal", *Frontline*, June, 1996.

Datta, P., *The Second Generation Panchayats in India*, Calcutta: Calcutta Book House, 1993.

Datta, P., "Rural Development Through Panchayats: The West Bengal Experience", *Kurukshetra*, April, 1996.

Datta, P., *Revitalization of Panchayats: The West Bengal Experience*, Calcutta: State Institute of Panchayats, Government of West Bengal, 1996.

Datta, P., *The Second Generation Panchayats in India*, Calcutta : Calcutta Book House, 1996.

Dreeze, J. and A. Sen, *India Economic Development and Social Opportunity*, New Delhi : Oxford University Press, 1995.

Dreeze J., "Poverty in India and IRDP Delusion" *Economic and Political Weekly*, September 29, 1990.

Ghosh, Arun, "Decentralized Planning : West Bengal Experience", *Economic and Political Weekly*, March 26, 1988.

Government of India, *Report of the Working Group on Block Level Planning*, New Delhi : Planning Commission, 1978.

Government of Kerala, *The People's Campaign for Ninth Plan in Kerala: An Introduction*, Thiruvananthapuram : Kerala State Planning Board.

Government of Kerala, *Power to the People's Plan - Ninth Plan*, Thiruvananthapuram : State Planning Board, 1998.

Government of Kerala, *People's Campaign for Ninth Plan in Kerala: An Approach Paper*, Thiruvananthapuram : Kerala State Planning Board, 1996.

Government of Kerala, *Economic Review* 1998, Thiruvananthapuram : State Planning Board, 1999.

Government of Kerala, *Interim Report on the Committee on Decentralisation*, Thiruvananthapuram : Government of Kerala, 1996.

Government of Kerala, *Committee on Decentralisation: Final Report*, Volume 1 (A & B), Thiruvananthapuram : Government of Kerala, 1997.

Government of India, Report of the Team for the Study of Community Development Projects and National Extension Service, Vol. 1, New Delhi : Government of India, 1957.

Government of Karnataka, *The Karnataka Village Panchayats and Local Boards Act*, Bangalore : Department of Law and Parliamentary Affairs, 1959.

Government of Karnataka, *The Karnataka Zilla Parishads, Taluk Panchayat Samitis, Mandal Panchayats Act*, Bangalore : Government of Karnataka, 1985.

Government of Karnataka, The Karnataka Zilla Panchayats, Taluk Panchayats and Village Panchayats Act, Bangalore : Government of Karnataka, 1993.

Government of Karnataka, *Report of the Expert Committee on Karnataka Panchayat Raj Act 1993*, Bangalore : Government of Karnataka, 1996.

Government of Karnataka, *Report of the Karnataka State Finance Commission*, Bangalore : The Karnataka State

Finance Commission, 1996.

Government of Mysore, *Report on the Integration and Coordination Committee for Local Bodies*, Bangalore : Government of Mysore, 1949.

Government of Mysore, *Report of the Local Boards Enquiry Committee*, Bangalore : Government of Mysore, 1953.

Government of Mysore, *Report of the Committee on Panchayati Raj*, Bangalore : Government of Mysore,1963.

Government of West Bengal, *Jyoti Basu Speaks*, Calcutta : Department of Information and Cultural Affairs, 1991.

Government of West Bengal, *Report of the State Finance Commission*, Calcutta : Government of West Bengal, 1996.

Government of West Bengal, *Anti Poverty Programme : The role of Panchayats Correspondence Between Rajiv Gandhi and Jyoti Basu*, Calcutta : Department of Information and Cultural Affairs, 1985.

Harris, R., "Centralisation and Decentralisation in Latin America" in G.S. Cheema and D.A. Rondinelli (eds.), 1993, *Decentralisation and Development: Policy Implementation in Developing Countries*, Beverly Hills : Sage Publications, 1983.

Isaac and Harilal, "Planning for Empowerment: People's Campaign for Decentralised Planning in Kerala", *Economic and Political Weekly*, January, 1997.

Isaac, Thomas, T.M., *People's Campaign for Ninth Plan: An Approach Paper*, Thiruvananthapuram : Kerala State Planning Board, 1996.

Isaac, Thomas, T.M., *Janakiyasoothranam : Sidhanthavum Prayogavum* (Malayalam), Thiruvananthapuram : Kerala State Planning Board, 1997.

Isaac, Thomas, T.M, *People's Planning: Towards a Handbook*, Thiruvananthapuram : Kerala State Planning Board, 1999.

Iyer, Krishnan, "Beginning of Revolution", *Mathrubhumi*, August, 1998.

Klibanoff, P. and J. Morduch, "Decentralisation, Externalities and Efficiency", *Review of Economic Studies*, Vol. 2, 1995.

Kohli, A., *The State and Poverty in India: Politics of Reform*,

New York : Cambridge University Press, 1989.

Lieten, G.K., "Panchayat Leaders in a West Bengal District" *Economic and Political Weekly*, October 1, 1988.

Lieten, G.K., "Rural Development in West Bengal: Views from Below" *Journal of Contemporary Asia*, Vol.24 (4), 1994.

Maddick, H., *Democracy, Decentralisation and Development*, Bombay : Asia Publishing House, 1963.

Mahipal, "Women in Panchayats: Experiences of a Training Camp", *Economic and Political Weekly*, January, 1989.

Mathew, George, *Panchayati Raj in Karnataka Today*, New Delhi : Concept Publishing Company, 1986.

Mathew, George (ed), *Status of Panchayati Raj in the States of India*, New Delhi : Concept Publishing Company, 1995.

Meenakshisundaram, S.S., *Decentralisation in Developing Countries*, New Delhi : Concept Publishing Company, 1994.

Mishra, S.N., Kumar Lokesh and Pal Chaitali, *New Panchayat Raj in Action*, New Delhi : Mittal Publications, 1996.

Mishra, S.K., *An Alternative Approach to Development: Land Reforms and Panchayats*, Calcutta: Department of Information and Cultural Affairs, Government of West Bengal, 1991.

Mohanti, Tushar., "Bengal Farm Labour Gains Little", *Economic Times*, July 12, 1994.

Mukherjee, Amitava and B.N.Yugandhar, *Methodology and Database for Decentralized Planning Studies in Multilevel Planning*, Vol. III, New Delhi : Heritage Publishers, 1991.

Nair, Adoor, K.K. Ramachandran, *Kerala, State Gazetteer*, Vol. I, Thiruvananthapuram : State Editor, Kerala Gazetteers, 1986.

Namboodripad, E.M.S., "Political Parties and Panchayati Raj", *Indian Journal of Public Administration*, October-December, 1996.

Oommen, M.A., "Development Experience, Development Priorities and Fiscal Resources of Kerala" in *People and Development*, Thrissur: Centre of Science and Technology for Rural Development, 1997.

Pai, Sudha, "Pradhans in the New Panchayats — Field Notes from Meerut", *Economic and Political Weekly*, Vol. 33(18), 1998.

Palanithurai, G., "Capacity Building exercise for Elected Representatives in Tamil Nadu", *Journal of Rural Development*, Vol. 16(4), Hyderabad : National Institute of Rural Development, 1997.

Paruthi, Renu, *A Study on Training Needs Assessment of Panchayat Raj members in context of Local Decentralised Development Planning including Health*, (Unpublished thesis submitted to the Faculty of Medical Associations) New Delhi : Faculty of Medical Associations, 1998.

Planning Commission, *Report of the Task Force on Agrarian Relations*, New Delhi : Government of India, Planning Commission, 1973.

Prashant, Prem, Suresh Mishra and Charanjeev Singh, Popular Participation in Rural Development, (Emerging Dynamics of Panchayati Raj Institutes in Haryana), Gurgaon : HIPA, 1996.

Pramanick S. and P. Datta., *Panchayats and People*, Calcutta : Sarat Book House, 1994.

Rajiv Gandhi Foundation, *Report of the Task Force on Panchayati Raj*, New Delhi : Rajiv Gandhi Foundation, 1997.

Ramachandran V.K, "On Kerala's Development Achievements", in Jene Dreze and Amartya Sen, (eds.), *Indian Development: Selected Regional Perspectives*, Delhi : Oxford University Press, 1996.

Reddy, Ram G., "Panchayati Raj and Rural Development and Local Organisation in Andhra Pradesh" in J. Milton and Norman T. Uphoff (eds)., *Rural Development and Local Organisation in Asia*, New Delhi : Mcmillian and company, 1982.

Sarumathy M., "Panchayati Raj in Andhra Pradesh" in R.C. Choudhry & S.P. Jain (eds), *Patterns of Decentralised Governance in Rural India*, Hyderabad : NIRD, 1999.

Sarumathy M., "Panchayati Raj in Andhra Pradesh A Democratic Step", *Southern Economist*, 11 (5), 1992.

Sastry, K.R., C.P. Vithal. and G. Ramachandriah, "Panchayati Raj in Andhra Pradesh: An Analytical Study" in NIRD (ed.), *Panchayati Raj Institutions in Selected States: An analytical Study*, Hyderabad : NIRD, 1995.

Sengupta B., *CPI(M) Promises, Prospects and Problems*, New

Delhi: Young Asia Publications, 1979.

Singh, Hargian, *Panchayati Raj Administration in Haryana*, Gurgaon : Indira Publications, 1985.

Sivanna N., Panchayati Raj Reforms and Rural Development. Allahabad : Chugh Publications, 1990.

Sivanna N., "A Fillip to Power to the People", *Deccan Herald*, April 27, 1996.

Sivanna N., "Amendments to the Panchayati Raj Act", *Deccan Herald*, September 28, 1997.

Sivanna N., "Decentralised Governance and Planning in Karnataka", *Social Change*, Vol. 28 No.1, 1998.

Slater R.P., *et al.* (eds.), *Participation and Development*, Hyderabad: National Institute of Rural Development, 1991.

Slater, Richard and John Watson, "Democratic Decentralisation or Political Consolidation : The Case of Local Government Reform in Karnataka", *Public Administration and Development*, 9(1), 1989.

Sreekumar T.T., "Neither Rural Nor Urban: Spatial Formation and the Development Process", *Economic and Political Weekly* September, 1990.

State Editor, *Kerala State Gazetteer*, Economic Affairs, Thiruvananthapuram : *Gazetteer of India, Kerala Gazetteers* Volume III, 1989.

Subha K., *Karnataka Panchayat Elections 1995, Process, Issues and Membership Profile*, New Delhi: Concept Publishing Company, 1995.

Sundaram., "District Planning Committee : Its Implications", *Journal of Rural Development*, Vol. 16 No. 4, Hyderabad : National Institute of Rural Development, October -December, 1997.

Sundaram, K.V., *Decentralised Multilevel Planning: Principles and Practice (Asian and African Experiences)*, New Delhi : Concept Publishing Company, 1997.

Swaminathan, M., "Village Level Implementation of IRDP: Comparison of West Bengal and Tamil Nadu", *Economic and Political Weekly*, March, 1990.

Webster, N., *Panchayati Raj and Decentralization of Development Planning in West Bengal*, Calcutta : Government of West Bengal, 1992.

Westergaard, K., *People's Participation Local Government and Rural Development - The Case of West Bengal*, Copenhagen : Centre for Development Research, 1986.

Woodcock, George, *Kerala - A Portrait of the Malabar Coast*, London : Faber and Faber, 1967.

INDEX

Aberrations, 50
Accounts manual, 170
Accountability, 34, 55, 60, 150,238
Adhyaksha, 204, 205, 208, 211, 236
Administration demonstration, 7
Administering social justice, 12
AIDS control programme, 219
Ambedkar Housing Schemes, 233-34
America, executive powers, 15
Amitava Mukherjee, 40
Anchal Panchayats, 19, 96, 97, 98
Anchalik Parishad, 96, 97, 98
Andhra Mandal Praja Parishad, 224
Andhra Pradesh Gram Panchayat Act, 242
Andhra Pradesh,
- Janma Bhoomi movement, 50
- Panchayati Raj Act, 242
- special features in, 260-61
- Panchayati Raj institutions, 259
- Rural local Government in, 242-269
- powers and functions, devolution of, 257-58
- State Finance Commission, 256-58
- Ward constituency, 243

Anti-defection law, 100-101, 172-73
Anti-poverty programmes, 50,130
Appelate Tribunal, 174-75
Artha-o-Sthayea Samiti, 112
Arun Ghosh, 37, 38
Ashrya, 233
Ashok Mehta Committee, 22, 23, 204
- recommendations, 23-28
- report, 203, 204

Assessment, 20, 44, 191
Audit commission, 54
Audit manual, 170
Autonomy, 148
- dimensions of, 148-48
- issues of, 259-60

Aziz, Abdul, 156, 201, 204

Balwant Rai Mehta Committee Report, 19, 21, 96, 202
Barua, S., 127
Basic amenities, 8
Bengal Local Self Govenrment Act, 94
Bengal partition agitation, 95
Bengal Village Self Government Act, 95
Bhuria Committee, 69
Block Development Officer (BDO), 101, 106, 203, 205
Block Level Expert Committee (BLEC), 179, 195
Block level planning, 151
Block Panchayat, 10, 44, 159, 160, 193
- fund, 164-65

Block Planning Committee (BPC), 49
Boraian, M.P., 83
Bottom-up approach, 84
Budget manual, 170
Bureaucracy, 16, 17, 37, 54, 127, 128, 131

Central Government, rural policies, 85
Centrally sponsored schemes, 130-33
Challenges, 77
Chandran, 203
Chandrasekhar, C.P., 133
Chandrashekaraiah, D., 202

Children, universal education for, 145
Chitradurga Zilla Panchayat, 210, 229, 230
  expenditure pattern of, 231
Chowkidari Panchayat, 94, 95
Chotuppal Gram Panchayat, socio-political scenario in, 267-68
Chotuppal Mandal Parishad, general body members of, 264-66
  Joint Mandal credit plan, 266-67
Chullas, 269
Clearing house, 90
Colonial Bengal, Panchayats in, 94-95
Community based organization, 46
Community development programmes, 84
Community project, 20
Consolidation fund of the State, 27, 31
Constitution of Finance Commissions, 27
Constitutional provisions, 18
Constraints, 41, 42
Corporation Level Block Committee (CLBC), 179
Corruption, 7
CPI (M), 99
Criticism, 98

Dahl, Robert, 60
Dalits, 84
DANIDA, 89
Datta, Chandan, 93
Datta, Prabhat, 93
Decentralization of Power, 3-6, 98
  administering development, 5
  concept of, 2-4
  democracy, 3
  objectives of, 3-6
  people's participation, 3-4
  planning, 5
  principles of, 148-150
  steps of, 36-37
Decentralised planning, 150-52
  experiment in, 152-53
  planning process, 57, 185
  steps of, 36-37
  present state of Art, 35-36
Deforestation, 77
Democratic decentralization, 73
  system, 54
Democracy, 3, 83
De Tocqueville, Willoughby, 16
Development distance, 85-86
Development Seminars, 187-88
Development Plan, implementation of, 195
Development programmes, 6-7
Dey, S.K., 21
Discrimination, 12
District Boards, 16
District Development Council (DDC), 203
District Level Expert Committee (DLEC), 179, 194, 195
District Panchayat, 10, 162-63, 193
  development plan, 193-94
  fund, 164-65
District Planning Committee, 13, 32, 36, 44, 49, 152, 184, 193, 210, 250
District planning, operationalisation of, 42
District planning and Development Council, 37
District Rural Development Agency (DRDA), 50, 76, 260-61
Donar agencies, 88
Dowry, 76
DWCRA, 138
Dwitiya Sansodan Adhiniyam, 75

Education, promotion of, 76
Election Commission, 27
  creation of, 12-13
Employment, 135
Employment Assurance Committee, 237
Empowering Local Bodies, 181-82
Enforced development, 84
Environmental problems, 7

Expert Committees, 194-95
Expert consultations, 88-89

Finance Commission, creation of, 12
Financial constraints, 42
Financial resources, devolution of, 222
Ford Foundation, 89
Fiedrich, Carl, 16

Gender discrimination, 147
George, Sunny, 141
Godwana Sangharsh Samiti, 254
Government functionaries, 107-110
  audit, 109-110
  budget, 108
  financial resources, 107-108
  job assistance, 107
  planning process, 109-110
Government policies, development distance, 85, 88
Gram Panchayat, 6, 10, 18, 19, 39, 96, 97, 98, 100, 101, 158-59, 244-45
  anti-defection law, 100-101
  distribution of, 159
  executive powers of, 106-107
  findings of 78-80, 164-65
  government functionaries, 108-109
  income and expenditure of, 222-25
  issues, 261-62
  meatings, 101-104
  performances, 278
  powers and functions of, 72-73, 218-19
  programmes of 127-128
  relationship, 117-18
  resource mobilization, 135-36
  revenue of, 255-56
  taxes, 160-61
Gram Panchayat Level, Standing Committees, 249
  staffing pattern, 253-54
Gram Panchayat Territorial Constituency (GPTC), 243
Gram Sabhas, 9, 10, 19, 21, 33, 45, 46, 47, 54, 70, 71, 204, 205, 243-44
  meetings, 105, 134-38
  powers and functions of, 71, 74, 166-67
Gram Sabha / Ward committees, 185-86
Gram Sansad, 104, 105, 134
  meetings, 105
  schemes, 104, 105
Grassroot dialogue, 87
Gujarat, 37

Hat (weekly markets), 111, 128, 134
Higher tiers, annual plan of, 193-94
Human resource development, 23

Illiteracy, 77
Improvement Trust, 17
Indira Awas Yojana, 219, 233
Industrialisation, 77
Informal interest groups, 48
Ingenuity, 45
Institutionalisation, 101
Institutionalized arrangement, 41
Integrated Rural Development Programme (IRDP), 70, 130, 219, 233
International Labour Organisation (ILO), 129
Irrigation management group, 48

Janata Party, 203
Janata Dal, 208, 212
Janma bhoomi, 269
Janpad panchayat, 70
  power and functions, 72-73, 80-81
Jawahar Rozgar Yojana (JRY), 104, 130, 132, 219, 220, 224, 225
  Action plan, 233, 234
  funds, 262
  income and expenditure, 227-28
  programmes, 236

Karmadhyaksha, 115, 116, 117
Karnataka,
  gram panchayat, 200, 204, 205, 206, 207, 208, 211, 214, 218, 219-20, 224, 230, 234, 235, 237

new Panchayati Raj System, 200-230
Taluk Panchayats, 200, 204, 205, 206, 206, 208, 211-24, 218-20, 229, 230, 234-57
Zilla Panchayats, 200, 204-208, 211-24, 218-20, 224, 230, 234-57
Zilla Parishads, 203
Karnataka Panchayati Raj Act, 206, 207
Kendra Panchayats, 19
Kerala,
Block Panchayats, 159-60
decentralisation, 148-50, 150-53
programmes, 45
democratic decentralisation, 141
development functions, 173-74
early demographic transition, 144-45
economy, 143-45
experiment, 45-46
geography and ecology, 143-44
gender discrimination, 147
gram panchayat, 152-53, 158-59
gram sabha, 165-66
land reforms, 147-48
Municipal Corporation Act, 164
new systems, expectations of, 153
Panchayati Raj System, 143, 153-54
plan grant-in-aid, 164-65
political panchayat, 172-73
public action, 144-45
public distribution system, 147
remittancies, 147-48
rural-urban continuum, 144-45
social infrastructure, 145
total literacy, 145
scheduled caste and scheduled tribes, reservation of seats, 176
state election commission, 175
state government, role of, 168-69
Kerala Panchayati Raj (Amendment) Act, 141, 142, 143, 152, 154, 155, 165-66, 174-75
features of, 141-42
recommendations, 155
Krishak Samiti, 134
Krishna Iyer (Justice), 197

Land Alienation Act, 74
Land reforms, 126-27, 147-48
Land revenue collection, 136
Land utilization pattern, 210
Left Front Government, 39, 93, 98
approach to panchayats, 99-100, 123-35
electoral slogan of, 123
rural development policy, 125-26
grassroots participation, 133-34
Lalithabhai, K.N., 141
Loans, 85
Local contributions, 45
Local development areas, 186-87
Local planning process, 34, 35, 50
instrumentalities, 46-48
Local Self Government, 2, 15
resolution, 16
Local Self Government Institutions (LSGIs), 57, 141
Ombudsman for, 175-76
power to, 148
structure of, 156-58
Lord Ripon, 17, 94
resolution, 94

Madhya Pradesh Panchayats, 19
Madhya Pradesh, scheduled areas in, 65-69
tribal zones of, 65
Madhya Pradesh Panchayati Raj (Dwitya Sanshodhan) Adhiniyam Act, 68, 69, 72, 73, 74
Mahaharashtra, 37
Mahatma Gandhi, 14
Mahila Mandals, 25
Mandal Panchayati, 19, 24, 26, 203, 204, 205, 245

programmes and schemes, implementation of, 205
sources of income, 256-57
Mandal Parishad, 292
administration, 252
level, Standing Committees, 249
Mandal Parishad Development Officer (MPDO), 252
Mandal Parishad Territorial Constituency, 243
Merxist Government, 99
Mc Iver, R.M., 15
Meenakshisundaram, S.S., 203
Melas, 117
Members of Legislative Assembly (MLAs), 38
Metropolitan Planning, 32
Metropolitan Planning Committee, 44
Midnapore experiment, 39
Mill, John Stuart, 16, 94
Mining Settlement Authorities, 17
Mishra, S.N., 56
MPs/MLAs representation of, 173
Municipal Corporation, 17
Municipal Level Expert Committee, 179, 195
Mysore Village Panchayat, 202

Nalgonda Zilla Parishad, administration of, 257
general body meeting, 264
Namboodiripad, E.M.S., 123
Narasimha Rao, P.V., 11
National Development Council, resolution, 21
National Extensive Service, 19, 20
recommendation of, 19-20
National Institute of Rural Development (NIRD), 36, 40
National Rural Employment Progammes (NRED), 130
National Sample Survey (NSS), 133
Nehru Yuvak Kendras, 25
New Panchayati Raj System, 2, 9, 13, 55
funding for, 51
New Rural leadership, 124-25
Nicholson, Russell, 201
Ninth Five Year Plan, 175, 176
people's campaign for, 179-80
Nominal Muster Roll (NMR), system, 263
Non-Governmental Organizations (NGOs), 52, 84, 87, 88
Non-land input support, 129-30
NORAD, 89
Nyaya Panchayat Act, 203

Octroi, 18
Official-non-official interface, 172
political economy of, 178-79
Ombudsman, 174-75
On-going programmes, 89
Operation Barga (OB), 127
programmes, 127-28
Organisational pluralism, 38, 50
Out-migration, 77

Pahari Korwas (tribes), 65
Palanithurai, G., 1, 56
Panchayat Audit and Account Officer (PAAO), 109
Panchayat Committee, audit system of, 170-71
Panchayat Development Report (PDR), 188
Panchayat election, 123
funds, 164-65
functional autonomy of, 109-70
leaders, 87-88
plan, 191-92
president, full-time role of, 163
Panchayat Samiti, 39, 54, 98, 110-12, 131, 177, 178, 179
audit, 118
functionaries, 111-12
funds, 117-18
planning process, 118-19
power and functions, 110-11
Panchayati Raj Bodies,
election to, 273-74

functions of, 246-48
gram panchayat, 246
mandal panchayat, 246-47
statement information of, 275-76
zilla parishad, 247
Panchayati Raj Election, 242
Panchayati Raj institutions, 14, 22, 37, 38, 55, 56, 200
financial allocations to, 277
role of women, 24
Panchayati Raj, organisations structure of, 250
Panchayati Raj System, 2, 22, 84
burning problems of, 74
pattern of, 67
regular election to, 13
structure of, 243-45
Partially tribal areas, categories of, 66-67
Participatory development, 84
Participatory Rural Appraisal (PRA), 89
People's democracy, 9
People's participation, 48
Phalias, 70
Plan Appraisal, 194-95
Planned development, activities, 34-35
Planning Commission, 40, 133
Planning process, transparency and accountability factor in, 51-60
Planning techniques, 41
Pochampally Mandal Parishad, funds allotted, 259-60
Policy Research, 89-90
Political mobilization, 127
Political Panchayat, 172-73
Poverty, 77
Poverty alleviation programmes, 224
implementation of, 258
P.R. Nayak Committee, 218, 222, 238
Pradhan, 106, 107
Present Panchayati Raj System, 155
Profession Tax, 135, 262
Public Distribution System, 147, 222
Purohit, B.R., 63

Query system, 54

Rajiv Gandhi, 11, 26, 28
Rajiv Gandhi Foundation, 54
Ramachandran, G., 19
Ramachandran, V.K., 54
Rao, G.V.K., 22
Ramittances, 147-48
Renu Purohit, 56
Resource mobilisation, scheme, 135-37
Resources management group, 48
Reservation of seats for *Dalit*, 11-12
Reservation of seats for women, 11
Rights to equality, 63
Robson, A., 16
Rock departmentalism, 99
Rural development programme, implementation of, 132
policy, 125-26
Rural employment, 152
Rural Landless Employment Guarantee Programme (RLEGP), 130
Rural Panchayat Organisation, 19
Rural policy forum, 85-86
aims of, 86
dissemination, 90
objectives, 86-87
programmes, 87
Rural-urban continuum, 144-45

Sananvaya (Co-ordination) Committee, 116
Sarumatty, M., 242
Scheduled areas, administrative and control of, 64-66
gram panchayats, 72
gram sabha, 71
institutional structure, 69-70
panchayats in, 254-55
power and functions of, 71-75
special provisions for, 69-73
possible hurdles, 75-77
tribal community of, 76
zilla panchayat, 72

Scheduled Caste and Scheduled Tribes, development schemes, 192-93
reservation of seats, 29-30, 70, 176, 202, 204, 243, 271-72
welfare corporation, 258
Seasonal unemployment, 77
Second Five Year Plan, 18
Self Help Groups, 269
Self-regulatory mechanism, 238
Sen, Abhijit, 133
Sepoy Mutiny, 93
73rd Constitutional Amendment Act, 1, 8, 31, 43, 65, 68, 154, 155, 254
recommendations, 31-32
74th Constitutional Amendment Act, 43
Sharma, S.D., 19
Sivanna, M., 200, 201
63rd Constitutional Amendment Bill 28
64th Constitutional Amendment Bill, 26
Social audit system, 171-72
Social infrastructure, distribution of, 145-46
Special Component Plan (SCP), 192
Standing Committees, 114-16, 163-64, 249
functions, 113-16
State Development Council, 58
State Election Commission, 175-76
State Finance Commission, 231, 256-57
State Governments, rural policies, 85
State Panchayat Parishad, 235
State Sponsored District Sector Scheme, 37
Steering Committees, 162-63
Subsidies, 85
Subsidiarity, 149, 181
Sudha Pai, 56
Sundaram, K.V., 34, 40, 50
Swaminathan, M.S., 131

Taluk Development Boards, 17, 202
Taluk Panchayats, income expenditure pattern of, 225-29
partiwise distribution of seats, 217
power and functions, 218-19
programmes, 219-20
responsibilities of, 220
Taluk Panchayat Samiti, 203
Tamil Nadu, Kamudi Town Panchayat, 21
Tamil Nadu Right to Information Act, 53
Task forces, 189-190
Task force on Agrarian relations, 127-28
Tax collection, 97
Taxes, 18
Technocratic, Academic and Democratic Mix (TAD) Mix, 49
Tenth Finance Commission, 257
Thimmaiah, G., 231
Three tier training programme, 183
Time constraints, 183
Top down approach, 84
Total literacy, 145
Training deficiencies, 41
programmes, 23-24
Training / empowerment programmes, 186
Transparency, 53, 60, 150, 171-72
democratic value of, 34
Tribal Advisory Council (TAC), 64, 65
Tribal districts, 66
Tribal population, 66-67
Tribal Sub-Plan (TSP), 192-93
TRYSEM, 219

Union Committee, 94, 95
Units of Local Self Government, 207
United Front Government, 97, 98
Un-tied funds, 37
Untouchability, removal of, 76
Upadhayaksha, 204, 206, 208, 211
Upa-pradhan, 106
Urban Local Bodies, 44

Vehicle tax, 255
Venkataramaiah, E.S., 14
Vilambara Jathas, 185
Village Panchayats, 17, 44, 47, 48